PRAISE FOR HOW TO TEACH

"Beadle is of course a 'one-off' charismatic and, so some would say, inimitable teacher. But here he puts together a rich array of delightful insights into the art of teaching in such a way that everybody will be able to take something to shape their own practice. It's one for the staff library and a must-read for all new teachers."

Sir Tim Brighouse, Visiting Professor at the Institute of Education London

"Teaching is one of the most cognitively engaging, emotionally draining, and physically demanding occupations there is. In fact, it is such a complex job that one life-time is not enough to master it, which is what makes it such a wonderful career. No matter whether you are a beginning teacher or a 20-year veteran, one can always get better at it, and this book is a great resource for helping in that journey. Beginning teachers will find lots of useful advice about this incredibly hard job; practical, sure, but also realistic about what is achievable in typical classrooms. And even the grizzled classroom veteran will find something new, or at least a new way of looking at old things, here. And this book is funny. It is laugh-out-loud, embarass-yourself-in-public funny. Every teacher should read it (in private)."

Professor Dylan Wiliam, Deputy Director, Institute of Education, University of London

"Shocking stories, fruity language, stand-up humour, gruesome anecdotes, and politically-incorrect hints – Phil Beadle takes the 'horrible histories' approach to the how-to-teach manual. The result is a funny, informative, practical and realistic book overflowing with memorable, cut-out-and-keep, easy-to-follow tips. Reading this book will be a whole lot more fun than your first teaching practice – and more valuable too. Beadle is the wise, but mischievous, old lag in the corner of the staffroom – pull up a chair and wonder at his stories of survival. They could save your teaching career."

Mike Baker, BBC News/*The Guardian*

"Here's the book that tells you everything that traditional teacher training courses don't – why 'pens down' and 'bags on the floor' may be the most important words you'll ever utter, how to build the respect of a class, how to survive those challenging first few days (or years) as a fledgling teacher. Conveyed with astringent honesty and directness, Phil Beadle's classroom wisdom cuts through the jargon and psychobabble of too many guides for teachers. His book is an intoxicating, often hilarious, and deeply wise reminder of why being a teacher can – if you get the essential ingredients right – be one of the most rewarding jobs in the world."

Geoff Barton, Headteacher, King Edward VI School

"I have been in education all my life.

"I learned first from my mother and father and, to some extent, from my three elder siblings. Subsequently, I attended schools from the age of three until my eighteenth year, college for three years and then commenced a somewhat chequered career as an educator. You would think that, by this ripe period of my middle three score years, I should know the craft... and I thought I did until I read this publication, the Phil Beadle Bible.

"Life is a learning journey and I thrive on learning. Google is possibly one of the greatest innovations for the learner that history has seen. I no longer have to go to the library and borrow three or five or seven tomes that are probably already three years or more out of date, in order to research new material for a customised conference or keynote speech. I now boot the P.C. and consult my pal, Google and he fills my mind with new knowledge and understanding.

"In the dawning days of this academic year Google enhanced my learning on language and words. I learned fascinating things about the number of words that different categories of human beings probably know and I learned how to find out how many words I probably know, which would appear to be in the region of 33,850! In addition, I learned that, to some extent, the nature / nurture debate with regard to the genders has been resolved with the determination to different behaviours (given that there is a continuum along which we all fall) from the moment the xx chromosomes divide to form the xy. Yet I still did not know *what I did not know*.

"This book is hilarious. It is controversial and it is irreverent. It provokes and, at times, it shocks, but above all it teaches. It exudes information, ideas and tips – some of which are tried and tested over the aeons of historic and emergent pedagogy and others which are new and amazingly enlightening and empowering. Like most professionals, I may not have used it all, I may have adapted and personalised strategies and techniques, yet the courage and wisdom of so much of *How To Teach* would undoubtedly have honed my craft in ways that can only be imagined. And it is all in one, personal, publication that I can carry with me. Unlike my Google, it can be annotated and highlighted, pages can be held by Post-its, passages can be underlined and items can be asterisked. It will become the teacher's 'best friend', a source of support and wisdom as the practitioner develops and refines his or her skills and expertise in this great craft of teaching.

"How I wish that I had had the full extent of this knowledge when I was in the classroom!"

Rosalind H. V. Wilson, Education Consultant, Andrell Education Ltd

"This book is that rare thing in education. Readable. Hugely readable. And necessary. Hugely necessary. It's also hip, sharp, sussed, funny and extremely practical – a scintillating, pedagogical romp, written by someone who knows. You want to be a 'phenomenal' teacher? Not just 'mediocre'? Well, this is indeed your bible.

"It's a happy mix of the idealistic and the tough. There are no short cuts to success. It's very hard graft. But get the basics right and the rest will follow. Get them wrong and you're toast. Teaching, for Beadle, is 'a performance art'. Dullness is not an option and his judgements are severe. Bore the kids and 'it becomes their moral responsibility to misbehave'.

"Oo –er! How to prevent this? With fierce subject knowledge, much passion and Beadle's Top Teaching Tips. These are many, detailed, inventive and practical.

"'Sweat the small stuff and the big stuff don't happen'.

"Small stuff like 'Turn up. Take the punches. Smile back.' There's hardcore wisdom about seating plans and hands up and shutting up (you not them) and the horrors of detentions (yours not theirs) and the need to get tough on gum and crisps and pens and not to be scared to cultivate your inner sadist. The section on the gradational levels of confrontation is a belter. You need to develop an extensive repertoire – from the Pinter pause, the mono brow, the micro nod, the eye narrow raise, to the 'extremely useful' borderline psychosis. Ho hum. He is Stalinist with marking and after reading about Cerise you will be too.

"He dismantles the Victorian classroom.

"'Desks are the enemies of learning'.

"He dismantles the teacher-led discussion. Children turn off after about seven minutes. It took me years to get this. They learn in groups – and in permutations of groups. They learn by DOING things. He's right! This section is again full of detailed, brilliantly classroom tactics. Apply these and 'the classroom's your playground'.

"You're now ready to be yourself. Passionate, larky, creative, risky – and to see off Ofsted and their often dreary criteria.

"These exhausting rigours are all in the service of the greater good – to teach children. 'Remember, it is for them you want to be a good teacher.' Beadle emphasises their fragility, their continuously threatened self-esteem, their daily humiliations. So many have had so much of this. They don't want more in the classroom. Especially working class children – especially white working class boys. Beadle 'gets' these often naughty boys and knows that education is their only weapon, their only break. The book respects children throughout without any tacky sentiment. 'All children', we are reminded, 'lie'. And 'all children are special needs'.

"Teaching, for Beadle is not a vocation for the idle, the craven, pansy liberals or, I'm afraid, north London social workers – or even Accrington Stanley fans. The rest of you should get it. This is the Knowledge. It's necessary. It's often hilarious. It works. For the new teacher it is indeed the Bible. And for old lags – I taught for thirty-five years and if I'd read this book I would have been so much better."

Ian Whitwham, SecEd columnist, journalist and former teacher

"Some time ago Phil Beadle came to see me with the idea of writing a PhD. As with all such applicants, I asked him if he really didn't have anything better to do with the next four or five years of his life. Luckily he did and this book is the result. It is much more readable than most PhDs since Phil's writing is as engaging as his teaching. It is also very funny; there is a chuckle or a hoot-out-loud on every page – and how many books on education can you say that about?! As well as its supreme readability in presenting a cast of characters in situations all too well known to anyone familiar with what Phil calls 'the surreal parallel universe of the classroom', it is also remarkably practical. For the trainee and newly qualified teacher it will, like *Everyman*, go with them and be their guide. At the same time, like the best of PhDs rewritten for publication, it presents a complete picture of what English state schooling has become in recent years. Not only in secondary but also in primary schools, in further education colleges and even in universities, where in seminars and lectures I find myself using many of the tricks of the trade that Phil imparts to the overwhelmed and overseen pedagogue. In this way *How to Teach* presents not only an invaluable practical guide but is also a classic source for those seeking to understand the strange version of learning and teaching that our society has inflicted upon its young in its persistent obsession with what it calls 'education'. 'Why are we doing this?' asks Phil's 'poor, industrially alienated student', accredited and assessed towards endlessly receding horizons from which any mirage of regular and rewarding employment has long vanished. If, as he admits, Phil is unable to answer this 'not unreasonable question', his book explains how the modernised and monitored, tested and target-driven culture of accumulating accreditation grinds on, 'gentling the masses' as it selects a one dimensional minority while rejecting the majority who fall at every fence. But more than that, it shows how – beneath the weight of centralised inspection and audit and beyond the latest snake-oil solutions of 'learning styles' or 'left and right brain gym' derived from dubious neuro-mythologies – teachers still strive to retain and develop their expertise in helping students to understand themselves and the increasingly mad world we inhabit. Together with our students we can then learn from the past to alter our behaviour in the future. This critical transmission of culture down the generations is after all what institutionalised learning at all levels is supposed to be about. With insightful humour and practical wisdom, this book offers methods applicable in any classroom to regain that purpose and hope for education."

**Patrick Ainley, Professor of Training and Education,
School of Education and Training, University of Greenwich**

"Phil Beadle is a legend. His appearance in Channel 4's *The Unteachables* was one of the iconic moments of television during the Noughties: his Kung-Fu Punctuation exercises and teaching *Macbeth* to the cows not only showed the public that difficult subjects could be made fun and easily accessible for the most challenging pupils, but also that great teaching can make a real difference. His new book develops many of the ideas and techniques that he revealed so entertainingly in the TV show. As he says himself, it is not a survival guide but the hard-won wisdom of a practising teacher who confronts the reality of the classroom still. This book is packed full of practical advice from someone who has to deal with pupils chewing gum, eating crisps, not listening, drifting off task, and generally getting up to no good on a daily basis. The solutions he offers are both imaginative, sensible and, above all, WORKABLE. Even though I've been teaching for twenty years, I found huge chunks of this book really useful. Even when I disagreed with him – there's a brilliant but controversial section on ICT in the book – I felt that I had to modify my teaching in the light of what he said. The advice isn't comforting, it's more of a wake-up call to the whole profession. To be honest, every teacher should read and act upon this book because there's a gem on nearly every page."

Francis Gilbert author of *Working The System:*
How To Get The Very Best State Education For Your Child

"... is quite simply the most fantastic and thoroughly realistic book for anyone embarking on a career in teaching. In fact, I would highly recommend it to any-one in the profession, however experienced they are! The book incorporates just about everything you need to know about current thinking, behaviour management, how to engage today's pupils and most importantly gives a true picture of the real-ity of classroom practice. It is a thoroughly readable and insightful book written with great humour and crucially shows a total empathy with pupils and how to help them reach their full potential."

Maggie Shevlane, Kent Lead Advanced Skills Teacher

HOW TO TEACH

PHIL BEADLE

Crown House Publishing Ltd
www.crownhouse.co.uk
www.crownhousepublishing.com

First published by
Crown House Publishing Ltd
Crown Buildings, Bancyfelin, Carmarthen, Wales, SA33 5ND, UK
www.crownhouse.co.uk
and
Crown House Publishing Company LLC
6 Trowbridge Drive, Suite 5, Bethel, CT 06801, USA
www.crownhousepublishing.com

Page 70, extract from the QCA's website has been reproduced with their permission.
Page 80, extract from *Standing on the Shoulders of Giants: Hermann Vaske's Conversations with the Masters of Advertising* by
Hermann Vaske has been reproduced with the kind permission of Die Gestalten Verlag GmbH & Co. KG, Berlin. (Published
2001, ISBN: 9783931126698).
Page 86, extract from *Teach-It* newsletter has been reproduced with the kind permission of Teach-It. (www.teachit.co.uk).
Page 186, extract from Murdoch University website has been reproduced with their kind permission.
(www.tlc.murdoch.edu.au/gradatt/verbs.html).
Page 192, extract from the Analyze Math website has been reproduced with their kind permission. (www.analyzemath.com/
calculus_questions/functions.html).

British Library of Cataloguing-in-Publication Data
A catalogue entry for this book is available
from the British Library.

10-digit ISBN 184590393-5
13-digit ISBN 978-184590393-0

2009936664

Printed and bound in the UK by
Gomer Press, Llandysul, Ceredigion

TO THE BOK FAMILY

Acknowledgements

I would like to thank all the mates who have made working in schools a laugh Zafirios Lastiotis, James Mackay, Roger Moisan, Phil McNortherner, Kevin Ducker, Superdooper Robbie Cooper, John Murphy and James Stafford.

CONTENTS

FOREWORD

This book will take you inside the mind of a teacher who break all the rules of conventional wisdom, while at the same time providing new teachers with a solid and timely scaffold of pedagogy for the post-Ofsted age.

You won't find Phil's rules for promoting good behaviour (and teacher sanity) in any ITT institution or DfE classroom management manual. Reading Chapter 1 made me laugh out loud on a crowded train full of strangers, travelling – as it happens – from one august training institution to another. Laughter caused by the joy of recognition that here was a teachers' teacher who really understands and likes children, empathises with the pain of growing up, recognises the natural urge to challenge authority if given half a chance, and who intends to stay on top and the adult in charge.

Although full of wit and humour, this is a deeply serious book written by a seasoned practitioner who has not migrated to academia, civil service or inspection, but remains in the urban classroom. No educational jargon, no tortuous theory – just sheer common sense and humanity. Any new teacher will tell you that it's not subject knowledge or lesson planning that keeps you awake at night – it's the sheer terror of being one against thirty, or more often, one against a few individuals who give you grief.

Any rooky teacher would do well to internalise some of this wisdom – such as that all children have 'special needs', the pointlessness of detentions and how to be assertive without being confrontational. One of Phil's best tips – along with "don't be too matey", "appear relentlessly happy" and pile on the praise – is "We are dealing with a generation of children who are used to negotiating with their parent/s and who find this a profitable way of doing business. Don't." There's an absence of panic about how difficult inner city children are to manage, just some common sense about how to stay one step ahead and the adult in the situation.

Phil's book provides novices with a practical toolkit, demystifying lesson planning and differentiation strategies, illustrating a comprehensive range of effective pupil grouping techniques designed to facilitate learning and subvert boredom. Old hands (and mentors to NQTs and BTs) will smirk at the irreverent swipes at current orthodoxy surrounding differentiation, gifted and talented provision and 'learning styles', assessment fads and political correctness, and welcome the emphasis on teaching as a craft, rather than an art or a science, that can be learned – but not without putting in time and hard graft. Phil also re-invents teaching as a performance art, rather an important message for new teachers bent on acquiring psychological presence and gravitas in the classroom – or 'acquiring rep' as he would call it.

The readability, wit and style of this book belie its seriousness as a guide to being the best teacher you can be. There are some great original and workable ideas in chapters on methods and organisation, lesson planning and assessment, the 'third hidden objective', the Harris Method and the many football analogies among them.

The cast of urban kids cited in examples have almost a cartoon-like familiarity but amongst the humour there are some profound truths about the vulnerability of adolescence rarely addressed in teacher training, the need to feel safe and fear of loss. In many ways this is an old-fashioned book, a refreshing change from years of government strategy documents and wordy university research papers. Simple truths about what children really want and need – permanent teachers permanently present and books regularly marked – and the essential mundane tasks that underpin the nobler aspects of teaching – rigorous attention to the marking, presentation and display of children's work, are articulated with passion and conviction, along with a welcome return to the primacy of and joy in subject knowledge.

Andrea Berkeley, Development Director, Teaching Leaders
26 March 2010

INTRODUCTION

Make no mistake. Your first year as a teacher is tough; nothing like the permanently uplifting stroll you may have been sold by glossy government adverts and brochures. Your days can be confusing, spirit crushing, depressing; frightening even, but you will also have moments of profound joy, in which you see why some regard it as being the best job in the world; moments where you feel 'part of the solution'. (These will last exactly until the next lesson when you are immediately and summarily turned over by year 4/6/8, and spat out shuddering.)

Over the next two hundred or so pages I aim to give practical solutions to help you be the best classroom teacher you can be as quickly as possible. This is decidedly not a survival guide. There is no advice contained in this book as to how you should deal with a difficult boss, or how you get the bloke who does the photocopying to respect you. There is no trouble-shooting session, nor any cod psychological cack about how to deal with stress. It is written assuming that, as an intelligent, graduate professional, you can work most of that stuff out for yourself, and that you are aware of your nearest licensed premises.

This book is a guide to doing infinitely better than just surviving. You will not revolutionise the life chances of the children you are to teach, or make a vast and seditious contribution to overturning the class system, one child a time, by merely surviving. It's a guidebook, the intent of which is to help you to fly; to be phenomenal. And it is a guidebook written by someone whose, admittedly over-hyped, reputation comes from being identified as being outstanding where it counts: in the classroom. Unlike many *experts* in education I am still a serving schoolteacher. As such, these insights are not something I once thought fifteen years ago that no longer apply; I am using the techniques in this book, in a school towards the bottom of the league tables, on the day you are reading this.

Organisationally, it is divided into five chapters: management of students, knowledge and understanding, methods and organisation, lesson planning and, finally, assessment. These subject headings are taken from the lesson observation sheet that I use when I am sitting in the back of other people's lessons tutting. The lesson observation sheet came from my time at Eastlea Community School, and is, I think, the creation of Linda Powell, my former head teacher, who was the first person ever to recognise that a haircut was not outside the realms of my abilities.

CHAPTER 1
MANAGEMENT OF STUDENTS

AaaaaaaAarGhhH!

How on earth are you ever going to manage thirty knife-wielding psychos on your own? What happens if they don't do what you say? What if they go completely hat-stand? Carroty even? Completely mental? My God, you're under-prepared. You're über-under-prepared. They'll kill you. You're not cut out for this. You're not in the right job. You're not in the right profession. Best you resign before it all gets too bloody.

The beginner teacher's fear of the unruly class is similar to the turkey's fear of Christmas, in that, not only is it entirely warranted, but also neither teacher nor turkey are anywhere near properly prepared for the full horror of what it is they are to face. PGCEs rarely give much more than a day's training on how to manage behaviour, and that generally consists of sitting mute, watching Antipodean behavioural guru, Bill Rogers, effortlessly controlling a class of miniature, compliant Aussies, as a room full of adults think, as one, "Well that's got to be a piece of cake, hasn't it? The kids in the Bill Rogers video are all well fed, clearly middle class and obviously easy to manage. I don't think there's going to be too many of those in the school that I've just signed on for."

This proved to be true in my first year of teaching. I thought I'd manage them purely on the basis of having nice(ish) hair for a thirty-two-year-old and being able to read books aloud in the stentorian, actorly manner of an amateur Kennneth Bran-argh. Wrong.

In my first year of teaching I was shuffled into a classroom far away from the rest of the English department and left to get on with it.

In no way did my PGCE prepare me for Rod freaking out and sobbing; for Lee threatening to chuck a chair at me; for the whole of 8M point-blank refusing to do anything I asked, nay begged, them to do, ever; for Mick pushing me; for 8S winding me up something chronic; for Mick pushing me again; for JK punching Cookey in the mouth in the first five seconds of my first Ofsted observed lesson; for Tammy and her mate to write me really scary love letters; for the whole sorry mess that was my desire to be a good teacher to teeter and threaten to topple into the abyss on a near daily basis.

It would have been much easier if I'd had some of the pieces of information, of which you will be in possession within a couple of minutes. Managing behaviour is actually fairly easy provided you observe a few rules (also provided that you haven't been gifted the most difficult class in the borough on your first day in the profession). You must observe them religiously though. Fail to do any of the following and you'll find that you are not in control of the class. And this is key: it's your classroom. You are the teacher. If you are not in control it'll all go to cock, the kids will learn nothing and, what is more, they'll have a deeply unpleasant experience, as they won't feel at all safe.

RULE 1 – TURN UP

One of the most difficult classes I've ever taught was in my first year as a teacher: En10a2. The worst you would think on seeing this seemingly innocuous set of letters and numbers is that they are slightly oddly capitalised. To me, in 1997, the merest flash of this set of signifiers would be enough to reduce me to shuddering, silent screams of, "Please. Don't make me go in that room with them. They are savages." It was in En10a2 that Mick, a bulky fifteen-year-old, pushed me, with substantial force, full in the chest, in front of the rest of the class. (He was taken to internal inclusion and told off. I was left to teach the rest of the class, hands shaking and pale as a sheet as I held grimly to the piece of paper I was reading to them in a quivering voice). And it was in En10a2 that the same kid performed the same feat two weeks later. It was in En10a2 that Tammy and her mate wrote the love letters, that JK punched Cookey when Ofsted were in, that Christelle informed me in front of a senior manager that she, "Didn't give a fuck" about my lesson, that the whole class came in sobbing after a funeral they'd attended that no one thought I should be told about and called me an, "Insensitive tosser" for trying to teach them afterwards. And it was in En10a2 that I was given the gift of being Coops's teacher, (which, if you'd met Coops, you'd understand is the kind of gift that would make you believe a brain tumour to be a birthday present).

In my first year as a teacher, every lesson with En10a2 was fretted about before, dismal and depressing during and, afterwards, often left me as a shell-shocked wreck, strung together with string and masking tape, barely suppressing the tears lining my lower eyelids, which were threatening to make me even more of a laughing stock in the staffroom than I already thought I was.

By the end of year 10 they were my favourite class. I adored them. And it was, they were fairly fond of telling me, one of the rare moments in my life where such affection was, at least partially, reciprocated. The next year, when HMI were in, En11a2 organised their own séance in class when my lesson was being observed, Coops taking his group and leading them brilliantly. My head of department witnessed a conversation between an inspector and the Principal, in which she pointed out Coops to be about the most challenging young man in the school, and that I had him, "Wrapped around my little finger." En10a2 were eventually the first step to me getting recognised as being alright in the classroom, as opposed to the borderline pass I'd been regarded as in my NQT year. But it was not always thus ...

In year 11, the class and I spoke about the early days. Oh, how we all laughed at how difficult it had been the year before. They remembered how horrific they had been in those first few half terms. They were sorry they'd been horrible but, as Danksy pointed out, I was about their fifteenth English teacher in the space of a year. They'd actually quite liked me (sort-of-ish-a-bit-but-not-really) from the first moment, but no English teacher had ever stayed around long enough to see their good side before and, quite reasonably, they saw no reason to think I'd be any different, and consequently, no cause for getting that good side off the mantelpiece and giving it a shine. They didn't want to get too fond, because that'd result in them being all the more disappointed when I left them, as I was inevitably bound to do, particularly as they'd behaved so awfully!

It is a sad truth that you will teach many young people in your career who are all too used to adults letting them down. Sadder still, many are used to the adults they care for the very most leaving them. Put yourself in their shoes. Would your response to experiencing such loss at such an early age be sane? In behaving appallingly in the first few half terms, En10a2 could at least draw some power from their teacher's inevitable chucking in of the towel. They had caused it. They were the hardest, the toughest and the meanest. Adults leaving them was entirely in their control. They were not helpless, or vulnerable, or any of the other things they feared they might be in their darker moments. They were captains of their own fate.

You may think you're a crap teacher doing a crap job when you are in front of the class, but you're worse when you're not there. Turn up. Take the punches. Smile back. Within six months you'll have achieved what some teachers refer to as the 'bowling ball effect'. You pick them off one by one. You'll notice a couple of kids initially (in the case of En10a2 it was Kelly and Sam) who are less resistant to learning, and to you, than the others. After a while a couple more might join them. Then you pick them off like pins at a bowling alley, until such point as you have a critical mass in favour of both you and your lesson. Eventually, even the hardest nut cracks and you have that profound moment of epiphanic teaching joy: the first good lesson with the truly hard class, in which you begin to see it *is* possible. You *can* do this.

The reason this is in the section regarding behaviour management is that kids like teachers who are there every day. One of my most weirdly proud moments came when, halfway through the spring term, Big Isaac (a charming and vastly proportioned naughty boy, who couldn't write that well, but was a very promising boxer) cried out to me, giving vent to an exasperation that had obviously troubled him for a while, "Christ! Beadleman," he exhaled, "Don't you ever take any time off? When are we going to get a break from you?" This, I think, was Isaac's backhanded way of saying that he appreciated my attendance record. (From my perspective I was very grateful he didn't punch me even once during our years together). If you get a reputation with the children as a good attender, it will pay dividends in terms of behaviour. You will always be on top of what happened yesterday, and the children will respect the commitment you show to them by always being there.

RULE 2 – SORT YOUR SEATING

A teacher without a seating plan is a dunce and is asking for it. Other than your own ability to charm, cajole and sometimes even confront, the seating plan is the single most important piece of behavioural modification equipment you have in your toolbox.

There are different schools of thought on this. I have a particular methodology, which I'll explain later, but first, a bit on why classroom organisation is the most important philosophical decision you will make in your career and why you should turn your face away from the darkness and towards the light.

Here's a shock. You are not necessarily the cleverest person in your classroom. You may not even be in the top ten. Yes, you are the one with a degree. You are the bigshot, for now. But, let's face it, you have no idea what the children in front of you may one day become. Something altogether more impressive than a piffling, cardigan-clad, Cornish-pasty-shoe-wearing schoolteacher, perhaps?

Any survey of students that asks them the important question, "How do you learn best?" finds the same answer at the top of the list. "Groups," their replies will scream, with one impassioned voice. "We learn best in groups. WHY WON'T ANYONE LISTEN TO US?" Having your desks set out in groups is the right way to organise your classroom. Period. No discussion. No arguing. Having the tables in groups allows you to set them the grouped speaking and listening activities that are the way in which they learn most effectively. Having your tables in groups lets them learn from each other. And having your tables in groups is a spatially symbolic move away from the Dickensian notion of the teacher standing at the front talking cobblers about really hard sums all day, every day.

Having your tables in five groups of six is the optimum classroom layout, in that it allows you to mix up the activities. You can do a paired activity, then one in threes, then one in groups without so much as a single moved chair. Not only is it convenient, but it is good use of the classroom space. If you ensure that each group of tables is positioned as near to the boundaries of the classroom as is possible, whilst still allowing the kids at the edge to be able to breathe, you are left with a space in the middle of the classroom in which kids can do exciting kinaesthetic activities, or you can stand in the spotlight declaiming your own shockingly bad poetry in a fruity RSC bombast.

Having your tables in groups also allows you to implement a quite interesting piece of methodology, which I'll explain now. Many years ago, when doing some work on boys' achievement, I chanced upon Ofsted's report on the same issue, and actually read the bloody thing. In it there was a fascinating section about the seating plan (Christ! I really, really must do something about my work/lack of anything anywhere near resembling a life balance). Ofsted suggest that the best way of getting serious work out of boys in a mixed school is getting them to sit with slightly lower ability girls. If they are sat with higher ability girls then they just go into learned helplessness mode and get the girls to do their work for them. If they are sat with girls of the same ability range they go all stupid and competitive. But if you sit them with girls they can help, they change character immediately: becoming nurturing, gentle, supportive and interested in their own attainment and that of others. I use this method now for every class I teach and, you know, it kind of works.

There are teething issues with implementing any new seating plan. This methodology doesn't take account of existing relationships, for instance, and it may be that you've sat people on the same table who pathologically detest each other or, worse still, are the best of friends. But with the odd tweak it can be made to work. It has, at its base, the important basic that boys and girls must always be sat next to each other, and is a defensible methodology in terms of Ofsted or senior management asking probing questions of you. Of course, it's useless in single-sex schools, and it relies on there being a critical mass of relatively high-attaining males in the class, which is not always so. It also condemns the highest ability girls to sit on a table with the three lowest attaining males. But this too has benefits, which you'll find out once you implement it.

The implementation of a seating plan can be bloody however, and you must be both rigourous and intractable, as the kids will seek to circumvent it. Any request from a student must be resolutely refused. "But Miss, I don't like ..." or, "We don't get on ..." must be treated as the irrelevant impertinence that it is. You decide where they sit, and you have arranged the seating plan to maximise their attainment not so they can sit gossiping with their best mate. You will find that within a lesson or so, they will attempt to just go and sit back in the place that they want to occupy, you have to call them on this immediately. Acceding to even a single request regarding where they sit will lead to chaos, and chaos is not what we're after.

RULE 3 – SWEAT THE SMALL STUFF AND THE BIG STUFF DON'T HAPPEN

There are certain 'tells' regarding behaviour management that will give any person observing that lesson a pretty well immediate sense of whether the teacher knows what they are doing or not. The first of these is obvious from the moment the observer walks into the class: if there are kids' coats and bags on the desks then the teacher is clueless and the lesson is likely to be a disaster. If the kids' coats are on their backs then the same applies, only more so.

The reason for this is that there are certain rules that children won't bother reacting against or calling into question, such as putting their bags on the floor and their outside wear on the back of a chair. I don't recall a situation in my many years standing in front of a class talking twaddle, in which a child has defended to the death their right to have their coat sprawled out on the desk. All children will obey this instruction. It is therefore senseless to bottle it because you are scared of an adverse reaction from them that they can't be arsed to summon up.

As soon as the children enter your class, insist that their bags are off the table and their coats hung up or chucked, gently, wherever those coats go. Insisting that this routine is followed without question at the beginning of every lesson does so much more for you, as a teacher, than just keeping the coats and bags orderly. It gives out a message: this is a classroom in which the rules are to be followed, and your insistence on such a routine sets the tone for the rest of the lesson. Because you have laid down the law first thing, you have asserted that you are not the sort of teacher who ignores behavioural infractions and, having established this with the class, you will find that there are fewer infractions. They don't bother committing them because they know you are going to call them on it.

RULE 4 – BECOME EXPERT IN THE TECHNICALITIES OF DEALING WITH CHEWING GUM

It's repulsive stuff, chewing gum. It performs no useful function other than allowing kids to believe themselves mini-versions of James Dean, 'rebels without an idea of how to mark off a subordinate clause'. It gets everywhere – into carpets, onto your best teaching trousers, and often into Hermione, the Pre-Raphaelite kid's, hair. Upturn any school desk and you'll find a 'tribble' of them nestling like guilty, germ-ridden, rock-hard glob-bogeys, festering and sneering at your utter impotence and inability to stop more of their cousins joining them next lesson. There are few things in British schools that bring out this teacher's inner fascist quicker than the wanton cud-chewer.

Some schools seem to have bigger problems with this issue than others. And if you are to teach in one of the schools in which gum chewing is endemic then, trust me, you will get heartily sick of instructing children to, "Spit it in the bin."

The same thing applies with the gum rule as with the coats and bags. If you ignore the fact that a child is chewing gum then you are setting a precedent for the whole class – giving them the message that it is OK to break school rules in your lesson. It may seem slightly petty dispensing summary justice to those who break the gum-chewing rule (see also packets of crisps, toffees, etc.) but, again, it sends a message that since the smaller infractions will not be tolerated, the bigger ones must not occur. Zero tolerance in small areas allows you to be utterly tolerant in others.

There are a couple of technical issues when dealing with the gum chewer that won't be apparent immediately, and which you should be hip to:

1. If Mohammed won't go to the waste paper bin, then the bin must go to Mohammed – In all things you should keep a sharp eye out for humiliating children. Public humiliation is no one's favourite diet, and if you accidentally humiliate a kid, then you will pay double for it in the fullness of time. Yes, they have committed the mortal sin of chewing gum. Yes, they are the criminal. And, yes, you are the law. However, if you stand at the front of the class and sternly

intone the phrase, "Mohammed! Gum in the bin. Now," you force poor old Mo to take the walk of shame in front of his mates and to lose face badly. He is likely to hate you for it, and may spend the rest of the lesson devising a cunning and unpleasant revenge. And should he choose to take vengeance against you, beware! As Charlie Bukowski said, "...beware the average man, the average woman, beware their love, their love is average, seeks average, but their genius is their hatred, there is enough genius in their hatred to kill you ..."[1]

Better, having noticed Mo's gnashers masticating up and downwards at metronomic pace, that you wait for some moment during which the class are involved in a task, take the waste paper bin in your hand, and quietly sidle up to him, saying in a near whisper, "Gum in the bin, please." (It is also useful reinforcement whilst intoning the instruction to point to your own open mouth, and from thence to the bin). Generally, because you have avoided publicly upbraiding the perp, he will obey without question. Unless he attempts the sleight of hand, which will lead you to the second technicality of dealing with the gum chewer, the phrase ...

2. "All of it." – You will find that the seasoned classroom criminal has many saucy and wicked ways of deceiving the stupid old duffer at the front of the class. One of these is related to gum. You will request that they dump the wad, and they will appear to do so. To the untrained eye a deposit of chewing gum has gone in the bin. Job done. World saved.

    To the experienced professional, however, a cunning sleight of hand has been used that may well dupe the gullible, but doesn't work with them, nor indeed with anybody who has read this book. Many of the more inveterate wad munchers will, when instructed to eject the offensive article, hold it between their teeth and pull off a token third or so. With a magician's dexterity, they'll then hide the size of it by concealing it, keeping the blim of gum between forefinger and thumb, and holding the hand downwards, so the back of it disguises

---

1 *God knows where this comes from. I've half-read several Bukowski books but, as I recall, left each one of 'em in the boozer.*

the size of the bitten off bit. This will then be deposited in the bin with an ingenuous expression convincing only to the untrained eye.

At this point the seasoned practitioner firmly utters the phrase, "All of it." Note, the really experienced professional doesn't even have to part their lips for this phrase to ring out straight and true. At which point your student will realise you are perhaps not the credulous fool they took you for, and will obey the instruction.

3. Trust yourself – You did see them chewing. The fact that they swear blind that they have an allergy to gum that causes them to go into anaphylactic shock the moment they smell it, is of no consequence. Trust yourself. You saw it. Yes, you may have been overworking, but you are not prone to hallucinatory visions on weekdays, particularly during the daytime. Trust yourself. You are not an idiot, nor are you blind (on weekdays: in the daytime). The child is lying. They were chewing. If they persist in calling you an idiot they should spend a brief time outside the class, contemplating the fact that teacher doesn't enjoy an eight/eleven/thirteen-year-old suggesting to them that they have lost it. (See Rule 4 – below).

4. Stay vigilant – You'll win the odd battle with gum, but the war is of an eternal nature and no one soldier is anything more than cannon fodder in it. You may be the most talented gum smeller in the school – sensitive of nose; perma-pricked of ear; ever-ready for the tell-tale rustle of silver paper, the sibilance of wad washing around in saliva, the slight smacking against teeth and tongue – but you will not have much time to celebrate whatever illusory and transient victory you achieve. Because the next day, the same child will pop the same substance into the same mouth, despite having been caught the day before, and having received the same instruction as every other sodding day. He will never be defeated. In fact, the war of attrition is more likely to result in you finding yourself gagging and sobbing against a wall, choking, as you soundlessly mouth the word, "Why?" and a drool of gossamer spittle attaches your lower lip, like a fine spider's web, to the classroom fabric.

You'll get bored to buggery of telling kids to spit the gum in the bin. There may well come a time when you ignore the odd infraction because you just can't stand to hear your voice intoning that same phrase, even one more time. But as with all of the small rules, it is pretty vital that you are seen to be the kind of teacher who doesn't ignore them. Your attitude to gum is indicative to the kids of your attitude to everything else. If you ignore the fact that they are chewing in your lesson, then the question that blossoms in their half-formeds is, "What else might she ignore?" Give them an inch on the small things and you'll end up having to go many an extra mile.

RULE 4 (SUBSECTION A) – CRISPS

Most schools have a 'no eating in lessons' rule. I'm not sure what I think of it. Personally, I wouldn't give a toss if it were allowed and kids delved greedy hands into crisp packets with the hand other to that with which they write. Indeed learning styles experts, (now there's an oxymoron for you) will tell you that these children have 'intake needs' and it will help them with their work if they are allowed to munch as they number crunch.

Whatever the truth of this, crisps can make speaking and listening activities messy, and if they are being assessed on these in front of an external moderator, then there's a good chance that they won't get the A* they so richly deserve. Moderators can be intolerant of being sprayed with the chewed up remains of potato masticated together with bad breath and saliva. So there's probably a very good reason that they're banned in lessons.

Given that this will probably be the rule in your school it is worth being hip to the major, crisp-related, wheeze kids employ: the *'hidingtheminajacketpocketand-pretendingtheyaren'ttthereatall,allthetimedelvingyourhandsurreptitiouslyintoa-forementionedpocketandbringingafingerfulofcrispstothemouththeneatingthem'* scam. To avoid being the dumb dupe in this affair, just be hip to it, and if you heard a rustle coming from someone's pocket, ask them for a crisp. This puts the child at their ease, thinking you are a card and will just take a crisp and return the packet to them, so they may munch away blameless for the rest of the lesson, now that teacher is complicit in their criminality. Surprise the perp by, just at the moment they offer the offending crisp packet to you, snatching it with lightning speed out of their hand and then performing one of three variations on a theme:

1. Eating the whole packet in front of them, then saying, "Thank you," perhaps even burping loudly afterwards to properly show your gratitude with the appropriate degree of ceremony.

2. Chucking the whole pack in the bin. (Reserve this 'shock and awe' technique for the utter scoundrel or serial recidivist).

3. Bringing the pack to your desk and saying they can have it back at the end of the lesson.

Which of these options you follow is entirely down to your professional judgement. Be wary, though, of eating the crisps of the very skinny kid wearing the haunted expression and the unwashed ankle swingers who thinks school dinners are great. It might be the only thing he'll eat all day. In this case, option 3 is the only morally acceptable path.

On this: it is worth having a few lunches with the kids in the canteen. Firstly, they're often better company than the staff and, secondly, it is well worth seeing which of the children tell you they love school dinners. Given that school dinners are generally prepared by people who think cigarettes are a vegetable, and are repulsive mulch you wouldn't feed to a pig, a child wolfing them down enthusiastically with snaffling relish will tell you something very important about that child: they are not properly looked after and you must take *extra-double, super-special* care of them in lessons, give them extra-double, super-special bucket-loads of praise, and allow them the odd occasion when they can take it all out on you without there being any reprisal from teacher whatsoever, because providing a distanced and self-protective form of love for those who don't get enough of it should be what you're there for, innit?

RULE 4 (SUBSECTION B) – FINISHING LUNCH AT THE BEGINNING OF THE FIRST LESSON AFTER LUNCH

This is one of those grey areas in which a teacher will be stuck with the 'allow it/ don't allow it' conundrum. I have given this issue due and deep consideration over the years, and my fruitily considered professional opinion is … allow it … grudgingly.

RULE 5 – NEVER EVER (AND I MEAN EVER) BELIEVE A SINGLE WORD A CHILD EVER SAYS TO YOU … AND YOU WON'T GO FAR WRONG

Children will defend any lie to any lengths. No matter how pointless the defence, no matter how little they gain from that lie, they will remain utterly tenacious in defending their innocence. They will run through a whole gamut of innocent, doe-eyed expressions and shrugs before going into grand displays of exasperation and indignation that their inviolable integrity has been brought into question by you, a lowly teacher, for God's sake!

It is disappointing when you finally realise the truth of this, but – and, trust me, I mean this – sadly, it is as certain as the fact that each crisp is made up of 0.015% of a potato and a full bucket of cooking oil. All children are born natural and extravagantly gifted liars. It is the one true talent that each and every one of them has been gifted by the gods in equal measure.

I witness the natural propensity for this gift in my own children. Bazzy, my eleven-year-old, has an uncanny ability at this complex talent. He will swear on his real dad's/granny's/dog's life that he didn't do it. He will defend the lie to the death. He will be utterly plausible. He will speak in measured and rational tones about why it would be pointless for him to do it. He will go into impassioned bouts of mock indig-nation. "So you are saying that if I admit that I lied, I won't have to go to bed early. But I didn't lie, and so you are asking me to lie to stay up. You are an unjust man. And

I shall not look after you in your old age!" he'll scream, tears flowing from his poor, gentle, innocent, oh-so-unjustly injured eyes.

The reason of course that I don't believe him is that I saw him do it.

The same thing applies with teaching. Children seem to think the fact that you were in front of them watching as, en masse, they put the pencil in Howard, the class victim's, ear and pushed – really hard – is merely circumstantial, and that no court in the land would even think of convicting them. They will be so utterly devout in their defence against the appalling violation in human rights that you have committed in calling the behaviour you witnessed, that you will begin to doubt your own eyes. Stop! That way madness lies. Trust yourself. You saw it. You are not an idiot. Be strong and carry through. Use a dismissive hand gesture, do not engage in any dialogue, be emphatic in your discipline, and then move on, quickly, to the learning.

The gentlemen and ladies who worship at the altar of neurolinguistic programming (NLP) have some insights into lying children which kind of work. I shan't go into the, cough, science of it, but NLPers claim that if someone right-handed is perpetrating a porkie, then their eyes will dart upwards and to the left before they answer (it is reversed if they are left-handed: their eyes go up and to the right). If you suspect a child is lying to you about something, then ask them first whether they are left or right handed (or better still hand them a pencil and see what hand they take it with, as they'd probably lie about that too), look directly into their eyes and ask them whether they did it. If their eyes dart upward and to the appropriate side for their brain organisation, then call them on the lie. If they keep your own eyes locked in a steely gaze, call them on the lie too (this is also considered to be evidence that they are constructing a memory).

It is entirely possible that this is all a crock. However, whatever the truth of it, gazing directly into a child's eyes with a sense that you have some methodology for doing so may well intimidate the errant little fib-monger enough for him or her to 'fess up. In any case it lets them know that you are not a pushover and you take lying seriously.

All children lie. However, kids' parents can find it very difficult to take in this ever so simple piece of information. I have lost count of the number of times I've heard a mum or dad passionately, and with fierce (not to say violent) conviction, intone this same phrase, "My Billy (it's always Billy) doesn't lie. He never lies. He's just not capable of it," to be greeted by a near imperceptible cough from teacher, and, an, "Erm. I think he is," or, "Well, we're all entitled to little one-offs, aren't we?" Stand your ground here. It can be easy to back down to the irate parent. (They rather enjoy scaring teachers, I think, particularly if they didn't much enjoy school themselves, or if they are middle managers in financial institutions and think that the multifaceted skill of teaching their children how to walk like men in the world is, in fact, far inferior to crunching numbers into a spreadsheet whilst wearing a Next suit that is the definition of average). If you back down, not only will you have done the child himself no favours, but it will be all over the school by break-time the next day, "Sir, you got bare[2] mash-up[3] by Billy's dad innit?"

What, then, is the correct answer to the appallingly aggressive question that you will most certainly be asked at some point in the first term: "Are you calling my son a liar?" It is, "Yes. Now sod off. I've got marking to do."

RULE 6 – ONE PERSON SPEAKING AT A TIME

This rule is cardinal really. It's where new teachers can really struggle. Its import is utter, and its implementation comes with a couple of hard and fast rules that you *must* follow religiously. It is of no use following the rules in a tokenistic manner, nor is it any use doing only half of it. If you want to be any good you have to do all the following.

If you allow a single child ever to speak at the same time as you do, then you are not going to be a good teacher. I'm sorry to be so emphatic about this. It doesn't sit comfortably with me, but you must trust teacher on this one.

---

2 Bare = street slang for "very."

3 Mash-up = street slang for "beaten up."

Let's put ourselves in one of those crass role-plays that bored-to-tears British Telecom clerks have to suffer on their rare customer service training days. You are the teacher.

Imagine that you are in front of a new class and are about to introduce a scintillating piece of knowledge. First, you share the lesson objectives with your class, "By the end of this lesson," you begin to declaim, a coiled spring ready to impart the joy of learning, "you will be ..." But before you get to the words, "able to" a boy in the back row turns to his mate and quietly mouths the phrase, "Your mum." His mate doesn't respond, and really you could get through the whole of the objective without there being any further infraction, and he didn't say it very loud.

Do you?

a.   Carry on.

b.   Stop.

The answer is implicit in the first paragraph of this section. If you carry on you have given the whole class a lesson you really don't want them to have learned. You have set up the expectation that it is OK for them to talk when you are doing so. This is the first miniscule chink in the dam that will inevitably lead, in four weeks time, to the tsunami of the uncontrollable class. You must call him on it. It may seem trivial to you. It may seem petty. But this is where you let it be known that you are serious about being a good teacher for them. (Remember, it is *for them* that you want to be a good teacher). Stop. Chuck a slightly astonished teacher look his way (you will become, within a short period of time, a masterful manipulator of the quizzical arch of the eyebrow), and then calmly intone. "OK. I'll start again." And go back to the beginning.

This technique requires nerves of steel and balls as big as Brazil. Because there is a good chance some wag will recognise that you are using it, and will exploit the opportunity, by deliberately coughing or by turning to their mate and emitting an utterance just so as to make you go back to the beginning. Do not panic here. It is a simple rite of passage. They are seeing how far you can be pushed before you crack. Much like gangland Los Angeles, the classroom is a region where the person prepared to go the furthest wins. It is the drug dealer who is prepared to dispense summary and brutal justice to his competitors who eventually runs the town; equally, the spoils of victory are available to the teacher who shows that they too have no limits. Remain utterly calm. Preternaturally so. The perp desires your anger. Give him none. Every time you are interrupted, admonish the perp and go back to the beginning, calmly starting again. Be prepared for this ludicrous ballet to play out four or five times before the class get the message. (There may be the odd occasion that, if presented with a particularly spirited class, you may have to be prepared to sacrifice a whole lesson of their education for them to learn the one lesson that will benefit all of you throughout the year's passage: that sir or miss is not to be interrupted when they are speaking). But go into the lesson assured of the fact that it will eventually play out.

This is not just a first lesson technique however. It is a career long challenge. There was a story put about by the French Decadents of an aristocrat who was so ennui-ridden at having to put on clothes every single morning that he committed suicide. There are certain aspects of teaching that will make you empathise with monsieur le froggy aristo. As with telling kids to get rid of the chewing gum, you will become heartily bored of telling children that they are not to speak when you are speaking. But you must do it.

The most important portions of the lesson for this mastery to be employed are at the beginning, of course, and, equally as importantly, when you are managing a transition.

The ability to manage a swift and smooth transition is one of the most important technical skills any teacher has in their possession. A transition occurs in the gap between one activity and the next, and being able to make these seamless is simultaneously much more difficult than you'd imagine and much easier than it feels at first.

Effective transition management relies on four pieces of expert technical knowledge:

1.   Recognising when it is time to halt the activity.

2.   Insisting on pens down.

3.   Insisting students look at you.

4.   Pause before speaking.

RULE 6 (SUBSECTION A) – RECOGNISING WHEN IT IS TIME TO HALT THE ACTIVITY

This is simple as Cup-a-Soup. The perfect moment to stop whatever activity your class are undertaking is two seconds after the first person has finished it.

Loads of new teachers get this so, so, so, so, so, so, so very wrong. They will rationalise, not unreasonably, that they should give kids the chance to involve themselves in the task, or for the task to develop, and will make a judgement call that they'll stop the activity when half of the class are finished. Whilst this appears initially to the initiate to be an entirely reasonable piece of thinking, when examined it becomes the quintessence of dumb-arsed. In waiting for half the class to finish you have, by definition, left half of the class, albeit for a relatively brief time, with nothing whatsoever to do. Here, the beginner teacher maketh a particularly spiky rod for their own back. It is either the bright, high-achievers, or the naughties who think that snotting up on a piece of paper constitutes decent completion of the work you have given them to do, who will have finished first, and of all things, beware most the clever, or the naughty child, who, in a room full of their mates, has nothing whatsoever to do. For they are creative of mind and will find something to do; something that is likely to be decidedly off-curriculum.

Think about it another way. In leaving kids with nothing to do you, the teacher, are perpetrating a crime. You are leaving a bright and lively young mind underemployed, fallow and dozing. Schools and lessons are meant to inspire, to stimulate, to excite and enliven passions and interests. They are not meant to leave kids sitting Scheiße-bored, in a room, waiting nearly half an hour for their slower mates to catch up.

If you do this, then you are playing to the lowest common denominator. And that's a particularly heinous crime in an education system blighted by what an American politician called, "The soft bigotry of low expectations." So, whatever the task, be it copying down learning objectives from the board, or translating Einstein's theory of relativity into Aramaic, either have some fruity extension work planned for those who finish first, or stop the activity the moment the first person finishes.

Both solutions have their attractions. However, since this book is about how to be a brilliant teacher without completely destroying your life, the second is the one I'd recommend. It has the side benefit that it sets up an expectation that all tasks will be completed with a degree of urgency: since we are working to the pace of Timothy, the boff, kids with a slightly less professorial bent are required to up their game.

RULE 6 (SUBSECTION B) – INSISTING ON PENS DOWN

In my first year as a teacher, as the school was in special measures, all the newly qualified teachers were subject to a series of observations from local authority advisors. Normally, more experienced staff will treat these people as if they are in possession of a particularly virulent form of leprosy. Many LA advisors are merely the automaton personification of the phrase, "A waste of tax payers' money." However, this guy, from the top of his shoulder-length, grey hair to the tip of his finely appointed pink cuff, was evidently something special. After witnessing a lesson I had taught, in which no one learnt anything at all, he leant over conspiratorially and breathed in my ear a piece of advice, which, he told me, many years previously, had been the best piece of teaching advice anyone had ever given him. He held it before me on a metaphorical platter decorated in ornate gold leaf, certain that he was inviting me into some arcane teachers' subgroup of the Magic Circle. And, many years later, I hold this self same piece of advice out to you, in the same spirit of the experienced, old lag giving the potentially talented initiate the keys to the kingdom of teaching heaven. You must take it as a very serious piece of advice from someone who has seen the depths of what can go wrong if you fail to follow it. And that piece of advice is (cue the roll of drums) …

When you are managing a transition, or when you are speaking, insist that not a single student has a pen in their hand.

Applause. Fanfares. Fireworks. "Yes" the dear reader cries. "It's all so obvious now. What an idea. The keys to teaching heaven are truly mine I tell you."

Yeh, I know, it's disappointing after such a build-up. But ...

It *really bloody* works.

It may seem counter-intuitive, but if a child has a pen in their hand, they are not listening to you. "How can this be?" the dear reader's inner monologue screams. "The hands and the ears are not connected. Surely this is rubbish." "Do not question, the truth," nods Yoda sagely. "It merely is. Your questions do not alter it."

I think how it works is that the pen is another focus point for the students. Pens are distracting. If you had a wheezy bore going on at you, and you had a pen in your hand, you'd probably, maybe unconsciously, do some thing (yes, I know it's ordinar-ily oneword)[4] with it. You'd tap it, put it in your mouth, catch up with recording the learning objectives, do a bit of scribble, write the name of the boy or girl you not so secretly fancy on the front cover of your book; you'd stick it in your ear, then stick it in your mouth, see how it tastes; you'd click the pen top with your thumbnail, see how far it stretches before it breaks; you'd stick your pinky in the pen top so it makes a charming, circular indetention at the top of your finger; you'd see if, by blowing in it and putting your finger over the single, small hole in the clear plastic, you could make it into a flute; or you'd contemplate the fact that writing with it distracts from its real function: that of blowing chewed up bits of paper through the tube onto Howard's bare neck. You'd do anything. Anything, that is, apart from listen to the teacher.

There's probably some sound neuroscientific reason why we don't listen too well when we've got a pen in our hand. All I know is that getting them all to put their pens down before I speak, is one of the best things anyone has told me about teaching. You should take it seriously. When managing a transition, or starting a lesson, insist that no child has a pen in their hands. Follow through with this. Kids won't challenge it, as politely intoning the question, "Could you just put your pens down for a second?" is not, in any way, an unreasonable or confrontational request. But you definitely don't

4 This a joke. I am aware that it is not even remotely funny.

go on with the 'teacher, she speaks' bit of the lesson until such point as all pens are out of hands. This sets up an expectation that carries through to all of your lessons: that when teacher speaks we put our pens down and we listen.

You'll find that some of the kids, particularly boys, cop a deaf 'un to your first request. Just repeat it to the whole class, and then pick them off one by one. "Ben, pen down please. James, pen please. Olu, would you be so kind as to put your pen down please, we're ready to move on." This is best delivered entirely sotto voce. Kids not doing it first time is not some wild act of rebellion, and you shouldn't get cross about it. They are probably just trying to catch up. In which case, recognise this explicitly, "I'm delighted that you're so into your work, but if you could put your pen down, now please ..." And sure enough with gentle persistence, you can launch into the next stage of managing the transition, which is ...

RULE 6 (SUBSECTION C) – INSISTING STUDENTS LOOK AT YOU

This goes hand in hand with the pens down rule. It follows immediately after, and further ensures that, when teacher speaks, it is not to backs of heads, but to faces and eyes lit up in rapt wonder.

It's quite simple. When everyone has put their pen down, you request that they look directly at you. The same thing applies regarding process: you start with a request to the whole class, then pick off stragglers one by one with gentle requests. With this, it also helps to use gesture and to employ a little of the technique Bill Rogers identifies as 'take-up time'. When a child's head is pointing the other way, you call their name, wait until they turn towards you, then waiting two seconds, before making eye contact and mouthing the phrase, "Turn 'round," and holding your hand out and making a gesture that, in the surreal parallel universe of the classroom would suggest that instruction, but anywhere else would be taken for a drunkard's poorly achieved impression of an epileptic spider failing to negotiate a hairpin bend.

HOW TO TEACH

Once you have all the kids in the class with their pens down and looking at you, you launch into the final technical stage of managing the transition. Which is ...

RULE 6 (SUBSECTION D) – PAUSE BEFORE SPEAKING

In teaching, as in life, you can get away with a lot if you've got a decent sense of rhythm. The rhythmic aspect of teaching is much underrated and little talked about, but it exists; expert teachers have an almost instinctive sense of the 'groove' aspect of their performance. They'll use pause and punctuation, consciously, in order to manipulate their students into certain modes of response. It is the use of the former of these that is the final element of managing a transition well.

It's this simple: once you have pens down and everyone looking at you, wait. Once you have waited, wait a little more ... then stretch the pause slightly ... hang around a bit ... wait a little ... then ... (long pause) ... speak. In doing this, you've assured that the focus is entirely on you, and that you haven't rushed it, losing the attention that has been so hard won before you've done anything with it. It also sets up the rhythm of your teaching. If you blast in, at a million miles an hour, you'll transmit nervousness or agitation to your charges and you'll get the same emotion back from them. If, however, you take a little breathing space before you start teaching, or introducing a task, then slide in, leisurely, laconic and quizzically interested at the fascinating fare you are about to deliver, again, you'll get back what you give out.

WHAT DO YOU DO WHEN IT ALL GOES WRONG?

Despite the fact that you have followed every suggestion contained in this chapter to the letter; despite the fact that you are the steeliest of all hands, sheathed in the silkiest of satin gloves; and despite the fact that you plan beautiful learning experiences, properly differentiated for every single lesson, it is guaranteed that something will go wrong. Every day.

Schools are great hubs of humans living far too close together. Some of these humans (mainly students) have lives outside of school, and these lives have a tendency to impinge on the way they perform in the school environment. I've written this book in the evenings after school, and just today I've taught a lovely sixteen-year-old-girl, who is pregnant, and whose weight loss issues worry me; a young man whose mother is dying; another young lady whose mother recently died and whose father is going to pieces; as well as countless children whose chemical addiction to PlayStation or XBox is keeping them up way past any reasonable person's idea of bedtime, and destroying whatever chances they had in life. (Nice one Sony. Another life ruined, another percentage point of a shekel on the dividend). And then they come to school, and we expect them to function, and are cross when they are unable to. The children you teach are human beings. They are fragile.

Here is a fact. Not every person who is married at the time of reading this book will still be married in five years' time. Imagine please: how would the medieval, emotional landscape of divorce affect how you perform at work? How about bereavement? How about not having a bed to sleep in? How about being pregnant at fourteen? How about being' routinely brutalised by your parents? How about having seen your parents murdered somewhere in Angola when you were six? How about being sexually abused by someone in your family? How about living on your own in a completely different country where you know no one and your whole family is dead?

Someone quite early on in my career asked me a taxing question, which caused me to chew my lips, for several minutes before they put me out of my misery. The question: "How many children in British schools have special needs?"

The answer: "All of 'em."

Remember this, and cut them some slack when you are able to. See your pupils as individuals operating under pressures unique to them. Look to find the person behind the behaviour: the person that you like, who made you laugh yesterday and who, you suspect, is having a tough time at the moment, and speak to them. There is a reason behind every piece of bad behaviour. Find out what that reason is before steaming in with punitive measures.

Other than attitude, there are a few tricks that you should learn. The first of which is:

GRADATIONAL/ASSERTIVE/NON-CONFRONTATIONAL DISCIPLINE

All school discipline policies are founded on the gradational nature of consequences. Do a small thing once, you'll get a warning. Do a small thing twice, you'll be told to move chair. Do a small thing three times, you'll be asked to stand at the side of the room. Four times and you'll stand outside it for a couple of minutes. Stab someone and you'll get excluded and sent to Feltham. (A word on Feltham. If you work in London you'll hear hushed whispers about Feltham. It is the schoolboy equivalent of Pleasure Island in *Pinocchio*, only there's markedly less pleasure involved. There ain't no entertainment and the judgements are severe).

Gradational/assertive/non-confrontational discipline (level 1) – The initial 'body language' telling-off

Where a student is talking when you are talking, or when they are off-task and you want them on, then it is time to dust off your array of telling-off techniques.

Dispensing a telling-off is actually a far more subtle and multifaceted skill than you might think. Just yelling, "Marcus, stop it with the talking already, you naughty boy," at the top of your voice isn't going to cut it. Firstly, in shouting not only do you add to the noise in the room, but you show that you have lost control, which is never a good signal to be putting out. Secondly, in upbraiding Marcus in such a public manner you humiliate him, and that too is bad. Finally, enough with the cod-Yiddish argot already.

The preferred options here rely on a variety of micro-gestures and moves that let Marcus know he is a wrong 'un, without you so much as emitting a murmur.

1. The mono-brow raise. Use your Irish heritage and your unpalatably high forehead to good effect by raising both brows in unison and crinkling up that forehead, so it resembles the contours of a relief map of a particularly high mountain. Combine this quizzical look with a slight micro-nod of the head

in the direction of the offender. He will rediscover a life-long love of learning instantaneously.

2.   Narrow your eyes. The Turks have a phrase for this, "Fazonki!" Which makes sense really. If a Turkish gent approached you in the street and uttered the phrase in your direction, you would, of course, immediately obey the instruction (whether or not you knew what it meant).[5] This technique is used for the more surreptitious or serial offender, and is appropriate for weaselling out if something naughty is going on. You point your gaze directly into the eyes of the perp. It lets them know that you know something is occurring. You might not know exactly what it is, but your spidey sense is tingling, and the fact that you don't know what it is shouldn't be any impediment to the perp stopping doing that 'whatever-it-is' soonish to now.

3.   Proximity. Otherwise known in professional circles as 'standing slightly too close to'. If there's a pair of naughties having a chat about the football when they should be having a chat about the phallic symbolism in the mise en scene of *Charlie and the Chocolate Factory*, then just go and stand in their immediate vicinity. They'll start talking about what they are meant to straightaway. It's a great one this. What is particularly brilliant about it is that it is entirely unconfrontational. Not even the hardest nut to crack is going to throw their rattle out of the pram on the basis that you have stood near them. Highly recommended.

If you are dealing with the kind of pupil who has a stubborn and righteous commitment to off-task behaviour, then it is well worth teacher's time to grab a chair, and to sit on it – all the while appearing leisurely and blithe, utterly comfortable and entirely unconcerned – in the vicinity of the offender. Use of this 'sitting slightly too close to' technique early on in your relationship with a class is, again, highly recommended. It sends out several messages. Not the least of which is that sir or miss is a seriously experienced professional and is not to be messed with: kids are hip to the fact that only teachers with a mature command of behaviour management ever use 'sitting slightly too close to', and

---

5 *This is all complete and utter cobblers by the way.*

its use suggests to them that you are wise in matters of off-task behaviour and will not easily be fobbed off. It is quite important here that you don't communicate with the student in any direct way, and that you give them a beaming grin as you are doing it. The smile lets them know who is boss in double quick time, as well as letting them know that you are so utterly experienced that you are aware of the mess that any unnecessary confrontation can get a teacher into, and you are not in a hurry to go there.

You must stay in position here substantially longer than feels strictly necessary. Smiling all the while. Sparing use of this technique will have you marked out as a top professional.

4.   Point them in the direction of the work. It's as simple as that really. This one is really effective and entirely reasonable. Just point at the work. It works well with a mini version of the mono-brow raise, and is doubly effective when combined with 'standing slightly too close to'. Kids know that they are there to work and will more readily accept this, throwing away their assumed right to misbehave, if you point them in the direction of the work. If you challenge the behaviour instead of the fact that they are not doing any work, then you are more than likely to be walking into a tinderbox, which could ignite things you'd prefer to stay inert.

Gradational/assertive/non-confrontational discipline (level 2) – The slightly more serious telling-off

This is best done outside of the classroom. To give a child a too-stern talking-to in front of his peers makes him feel 'boyed',[6] and there is a good chance that his mates will strike up into a chorus replete with vicious, see-saw mockery. "You've been *told*," they will taunt. This is not a pleasant thing for any child to undergo, and you should do your best to avoid walking into any situation that will cause a child to feel

---

6 Boyed = street slang for 'treated as if he were a small child'.

humiliated. Far better you take them briefly outside of the classroom and speak to them like you would speak to a normal human being. Speak calmly, but firmly. Look them directly in the eye and point them back in the direction of the work. Start with praise, "Last week the work you produced in the lesson was absolutely phenomenal. But I don't feel you are properly focused on your work in this lesson. I'd very much like the young man I enjoy teaching back in this lesson, please. Are we agreed? Or do you need to wait outside to think about things?" Pause briefly, then recap. "So we are agreed that when you get back in the lesson you are going to get cracking (pause) with (pause) the (pause) work? (Double pause). Good."

This way the child has not been made angry, has not lost any face and has been treated by the teacher as a human being worthy of respect. Often they will go back in and get on with things.

However, this is the point at which employing the persona of Mr or Miss Lovely-person stops. You have behaved professionally and have given the student the option to correct their behaviour and return their focus to the work. If they reject this opportunity, you have little option but to ramp it up a bit further, using the all-time teacher classic technique of ...

Gradational/assertive/non-confrontational discipline (level 3) – The either/or rule

"Either you take your finger out of his ear, or I am going to break all your fingers." Works every time.

Actually, it's not much more sophisticated than that.

If you have had sufficient respect for a child's human dignity to have a chat with them outside the class and they immediately renege on their promise to behave, then you must give the perpetrator a choice. "Either," for example, "you desist with your continued, wilful and conscious sabotaging of everyone else's learning, consequently their education, consequently their chances of a happy and successful life; or I am going to break your fingers with a blunt metal implement." Works every time.

They don't stop until such point as they've been given a hearty sandwich of knuckle, but on receipt of such you'll find they're less inclined to interrupt.

The point of this is not to lever yourself in the position where you get to dust off the thumb screws (you'll most likely get called into the head's office if you do), but to ensure that it is the child who has the power over their decisions. None of us enter teaching to be nasty to kids, and the teacher who actually enjoys punitive discipline is relatively rare, thankfully (though not as rare as you'd hope), and so giving them the choice to avoid it, to dig themselves out of the hole, is only right and proper. The finger action bit is to be used less than never. Generally speaking, it is considered more professional to offer the option to quit the disruptive behaviour forthwith, or you'll compel them to move seat.

Gradational/assertive/non-confrontational discipline (level 4) – Moving seat

Provided it all goes smoothly, this is the most ruthlessly efficient of all classroom management techniques. In an ideal world, if you have already given an initial 'body language' telling-off, you've had a word outside the classroom and you've dispensed a final warning in the form of an either/or choice, and the child has chosen the 'or', then you would simply instruct them to move seat, and they would meekly comply. In truth, this is what happens *some* of the time: the child silently crosses the room and takes their place in the chair on which you have asked them to sit. And, from thence, the mild behavioural issues they have presented in the lesson disappear.

There are steps that can be taken to ensure this is the most likely path, using the silent and deadly communication art of body language. Body language works best in such areas because we are moving into shallow seas, under which lie the rocks of potential confrontation, and whilst as a teacher you must be prepared for confronta-tion, you shouldn't be inviting it in and making up a spare bed for it. Using your voice in giving a student a firm instruction that is expressly *not* to be disobeyed in public lets the whole class know what is happening; therefore it causes the student to lose face in front of their peers. They are instantly under threat of public humiliation and will go into fight or flight mode. We don't want that as teachers. We lose then. The kid disappears into anger, and all hell can break loose.

Communicating with the body alone is secret. The rest of the class don't necessarily pick up on it, the student in question is not humiliated and is, therefore, more likely to accede to your instruction. If instructing a child who has broken the rules three times, despite the fact that you've been nice and understanding and given them chances and all that, then you should hold the chair out you want them to sit at, beckon them with one forefinger, pointing to the seat of the new chair with that same finger. Most times they will do what you have asked them to, because you have asked nicely.

However, it doesn't always work. Where the instruction has not been obeyed, then a very good (though occasionally risky) option, if you perceive it to be safe to do so, is to gently and calmly take their exercise book and to put it onto the desk at which you want them to sit. If they stay stubbornly seated, then they are explicitly breaking a school rule. It is the teacher who decides who sits where and not the student. If they remain dogged in their desire to subvert this rule things get serious. If a child point-blank refuses to move chair, then you must skip three levels and go immediately to level **8**.

Gradational/assertive/non-confrontational discipline (levels 5, 6 and 7) – Moving away from the table/standing up/moving to the corner of the room

All the classroom discipline manuals will tell you (so I've heard; I've never read one) that if you have asked a child to move seat and they have been compliant, but it has not altered their penchant for low level disruption, then you should then ask them to move their seat away from the table at which they are now sitting. You can try this. It might work. I tried this occasionally in my early years in the classroom. It did work sometimes. But it's a bit babyish.

If you do this and they still manage to be disruptive, you should ask them to stand up. If they have stood up and they are still naughty – perhaps they do a sarcastic dance in the style of your most easily satirised traits at this point – then you should ask them to take their chair and sit in the corner of the room.

I tend to skip these stages in assertive discipline. They are a step too far in the direction of teacher-as-Supernanny-wannabe to be employing with kids who already have profitable careers in black market, smokeable items. Besides, if the student has moved seat and continues to chat about how brilliant his XBox is, then they are clearly taking the piss, and level **8** is now to be got out of its box, dusted off and employed with both vigour and fortitude.

However, if you are to be the kind of teacher who finds it relatively easy to have a comfortable, positive, jokey relationship with their students, then you can employ a correlative of these techniques with some success. Getting a student to stand looking out of the window for a pre-defined number of minutes (two-and-a-half is a useful amount of time here) focusing intently on a piece of dirt you have identified for him as being of particular noteworthiness, can pay substantial dividends. It lets both him and the class know who is boss; and it does so without unnecessary conflict. The perp will think focusing on the piece of dirt to be a perfectly happy alternative to the boring work they would otherwise be required to do, and will happily accede to your request. The fact that you have asked him to do this brings levity where ugliness might have reigned, and you will have made your point.

Gradational/assertive/non-confrontational discipline (level 8) – Standing outside the classroom

Level **8**. The nuclear option. If you have been either absurdly patient to the point of shooting yourself in the foot, all to no reward, or you have got pissed off at level 4 and jumped right into nuclear mode, then you are left with little option but to send the perpetrator outside of the classroom, so that they may contemplate their behaviour and its impact on others.

As with all behaviour management techniques there are two lines of possibility here: either it works, in which case, award yourself three gold stars and enjoy a silent shout of, "Yippee," or it doesn't, in which case several demerits and a loud chorus of "Boo."

Because when this one doesn't work it bombs with a vengeance. This one has to be treated with a real sense of what can possibly go wrong here, and what you can do if you have accidentally manoeuvred yourself into a lose-lose situation.

First, the positive. Generally, you will give an instruction in a firm tone, accompanied by emphatic body language (the 'single hand cutting the air in a downwards motion' hand technique patented by Lionel's brother, Tony, at various party conferences, stating emphatically that a series of heinous war crimes perpetrated on innocents was the only morally valid decision, is of use here). That instruction might be, "OK. Could you step outside for a bit please Michael?" Or it might be, "Right. I've had enough. Outside please." Note the politeness of the request. There is a school of thought in behaviour management circles that such politeness makes it a request rather than an instruction, and it is therefore more likely to result in the child turning that request down. This is cock. Manners cost nothing. The use of "please" here gives you a very useful backup argument: "I've been polite to you. I've been respectful. You are not treating me, a teacher, with the same respect that I am giving you." This can be a useful way of dealing with what are known in the trade as 'secondaries' (arguing, not with the fact that they have been badly behaved, but with the way you are managing the incident). Besides, being polite is actually a veil over the fact that you are actually ordering the student to do something, with very little 'or else' with which to back yourself up. If you are confrontational it is always wise to sheathe it in something more attractive. A polite, but emphatic request is more likely to achieve your aim than a confrontational instruction. You catch more flies with honey than with vinegar, as my dear old mum never said.

An important note here: if you have a pupil standing outside of the room, do not leave them there for a half hour, and don't, under any circumstances, entirely forget that they are there. This, and I don't believe I've used this word since I was seven, is nincompoopery. A beginner teacher who routinely leaves kids outside of the class for way, way too long quickly acquires a reputation as a teacher who is not coping well with behaviour, and you don't want this. In many ways teaching is quite an unpleasantly macho profession. If you are seen to be someone who is not managing behaviour, then, in today's climate, it will not be very long before you find you are in receipt of a slew of 'developmental' observations, which have a reporting structure up to the boss; the intent of which is to gather evidence as to whether you are not up to the job and have to be dispensed with.

If you send a student outside and they consent, then at the first possible opportunity (for this, read more or less immediately) go outside and have a chat with them. You leave the door ajar, and attempt somehow to place yourself so that you still have one leg in the classroom, and can still make your presence felt on the behaviour of the rest of the classroom. In speaking to the offender, be emphatic, but reasonable, and remember you are talking to a human being (no matter how dodgy their behaviour has been). "Right. You have been completely off it in this lesson. You haven't given me your best at all. What's wrong?" You may find that by asking a reasonable human question that you get a perfectly reasonable human answer, "I'm sorry, sir. I'm really tired today. There's loads of bad stuff happening at home." Or, "I don't know what's wrong, miss. I'm just having an off lesson." Often the slightest scratch of the surface will find that the child has either been getting up at five-thirty am for the past five weeks because their parents have moved away from the catchment area of the school and can't get them into another one, or you'll find that they are now living with their grandmother because their mum and dad have split up, or something equally horrendous. More often than this, however, you'll find out that they have no parental control at all and they have been playing PlayStation until three o'clock in the morning. Whatever the reason, once you have found it out, you have to use your professional judgement to decide on how you proceed.

This, of course, is when it all goes right. But sending a child out of a room is a path riddled with potential potholes, the first of which it is best to be forewarned about, as forewarned is better than ... y'know.

Gradational/assertive/non-confrontational discipline (level 8) – Standing outside the classroom. Subsection 1: The coat, the bag, the push in the chest

If you have instructed a child to stand outside of the classroom, and they pick up their coat and their bag, you've got trouble. This will happen a lot. And you need to have a plan for it. The plan may not work, but being aware that it is likely to happen will save you the shock on its first appearance as the serial recidivist's naughty boy tactic of choice.

The first key thing here is to be hip to it early on. If a student is intent on taking their coat and bag outside, this is a very serious message to the teacher; a message which says, "If you think I'm going to stand outside waiting for you, you've got another thing coming, you ragged bag of spanners. I'm offski." It is a way for them to save face in front of their peers. They have acceded to your request to step outside of the room but, in very publicly taking the means of running off home with them, they've also left a parting message that the teacher is a twat. If you let them go outside having won this battle you will lose face yourself and, just perhaps, some respect from the rest of the class. But it is very difficult to win this one. A naughty boy or girl who immediately reaches for bag and coat at this point is committed to rebellion and you will have to be very sharp indeed to shake them from their foul purpose.

The very moment they reach for their bag hold out your hand and offer to look after it for them. This immediately removes their prepared objection to leaving it. They were planning to say that they were not prepared to leave the bag in the room with their classmates because they feared theft from (or of) it. This is a sham. They were intending to bunk. Be plausible, open faced and genuine. Say, "No. Honestly, I wouldn't want anyone to mess with your stuff. I'll look after it."

This is your best chance of winning in this situation. If it works, and you get the bag, then don't worry about the coat. They'll probably leave this behind as well. If it doesn't work, then you have two options:

a.   You block the door (don't block the door).

b.   You let them leave (don't block the door).

If you let them leave, what is lost? Little. A child has walked out of your class to God knows where, hopefully to calm down. It is possible that they may return (possible, if unlikely). If you block the door, or their path to it, you are in a cage with an angry animal who clearly has no respect for the rules, who has just been put into fight or flight mode, for whom the flight option has just been blocked off and who will not lose their job if they get physical with you. If this happens it becomes a possibility that you may lose yours.

I mentioned earlier on in this chapter that I was physically assaulted twice by the same pupil in my first year of teaching. (The fact that it had to be twice before he was excluded is a sad indictment of the lack of respect for teachers in this country). But it was my fault. I blocked the door.

There are points in every teacher's professional life when they see their career flash before their eyes. The times this has happened to me have been caused by one particular mistake: blocking the door. It is tempting, given that the student child is publicly undermining your authority, when they attempt to leave the room with coat and bag in hand, to make a vain attempt to re-assert that authority. And it works sometimes. You block the door. The child is duly humiliated, and they return to their seat, perhaps exactly as humbled as you might think it is only right, just and proper that they be. This is what happens when it goes right. But when it goes wrong, it goes very wrong indeed, and you are in serious danger of losing your job!

If you are male, your instinctive reaction to someone pushing you in the chest might be to lamp them one. (If you are female you might feel inclined to tell all their (or better still, your) friends that they are an incompetent lover). This was how my body would have reacted when Mick pushed me if the mouldering, cranial, cauliflower part of it hadn't overruled it; I felt the urge, for a split second but, thankfully, in the process of raising my hands, the brain got a danger message through to the hands. So that rather than curl up into a fist, the fingers splayed, and I held them up, just as a prisoner at gunpoint might do in a 1950s' western. It is an unpleasant feeling to have your hands held up as someone who has just assaulted you takes another potshot. It is a deeply unpleasant feeling to have this happen in front of a group of young people who you are meant to be educating. It is even more unpleasant to be perceived a victim when you have the tools to correct this assumption but are not allowed to use them. But be assured you cannot.

None of this stuff would have happened if I hadn't tried to snatch the coat from Mick and, absolutely, it wouldn't have happened if I hadn't blocked the door. Don't do it. It isn't worth it. Let 'em go.

Gradational/assertive/non-confrontational discipline (level 9) – Detenzione

In the first school I taught in I think I went through a period of about three or four years without ever setting a single detention. I could never get teachers' fondness for them. "What? A kid misbehaves, and I have to stay late. Rough justice indeed milord."

Don't get over-attached to detentions. They don't really work. Sure, if it's the lesson before lunch or the last lesson before home time, then it's OK to keep them behind for a bit and let them stew, but the administrative side of setting detentions for any other class is a nightmare, and you can bet your backside kids will bunk them, causing you no end of grief, paperwork and hassle in a futile attempt to ensure that the recidivists are punished. The solution to this is don't set them. They are too much of a nuisance.

If, however, the occasion presents itself and you are in a position, with the last class of the day, to detain serial offenders, there are a few secrets that are worth knowing. Firstly, be assured that detention is a time for you to be an utter fascist. Sitting in a classroom with the naughties is not your preferred choice of things to be doing after school, when you could be either marking, laughing with your colleagues, or on the bus homewards. It is not something you do for the pleasure of it …

But you must make it appear as if it is. One of the most useful things an old lag ever told me about teaching was the following phrase, "If you're not enjoying their punishment, it isn't working."

"What?" I hear you scream. "I bought this book because I believe in the innate goodness of children, but the bloke who's written it is clearly a psychopathic sadist!" In schools, the uncomfortable idea of sadism being the new liberalism actually has some purchase. Allowing your inner sadist to inform your approach in detentions (and in detentions alone) can pay substantial dividends.

Detenzione is the arena in which the tables are well and truly turned. Dismiss the ruly members of the class in the order of their ruliness. Howard first, so he can rush home before the school bully catches him to dispense yet another brutal wedgie; then the kids who have done particularly well; followed by those who've done adequately;

decidedly not followed by those who have sabotaged everyone else's learning and, in doing so, lost the right to being treated like normal human beings – along with the right to go home on time.

At the point you have just the naughties remaining sit down on a chair near the door (not directly in front of it – remember, don't block the door) and instruct them either to get back to work or to get busy on some suitably thankless task that you have designed especially for just such an occasion. (Getting them to sharpen a whole box of coloured pencils is pleasingly soul destroying and comes with the added advantage of getting your coloured pencils sharpened. The truly consummate professional will ensure that all the leads are broken, giving the task has a gratifying impossibility).

We are dealing with a generation of children who are used to negotiating with their parent(s) and who find this a profitable way of doing business. They will attempt to negotiate with you. Don't. Detention is a scenario where the teacher's demands are non-negotiable. You must, however, be prepared for their laughable, stock attempts to get out of it.

Laughable, stock attempt to get out of detention 1 – "I've got to go to the dentists/doctors/opticians."

Suggested teacher response: "No you haven't. Sit down." They haven't. And even if they did, well these things are rarely a matter of life and death, and can be easily rearranged.

Laughable, stock attempt to get out of detention 2 – "I've got to pick up my baby sister."

Suggested teacher response: "No you haven't. Sit down." It's more difficult this one. Often, kids will have to pick up their younger siblings from school. It pays to do a little research on this. Ask two other children outside of the class whether it is the case. It is most likely, however, that it is a ruse, and most of those baby sisters will be in the safe, warm and comforting hands of a primary school in any case. Unless you have serious evidence to the contrary, don't allow it.

Laughable, stock attempt to get out of detention 3 – "I've got to go home."

Suggested teacher response: "Yeh, me too. Sit down." This is the phrase that accompanies the angriest outbursts. Here the kid is testing their will against yours. If you back down at this point you are handing over the keys to the kingdom to the instruments of darkness. Don't. They are seriously misbehaving at this point, and you should extend their detention by two minutes or so every time they utter this line.

Laughable, stock attempt to get out of detention 4 – "You can't keep me for longer than twenty minutes."

Suggested teacher response: "And those twenty minutes start the moment you are sitting down quietly. Sit down."

In the vital first few minutes of the detention it is of utter import that you stay, at all points, the consummate Nazi. The kids will test your resolve with every possible challenge to your authority they can muster; it is highly likely they will get quite passionate about it. At this point, they will show you their teeth in anger and some of these displays can be awe inspiring, even scary. You must show yours back. Smile at their worst excesses. Smile like you are enjoying it, and give no quarter. Your best technique is always to appear unthreatened and in control. No matter how extreme their behaviour gets, do not appear flustered. Gently and smilingly intone, "You wasted my time during the lesson and it is only fair that I waste your time now, I think." A slightly patronising half mono-brow raise works well here too.

Once you have all the perpetrators sitting quietly (and be aware that you may not be able to achieve this easily; you must tough it out) you speak to them individually. The form here is to dispense a quick telling-off that is in no way unfriendly, but is suitably stern and outlines your expectations for what goes on in your class. Having given the telling-off:

1. Ask for an apology.

2. Having received the apology, then ask them what they are apologising for? Everyone does this. I am not sure why. I think it serves a further twofold purpose: it's like a behavioural plenary in that it lodges both the nature of the crime and its future unacceptability in the criminal's head. Also, getting the child to clarify the apology they have just made seems unnecessary. And that, I suppose, is the point. In doing this you are giving a final cherry on the top of the 'don't sod about with sir or miss' cake.

You have an individual word with the kids in the reverse order of their unruliness. Unless, of course, someone has behaved appallingly during the detention, then poor behaviour in detention trumps whatever they may have done in lessons. Where you have several detainees and it has been a difficult and precarious session to run, it is time to play seriously dirty and to grope in the direction of 'extra'.

ON BEING 'EXTRA'

If it is your lot to work in the inner city, you will chance upon several phrases that will, initially at least, make no sense at all as they appear to be in an entirely new language. They are. One such is the concept of being 'extra'. Being 'extra' is a child's-eye understanding of the 'if you're not enjoying their punishment it's not working' maxim. If you have been seriously messed with during a detention, if kids have made bolts towards the door, have hidden under tables or have shouted at you, then you are in a worrying position. They are pushing you as far as they can to see what you are made of. The correct response here is to go 'extra'. This involves deliberately messing with their heads to prove who is boss, and requires a degree of mental dexterity. Ignore the twenty-minute detention rule, as this only starts when they are sitting quietly. In such a situation you are required to go (just a little) too far!

Ask a blinding series of questions that never stops. Ask the same question in subtly different ways for ten minutes. Launch into a lengthy and amused monologue about what you had for breakfast; alternatively, a tedious disquisition about what you think they may, or may not, have had for breakfast themselves. Talk about socks. Get them drawing a series of pairs of socks. Ask them to wonder aloud which socks would best suit which teacher. Have a discussion about who they think will be the first person you absent from the detention and why? Get them to guess your favourite tree and don't say yes until the fourteenth answer. Anything, in short, that is a total waste of their time, but is delivered as fun is what being 'extra' constitutes. When you are accused of being 'extra', apologise for your ignorance and, in a cut-glass, middle class accent say, "I'm genuinely sorry, but I really don't understand that term. You'll have to clarify it. By the way, how many cheeses can you name? The first one to write down ten gets out of detention straightaway."

When they have got the message you can flip from smiley maniac dispensing absurd tasks into stern teacher, and inform the miscreants that, in future, you expect the class to pay a great deal more respect to both you and to their education. Hold out a little longer, perhaps suggesting that once they have all been silent for two minutes they'll go home, then dismiss them individually. No blood has been spilt and you have sent a serious message without having been caused to lose the plot with the kids. The next day they will not hate you, but will have the message that they are not to behave like savages in either your lessons or the detentions you so rarely ever set.

EXTENDING DETENZIONE

It can be useful to write the kids' names on the board and alongside these the length of the detention they are to suffer: i.e. Jimmy – 7 minutes, Reg – 9 minutes, Amber – eternity. This is particularly worth doing in a fractious detention session. Remember to remind kids that the detention starts at the moment that they are seated quietly, and if they are not, then you start adding to the numbers on the board. Where a child is not settling at all or is seeking to negotiate with you, add two minutes, going to the board and crossing out the 5 next to their name, replacing it with a 7, then a 9 if they still fail to settle. Where behaviour is outrageous go straight in with the heavy guns and add five minutes on.

THE ULTIMATE SANCTION

Is ringing up their parents. You will find a variety of reactions to this threat which are broadly dependent on the ethnicity of the child. If you are working in a school where there are children of African heritage, often the threat of phoning up their parent(s) will be enough on its own. And you should think fairly long and hard before you actually pick up the phone. Without wanting to be too stereotypical, many of the taboos that, say, middle-class whites have regarding physical discipline can be regarded, somewhat paradoxically, as a form of child abuse in some communities. And if you ring the parents of some children you may be the catalyst to a fairly seriously unpleasant experience for them. Think before you do it.

There is a standard form when ringing home that will generally work to ensure that you don't get a mouthful of abuse when you call a child's parent(s) or carer(s). Praise first. It may be that the student in question is a complete horror who makes every teacher's day-to-day life a harrowing circle of hell, but remember, it is unlikely that this is what their mum or dad thinks of them. You would do well to remember that parents love their kids unconditionally and will not be grateful to you for storming straight in with a list of their faults. Broach these with some positive comment first, "Hello Mrs Thug. I'm Dave's embroidery teacher. He's been doing some fantastic work for me recently, and I love his cheeky sense of humour, but he's taken it a little bit far with Howard this lesson. I wonder whether you could have a little word with him that, perhaps, giving another student acupuncture in the eye isn't really what I expect from a nice young man like your son."

It pays to be nice. Mrs Thug will recognise that you like Dave, and that you have his best interests at heart and, as a consequence, will be more inclined to have a quiet word in his shell-like when he gets home. Whatever the result for Dave of you phoning home, the result for you will be indubitable: he will know that you carry out whatever threats you make, and will be less inclined to stab Howard in your next lesson.

On this point, it is vital that if you threaten some kind of sanction you carry through. Kids get hip pretty quickly to which teachers' threats mean something. Do not, at any point, say to a child, "And you know I mean it." If you say this, they will know you don't.

IN DEEPLY SERIOUS SITUATIONS

These happen. You may be lucky enough to work in a school or amongst students where the mortal sin is rare. It is within the bounds of possibility, however, that you will come across some pretty taxing moments early on in your career.

It is an entirely unreasonable expectation that teachers should allow themselves to be assaulted without any defence at all, and it may be that the difficult situation in which you find yourself is with a year 6 or 7 pupil whom you could take out quite easily, and who doesn't scare you at all. In this instance, you are legally allowed to use physical restraint.

If the child is going to damage themselves, another pupil, the school fabric or, most importantly, you; then you approach them from the back and wrap your arms around them. The idea here is that you are restraining them for their own good. Hitting, pulling hair and grabbing appendages are all out. If you are in this situation it is potentially career threatening. You must follow the letter of the law. Though, in such instances, you will generally find that your colleagues and the senior management team at the school are extremely supportive, you cannot afford any of the false allegations that may result as a result of your action to have any substance.

You are also legally allowed to use restraint with bigger kids, but it is inadvisable, as some of them can be very big indeed. I was advised once by a very experienced deputy head that if a child is invading your personal space in an aggressive and threatening manner, then you are within your rights to place both hands on their chest and push them back. This seems reasonable but, again, it is a risky strategy. Your best approach in moments of danger is to get into the corridor where any actions are public and can be seen, hopefully, by another member of staff. In extreme cases, you should also bring the class with you. If a kid has seriously lost the plot and is throwing chairs around, you have a duty, in loco parentis, to protect all the children in the class. By absenting all the kids, apart from the one who has lost it, and sending for senior management, you are providing that protection for all of them, including the kid chucking the chairs.

Many is the teacher who will tell you that you should never touch a child. And they have a point. You have no idea what that child's experience of the physical has been:

it may be an area in which they have had past trauma and, in entering that realm without permission, you are further damaging them. You will be protecting yourself by following this rule. However, in practice, it can be quite difficult to hold to this law in absolute terms. It may be that, after your relationship with your students has become one of trust, a guiding pat on the shoulder to congratulate a child on a great piece of work just seems to be the right thing to do. This, again, is down to your professional judgement. But it is probably advisable in your early months in the career, before you have actually managed to acquire any such judgement, that you obey the never touch a kid rule. And once you have acquired professional judgement you will realise that a key part of this is that you should certainly avoid touching a child who is not of the same gender as you.

One very useful technique when faced with a young person behaving completely beyond the pale, swearing at you, calling you names you would never have expected to hear coming from such a young mouth, is staying completely impassive and taking notes. This way you have a record of their manifold crimes that you can refer to when writing up the incident later. It also serves to put the power back in your hands. When a kid has gone completely rogue the worst part of it is the feeling of utter powerlessness: nothing you do or say has any impact, and it is generally in front of a group of young people whose respect you are going to need if you are going to teach them. By taking notes you are doing something that the rogue child realises is going to have some impact upon them. It also has a further pleasing element in that it infuriates them. Part of their going rogue was a display designed to show you up as powerless. By recording everything they do you put the power directly back in your hands, and the rest of the class will be able to see this.

CORRIDORS AND FIGHTS

There is a rule of thumb in British schools that your reputation in the school is made in the corridor, and it will be pretty obvious in your first few days at your first school which of your colleagues have acquired the kind of reputation that you would want. If a teacher is standing in the corridor and those wearing hats, immediately on seeing that teacher, take them off, then you'll know they have it pretty well cracked as regards behaviour. Achieving this status, however, is the result of hard work, and it won't come to you in the first week at a school. The temptation can be, on recognising that the senior teacher who appears well respected by the students is strict on every minor infraction in the corridor, to copy them. Don't (not immediately anyway). They may well have been at the school for a number of years and will have won their reputation over that time. You do not have the same status with the kids as a senior teacher, and there is a good chance that, in diving in and challenging every tiny piece of behaviour in the corridor, you will have manoeuvred yourself into a series of situations in which it is unlikely you'll win.

With building a 'rep' in the corridors, take it slow. In your first weeks experiment with challenging younger students who are wearing hats or indulging in bouts of horseplay. Experiment with intoning the word, "Hat" sharply, loudly and abruptly in no particular direction. See whether it works. Where there is horseplay, approach those indulging in it with a smile, placatory, both-palms-downwards gestures and politely request that they desist. Observe how the teachers you admire work the corridor and ease yourself into your practice in this area slowly. Above all, don't go in on your first day with all the restraint and subtlety of a Simon Le Bon vocal performance: it'll blow up in your face if you do.

One of the other things that can happen in the school corridor or playground is the fight. These separate into two subsections that require entirely different treatment: those in which only males are involved and those where the female of the species has unleashed her claws. The first is relatively easy to deal with. Make a double quick judgement call as to who is losing. Get between the two kids, wrap an arm around the one who is losing and take them away from it. Most boy fights feature two very scared young men who have been spurred into something they really don't want to be doing by their peers, and are absolutely desperate for the fight to be stopped. The one who is losing will not in any way seek to continue the fight, or resist your intervention once your caring and rescuing arm has intervened. They will be profoundly grateful – though they may not show it. You have probably saved them a serious beating and utter loss of face; take them right away from danger, and then you can mop up the afters and write a report as to what happened. Both kids will be temporarily excluded (which is madness, but seems to be the form in every school I've ever worked – institutions do not seem to care who started it) and you can go back to your work.

Girl fights are markedly different. If you storm into a girl fight without a bit of strategy it is highly possible you are going to get very badly hurt. In my career I've had the misfortune to witness a saintly EAL specialist have half his arm ripped off by a displeased young lady; I've seen pools of blood on the classroom floor spurting from the ear of a young man who had made the mistake of coming into too close contact with an angry pair of talons and I've accumulated a charming number of deep wounds on my own forearms which came with the added bonus of writing off a favourite shirt. In this realm the female of the species is indeed far, far deadlier than the male and your options are twofold:

1. Just let them kill each other.

2. Pause – think – act.

The first one, tempting though it may be after you've been in the middle of your first pair of spitting banshees and attempted, vainly, to protect your face from the dervish-like whirl of teeth, nails, spittle and hair, is not really an option. But, if you are going to intervene, don't do it immediately. You have only one chance, and so your intervention must be decisive. Pause briefly, locate the hands of the girl who is winning, and make a decisive grab for her wrists, using your weight to push her away from the other girl. It might work. If it doesn't you're probably going to need stitches, so don't just fire in blindly.

KNIVES

I have never come across a knife in a school, although I've heard of them being used. It is unlikely that you will ever have to deal with one of these. If you do my advice would be to walk away. The government expects an absurd amount of teachers; being murdered on the job is a request too far.

FORMING POSITIVE AND PRODUCTIVE RELATIONSHIPS

There are two adjectives in this heading, and the first isn't of any real use at all if the second is absent. Where one should draw the line is between being friendly and matey or stern and unpleasant is a matter for the individual. Whatever you are comfortable with is probably what will work for you. However, a warning – some younger teachers can make the mistake of getting way too involved in the world of the teenager. This is an understandable and easy mistake to make, but if you lose your authority with a class and they start seeing you as someone who is just there to have a laugh with, you will spend a long and thankless time trying, and miserably failing, to re-establish the professional distance you should have marked out at the beginning. You may only be a few years older than them, but it's not another mate they need: it's a responsible guide who is fully in charge of the environment in which they learn, and so is able to keep them safe.

HOW TO ACHIEVE POSITIVE RELATIONSHIPS WITH STUDENTS

Let's take it that all emotion is viral. Because it is. If someone shouts angrily at you, does it have the effect of making you calm? No. Not at all. It is vastly more than likely to make you angry in turn. If someone next to you laughs, is it likely to send you into a fit of strops or is it more likely to make you predisposed to laughter yourself? The latter, of course. Accepting that you can catch emotions as surely as you can catch a cold, is it a better classroom management technique then to always be in a bad mood, or to be little Miss Sunshine? The answer's obvious.

There is some science to back this up. In the United States they did an experiment on a guy who'd had two strokes, which meant that, although his eyes could still take in the signals (and to all intents and purposes actually worked), his brain couldn't process them, and so he was totally blind. Some stunningly clever and pitifully autistic scientists showed the blind man a series of pictures in order to learn more about his condition. Why someone thought it would be a bright idea to show a blind man a series of pictures and ask him what he could see, I don't know. It seems to suffer from a quite obvious fatal flaw to me. But, still, they did it.

First of all, they showed him a series of shapes, asking what he had seen, to be greeted with the tired and soulfully glum response of, "Erm. Look. As much as I respect your professionalism, I am, as you well know, completely bloody blind, and therefore find the question an offensive exercise in futility, which serves only to remind me of my current diminished state. I can't see anything at all." The square, the triangle, the circle, all the way into the mortifyingly glamorous outline of the dodecahedron; no change whatsoever in matey's response.

And then, in frustration, they'd show him pictures of a series of faces. Sure enough the same response: "Erm. Look. As much as I respect your professionalism ..." But with an important difference: though he would swear blind that he couldn't see anything at all, and certainly couldn't identify what he'd just been shown as a picture of a face, he was able to tell the scientists, with 100% accuracy, exactly what emotion was on the face that he hadn't seen. The clever people in white coats concluded from this that he was taking in information, but that this information was being processed somewhere other than the visual processing system in the brain.

They concluded from this that the brain actually has two perceiving systems: the first, which Daniel Goleman, in his book *Social Intelligence: The New Science of Human Relationships*, identifies as the 'high road', is your executive system – controlling rationale, higher order thinking, and comes in through the eyes. Goleman also identifies the perceiving system that the blind man used to identify the emotions on the faces he could not see as being the 'low road', a sensory system that operates far quicker than the 'high road' and is based on feeling. Picture a row of several meerkats on the lookout for predators.

How does the feller on the right, Sidney, tell that the little one on the left, Egbert, has seen an eagle? He is looking the other way.

He senses the far-left meerkat's distress through the 'low road' perceiving system.

As an example of how this works in humans, when the Lumiere brothers showed the first ever example of a moving picture, the arrival of a train at La Ciotat station in the South of France, in a Parisian café in 1895, (I don't know whether you've ever seen it. It's rubbish. The narrative structure, in summary, goes something like this: train is in background, train moves to foreground, train stops, people get off train). The first ever cinema audience, who had been briefed on the idea of a moving picture, all screamed, "Merde! Le train! Le train!" in terror as the image of the train came towards them and dived under the café tables for cover.

Whilst cognitively the Parisians' 'high road' would have rationalised that it was only a film, and that Stan and Reg Lumiere had already told them what was going to happen, and they shouldn't panic and that they would most certainly spill their foul tasting and ridiculously small coffees if they dived under the table, by the time they had gone through this process, their 'low road' had already made the decision for them.

How does this apply to what you do? You are the person at the front of the class. You are attempting to engage your students' 'high road'. But, before this even engages, their low road has kicked in. And they're having a reaction to what you wear, to what your facial expression is, to your body language, even to your choice of scent. There is a great saying found in Ian Gilbert's *Essential Motivation in the Classroom*: "Teacher, I can't hear what you are saying, because what you are is screaming too loud."

Emotion is viral. Think please. How many of the Mr. Men can you name in thirty seconds?

Now, which two of those you can name would make the best teacher?

(Note, if you identify Mr. Tickle as being a potentially great teacher you should, perhaps, be considering a different career).

Most people, when asked this question grasp in the direction of Mr. Happy. And they've got a point. If emotion is viral, then you can imagine that being in Mr. Happy's class would be a place that children could grow in, comfortable, happy and stable.

As an experiment, grab a mirror and put a picture of Mr. Happy in your mind. See what happens to your mouth and to your eyes. Emotion is viral.

To achieve a positive relationship with your students all you have to do is give of yourself. Be human. If there are issues you are struggling with, tell them. If you have a particularly interesting anecdote from your life that illuminates the concept you are teaching, tell them it. Be open. Be emotional. If you are hurt by a piece of behaviour, be honest about it. Be yourself. Kids can smell a fake a long way off, so don't start trying on clothes that don't fit you at all well. The teacher you are going to be is a version of yourself if you were, to quote Lou Reed, "Someone else; someone good." Be that person.

However, there is no point being popular with your students if they are using the fact that they like you as a means of ensuring they don't actually do any work at all. Every school student in the world is a past master at the distract-the-teacher technique, and given half a chance any school pupil worth their polo shirt will entice sir or miss into the realms of the off-task. Be wary of this. You'll be fooled once, maybe twice, but don't be an all-day, everyday sucker. Be aware that at any point every child in the room is waiting for a window to distract you from the ways of the righteous, and ensure that you are vigilant not only with them, but with yourself on this.

WORK AVOIDANCE TECHNIQUES

Rather than list the advanced work avoidance techniques that I have noticed in the classroom, I thought I'd go to source. Francis Prince is a sixteen-year-old young man who I have greatly enjoyed teaching this year. Hopefully, we have managed to get him a decent grade at English, but I've had to drag him every step of the way. You see, Francis, of every child I have ever taught, is the most masterful work avoider I have ever encountered. He is a complete genius and, as Ian Gilbert puts it, "A significant overachiever in underachieving." The amount of effort and intellect that Francis puts into being lazy, if translated into positive action, would have gained him eight A-stars.

I've approached Francis and said to him. "Francis." Because that's his name. And he's said, "Sir," because that's my name. And Francis has gone into his patented 'oi oi oi' dance, because he's always looking for an angle, a way out. As Francis comes from a community (white working class boys) in which paid work is the only kind with any status, I've bribed him. "Francis, you know you've got all these techniques that you stitch me up with, how about I give you thirty quid to write em all down?" And it's on my desk the next morning. Here are Francis's work avoidance techniques.

"My name is Francis Prince. Personally, I think I am a relatively bright student but, as every teacher I ever meet realises after about two weeks, I'm not too keen on school life. Generally, I hate school. Most of my life I have tried to avoid school work and many days I try and avoid going to school altogether. I think I have been influenced by my family on this, who are working class. My family haven't achieved the best grades. My dad didn't even finish school and my mum only left school with a cooking certificate. I have many techniques that I use to get out of lessons and out of learning. Here they are:

1. When a teacher has asked me to do something and I don't understand, I either go onto something outstanding, or move on to something else entirely. Then when the teacher comes back around, I act totally normally and ask a question about the work they've given me.

2. I do as much work as I can on the computer, making sure I always get to start a piece of work on computer, so that when the teacher says, "Where's your work, Francis?" I say I've started it on the computer, and then they have no choice but to let me work on the computer.

3. While working, I quickly change the subject and start going into detail on the new subject, so that the teacher gets distracted from teaching.

4. I am always very generous to everyone in the class (teacher, as well as students). If someone needs to borrow a pen, a book or a computer, I give it to them. That way, I don't have the stuff with which the teacher can make me do work.

5. If I have a lesson coming up that I don't like, I deliberately leave my bag somewhere and pretend that I've left my homework in it. I convince the teacher that I need to go and get it, get a note and then just walk around the corridors for a while. As I've got a note, the teachers who ask me what I'm doing are easily fobbed off.

6. I randomly talk to someone about the work and pretend that I am really thick. They feel sorry for me and help me with my work.

7. If I have not got enough space to work, or it is too noisy, I pretend that I am getting distracted and can't work because of it. I quickly raise my hand and complain.

8. I sometimes pretend that I'm ill and I seriously can't work. I put my head in my arms and I'm really quiet for about half an hour. Then I ask to go and see the school nurse.

9. I always exaggerate and go over the top. When someone accidentally steps on my feet, or something hits me I shout and I scream; almost demanding that the teacher sends me out.

10. I say I will do my work at home if I can't be bothered to do it in school. I have no intention of doing it, of course. The next time I see that teacher I pretend that my computer facilities at home have broken down, and I forge a letter from my dad.

11. When I have forgotten my PE kit I pretend that I have left it on the bus, and I also pretend to phone the bus company and say I've left my bag on the bus.

12. This one is simple. I simply sit there and stare into space and just don't say anything to anyone. I pretend to the teacher that I am thinking.

13. If I'm having a bad week, I will do something which will cause me to be sent into isolation, so I have got a full week out of lessons.

14. When I am on the computer I get a piece of work that I had done in the past, minimise it and go on games. Then, when the teacher comes back round I maximise it, then the teacher thinks I'm actually doing work.

You may be asking yourself, "Why? Why is he trying to get out of studying? And why is he not trying to get the best grades possible?" Well, I'll tell you: I'm not an academic person. Mr Beadle says I'm extremely talented, but I'm not too sure about that."

You will encounter every one of Francis's techniques in your first few weeks as a teacher. His particular genius is in synthesising them into one lovable, cuddly bundle of lassitude. But the techniques are common the world over. Be prepared.

Not all students are like Francis though – most know what they are at school for; and they actually prefer it when they have a teacher who is insistent on the fact that they work hard. They will be complaining to the head about you pretty soon if they do not feel you are making them work hard enough. How though, to ensure that grinding out the graft is the default setting of the class? What techniques are there?

Sadly, there's no quick fix technique for this. It is about attitude as much as it is about a set of skills you can learn. You have to model that attitude. If sir or miss comes in every lesson determined to get the best out of their pupils, then this expectation will transfer to the class. And it is about being merciless in your pursuit of their best.

One technique that you can employ here is being first to the plate on every piece of low-level behaviour. When you have set kids to task, remain at the front of the class and shoo off any initial requests for help that involve you going to where the child is sitting. Ask them to wait briefly. Your focus, once the kids have been set to task, should be on ensuring that they settle quickly and with proper engagement, and you do this by calling the first few minor offenders on anything that looks like even the shadow of off-task behaviour. Gently call the first three offenders on it by quietly, and in a fairly friendly manner, saying their name and making some subtle finger gesture pointing at the desk, indicating that it is now time for them to focus. After you have done this, and have a class beavering away happily, then you can ask the kids who have queries to come to you, at the *front* of the class.

Where you lose a class during a task is when you do the, 'let's show the Ofsted inspector I am supporting all the kids really eagerly tour'. In touring the class, and deserting your place at the front (your symbolic position of scariness), you become, to some daft pupils, an absence, and as such they feel that it is OK for them to sod about. Stay at the front, from whence you will be able to dispense mono-brow raises, micro-nods and eye narrows to your heart's content, and, since you have remained at the focal point of the class, these will be picked up on.

Where kids go off-task en masse is when you are supporting other pupils. It's a tough one this. If a kid needs clarification of the work, or if you have a child with special educational needs who really doesn't get it at all, you would be unwise and unkind to just leave them stewing in a suppurating vat of their own lack of self-worth. But, be aware that when you are supporting specific pupils, others will take it as a message that it's time to go off on one. The noise level will rise quickly, and if you don't nip it equally as quickly, everyone in the class will be talking about their social lives within the space of a bare minute.

One of the keys here is positioning: if you are going to go on tour around the class, checking that everyone understands and is able to engage with the work then, like a repertory actor in a regional panto, you need to be always aware of not having your back to the audience. Position yourself so that you can have half an eye on the student you are aiding and the other half an eye on the rest of the class, so that you may dispense the line, "Joseph, I am watching you" just at the point Joseph least expects you to be on top of your game.

It helps here of you have your tables in groups. It makes it far easier to support students with their work and, at the same time, keep your eyes on the rest of the class.

Where kids are trying gamely to go rogue when they should be working, do not challenge them on their behaviour. "Joseph, you are talking" can lead to the response, "No I wasn't." And then you're in a stupid and pointless argument about nothing, which disrupts everyone else's learning. "Joseph, can you focus on your work please?" is not an accusation and can't be argued with. In all such situations gently guiding them back in the direction of the work pays more dividends than challenging them. To work is, after all, what they're there for.

USING PRAISE APPROPRIATELY

Praise is the most valuable and powerful tool in the whole of your toolbox. You must become fluent in its use if you are to be the kind of teacher whose lessons kids adore. You must also be able to use it as a behaviour management technique.

Let's put ourselves in a scenario that you will most likely encounter on every day of your future working life. You are the teacher ...

The class comes in. Most students sit down, get their equipment out and await the bright light of learning with alert, smiling eyes. Charlie, on the other hand, does not. Charlie does not recognise the demands of the situation. He believes that now is the time for the horseplay. Charlie is six foot four, built like a brick outhouse and is uneven of temper.

Do you?

a. Tell him off.

b. Ignore him and start praising someone else.

What happens if you tell Charlie off is this. As you have, somewhat unwisely, chosen to do it in a public space, and have caused him to lose face, you have put him under threat. When a child, particularly a boy over the age of thirteen is under threat, either of physical danger, or, in this case, of humiliation, his reptilian brain clicks in and he goes into fight or flight mode. When the reptilian brain is activated the child is in a primal state. His higher level reasoning is no longer in operation and he will rapidly decide which of the two options he has to take to deal with the threat you have just put him under. He will either come back at you, guns blazing, and regain some of the status you have just taken off of him, by arguing with you, facing up to you or indulging in some other primeval response, or he will storm out of the classroom, not forgetting to slam the door so hard as to nearly break it off of its hinges. You don't want either of these options.

So ...

Rather than pick on Charlie, who's not doing what you want, you turn your attentions towards Johnny, who is. You don't do this because Johnny is a shyer, more malleable, more biddable human being and is therefore far easier to pick on. You don't humiliate Johnny. You're nice to him. Focusing entirely on the compliant child you go to town: "Well done John. Thanks for getting down to it so quickly, and I've noticed, and this is fantastic, every lesson you always get your stuff out straightaway, without me ever having to ask, and you've always got the right equipment, and what lovely equipment it is! Love your shoes by the way and are you doing something different with your hair this week?" Witness the good guy swell with a mixture of pride and slight embarrassment as he bathes in a sea of focused teacher attention, positive affirmation and all the good stuff that kids really need, but would never admit to wanting, just for doing what is expected.

And you turn round, and, sure enough, Charlie is sitting there, his equipment out for the first time in years. He's sitting up straight and has even rubbed his trainers against his trousers to give them a little shine.

Praise envy exists. Use it. It can be used individually or, equally as effectively, with groups. When it is getting difficult to settle kids at the beginning of the lesson, and only a few have managed the evidently difficult task of sitting down, go to town on those that have. "Well done Jim's table. You're doing what's required. Thank you too to Funmi and her mates. Who else is ready to start the lesson? Little Jim? Well done. Tracey. Good stuff." You praise those who are doing the right thing and eventually all groups manage to accede to the expectation that they will sit down and ready themselves to start the lesson. This is far more effective than screaming "Sit down you errant swines!" at the top of your voice and having everyone ignore you. Less soul destroying. Easier on nerves and vocal chords too.

You should not only use praise to manage classroom behaviour. It is to be trowelled about all over the place for the simple reason that it makes kids feel good about themselves. And if you are able to make kids feel good about who they are, you are doing your job well, and will find they have a vastly more positive approach to learning in your lesson than they would in a lesson where they are continually criticised.

When I'm training other teachers, I do an activity where I select five people and write complimentary things about them on Post-it notes, which I then proceed to stick on them, reading out the positive comments. They may be five people out of an audience of two hundred, and despite the fact that these teachers are usually sentient, intelligent people who can see through a bit of blather and slime, I can guarantee that, on receiving the Post-it note, they are thinking, "He ... noticed ... me. Not all you others, you tossers. I told you I was special." Everyone else is thinking. "Why's he got one and I haven't? He's an idiot. I'm much better than him." Praise envy exists even amongst a room of near middle aged professionals who should know far, far better.

Following this, to give them practice at finding something to like in people, and telling them about it (which is a key to being a decent teacher) I give them all five Post-its and ask them to record positive stuff about five random people in the room. Come the 'sticking-on point' we notice two things. Some people discover themselves to be extremely popular. The day is made for those who find themselves covered with a whole raft of Post-its suggesting that they are great. They skip home from the training sessions and find themselves being unaccountably nice to their partners.

What happens, though, to the self-esteem of those few wallflowers whom no one notices? How do they feel?

Worse than God-awful. They go home thinking, "I hate the other teachers. They are all bastards." I've done this exercise countless times and, on one particular occasion, only one person in the whole room did not receive a single complimentary phrase. Her entirely reasonable response? To run out of the room in sobs of tears. If praise is incredibly powerful stuff, then lack of it even more so. You have to be equitable with praise: spread it around a bit. It is of no use throwing it solely in the direction of the naughty boy, or only in the direction of the clever kid. Make sure it reaches every corner of the room.

There are shy, retiring wallflowers in every class. They ask for little and are always good. Many teachers will just ignore them. Make it a policy that you will not perpetrate this crime. Chose a quiet child and praise them publicly all lesson, even all week. Pick out the speccy boy who has an obsession with dinosaurs and make him feel that he is unique and special. Take a leaf out of Simon Cowell's book: when asked the secret of his success, he replied that he imagines everyone he meets has a huge sign on their head saying, "Make me feel important."

There will also be kids in your class who have not heard a great deal of positive talk throughout the passage of their young lives. A study in the United States showed that children from middle class families hear seven words of praise for every word of censure. In 'welfare' families it was almost exactly the opposite. For every one word of praise they were required to suffer eight admonishments. Many of the children you teach will have had an upbringing that differs from the American welfare family in accent alone. They will have, since birth, been force-fed a daily diet of their own wrongly perceived uselessness; their 'wrongness'; their inability to get anything right. School *should* be at least a *partial* antidote to this. In a decent teacher's class kids will be given exactly the opposite experience. When they have achieved, praise them; when they have struggled, praise them for having done so; and where they have failed, double praise them for having had the guts to try. Call them clever. Let them know you think they are special and have special talents. Children live up or down to the expectations you set for them. Let them know you think they have the capacity for genius and will one day reach that capacity. Give yourself a hard and fast rule. "No child who has come up with something of brilliance, be it in terms of their written response or just some chance remark they have made, will ever leave my class feeling anything other than ten feet tall."

However, praise has got to be judicious. And most of all it's got to be descriptive. Otherwise you find yourself in the position of the deputy head, who, standing at a lectern every Monday morning for the space of five years as the year group he supervised assembled for the morning act of worship of the secular educational gods Nelson Mandela, Rosa Parks and Jonathan Livingstone Seagull, would serially announce, in no particular direction, "Yes. Very good. That's great. Very good indeed. Excellent even.

Well done." Once a week, forty weeks a year over the passage of a half decade, until such point as towards the end of our charges' time at the school one bright spark had the temerity to pose a question of him. "Mr Popman," queried the wag, "for five years now you've been saying, 'Good. Excellent. Very good,' as we've come into assembly. What, exactly, is it that's very good?"

"Well, erm," blushed the deputy head as two hundred or so sharp sixteen-year-olds drank in his embarrassment, "... Erm. I, erm. Mmm. I don't really know. But it's very good isn't it? Excellent even."

There's no point in flannelling kids with meaningless nonsense – you'll get found out. Nor do you over-praise every action so that eventually that praise simply becomes just another flavour of the white noise that many students experience their teachers' voices to be. If you are going to praise you must take it seriously. Make eye contact with the child. Maintain that eye contact and describe exactly what they did that you thought was great. "William, I thought your listening skills throughout this lesson have been fantastic. You've kept your eyes on me, your body language is inclined towards me, and it's really helped me, throughout the process of the lesson that you've been able to do this."

There's also an argument that it should be in the language that the students relate to. Since I am not religious and have no God to turn to in tough moments, often in life, when in a difficult situation, I find myself asking the same question: what would Terry Venables do here? Generally, Big Tel will have the answer to most of life's quandaries, and he has very interesting things to say about the language of praise.

This is how Terry conjugates the verb phrase, 'to do well':

I done good.

You done good.

He/she/it done good.

We done good.

You done good.

They done good.

But the boy Rooney done magnificent.

There's a few secrets in Terry's conjugation that can be applied to teaching and, specifically, to praising kids. Football managers and pundits never put the 'ly' bit of the adverb on. Try it yourself when praising the kids you teach. It works. Don't tell them they have done well; try "You done magnificent there" on for size and see the difference in the size of their pride in themselves. Speak to them in the voice and the language of their fathers, and you will be hitting them where they live.

CAREER THREATENING ERRORS

I've witnessed some fairly foolish failings in this area from teachers in the past. Youth is an attractive state, but taking anything other than a polite and jokey (utter lack of) interest in teenagers' love lives will have you talked about in hushed and harpy-like tones; and whether it is for decent reason or not, getting a reputation in the staffroom as 'failing to maintain professional distance', is basically shorthand for being potentially a really scary paedo who must be made to go away soon.

On this subject, kids sometimes fancy their teachers. Be aware this happens. Thankfully, once you get past a certain age it goes away, but if you are lithe of limb and pleasing of face, it is likely that you will be the recipient of such glowing looks. How you deal with this is gender specific. A male teacher has the luxury of being able to treat his admirer with humanity, thanking them for having made him feel so nice about himself. For the female teacher, this arena, particularly with older boys, can be threatening, and you must stamp on it, reporting any incident, directly to your line manager.

Above all, be careful here. That is not to say you shouldn't be friendly, or that it is illegal to like your students, but professional distance, though it is a concept you may find a bit stuffy at the beginning, is there for a reason – to protect everyone, students and teachers alike.

CHAPTER 2
KNOWLEDGE AND UNDERSTANDING

CULTIVATING THE PASSION

If you haven't got passion for the subject you teach, then you should probably have stayed in office work. Spouting on interminably about how brilliant something is when, in truth, you think it's really a load of old toilet, is difficult to sustain over a career that could last forty years, and is a bit too much like being back in the PR or marketing job you might have just run away from – screaming. Passion in the classroom is vital. There is, however, something of a difference in this area between sectors.

As my next door neighbour, a retired primary school SENCO, is fond of telling me: a primary schoolteacher teaches kids, a secondary schoolteacher teaches a subject. And there's some truth babbling away beneath the surface of this clumsy looking maxim. Your first love, if you are to be a great primary schoolteacher, has to be the children you teach. Given that you, the fledgling primary practitioner, will have to teach thirteen or so different subjects in a day, it's perhaps too big an ask to hope that you'll develop and nurture grand passions for each and every one of them.

However, if your aim is to be a great secondary schoolteacher, you must have passion for what you are teaching, whatever that subject is. Great secondary teachers have subject related passion pouring from every pore.

In the most part, and provided you are teaching the subject you've trained for, it is pretty much a given that a secondary teacher will possess this love. I've seen derivations of it in ICT teachers who bring pulpit-style proselytising to their subject;

geography teachers who have so much love for volcanoes and plate tectonics that they even go so far as dressing like geography teachers (which is devotion beyond the call of duty) and adopting the patent humanities teacher walk: feet splayed, head back – quick march; and, of course, in every staffroom you'll also will find a mincing cabal (flounce is, I think, the correct collective noun) of language loving, extravagantly-shirted, English teaching fops who find nothing more glorious than going into grand guignol raptures about a prose paragraph containing an overlong description of a flower or a white horse.

It's one thing to have a passion, though, it's another to be able to convey it credibly; to manifest it so that it is transmitted to your students and they wait in lines outside your lesson jumping up and down in a feverish state of excited anticipation, devising sweetly sung, musical couplets in your praise.

"Yeeeeesss! Let joy be unconfined,

Double physics with Mrs Hardgrind."

Many of us are so used to keeping our passions hidden from our mothers or our partners, that when it comes to the classroom environment our stiff upper-lipped reserve clicks into gear and we are wary of going over the top, in case our students find us too gushing, too embarrassing – too whatever. Dismiss this thought as soon as it arrives. Firstly, giving two figs about whether thirteen-year-olds think you are maintaining an exquisite disinterest is, in itself, an affectation. For most kids 'teacher' and 'cool' only ever appear in the same sentence if the latter term is prefixed with the words, 'pathetically', 'bloody' and 'un'. They see us in more easily factored terms: we are either 'good', 'crap' or 'alright' ('alright' being, paradoxically, the highest level attainable). Secondly, if you entered the profession to be seen as cool by thirteen-year-olds, you do need to get out a little more. Thirteen-year-olds think, en masse, that the baseball hat is the height of sartorial elegance. Their idea of cool is not the same as yours. Don't pander to it.

So, don't beat yourself up for getting into it. It is only when you lose any sense of self-consciousness that you will really teach up a storm, and don't let a thirteen-year-old child's embarrassed chastening alter you from your course. It is far easier to tone a thing down than it is to turn it up, so go into your first lesson with a sense that you are going to enthuse your students into developing a life long passion for apostrophes, or algebra, or Gamelan music; whatever it is that you are going to teach them. If you have gone way too far over the top, the kids will soon let you know and you can bring it back in the direction of vanilla. Go into a lesson displaying a meek and worthy lack of ego however, and it is likely you will bore the kids so badly that it becomes their moral responsibility to misbehave, to give you a good chewing up and to spit you out, bedraggled and bemused.

(A warning here though, there is an empirical point at which what you think is Byronic flamboyance becomes upsetting eccentricity; you may think that you are starring in a never ending re-run of *Dead Poet's Society*, your students will not share this idea. Moreover, they will think you are a nutcase.[7] (Besides, and as no one ever points out, one of Robin Williams' pupils in that film killed himself. This is not what we are aiming for.))

So, bearing in mind that you should not be so big that there is no room in the classroom for the kids, you should attempt to rid yourself of reserve. To transmit the 'wow' to the kids you teach, you must be the 'wow' – the, "Wow. Look at that! Isn't it fantastic? Isn't that, unbelievably and utterly and endlessly and completely and amazingly and totally and unutterably and continually, endlessly fascinating?" If you are able to do this, credibly, then the classroom's your playground.

How then, do you go about transmitting such enthusiasm? The answer is in the question, really. You find a way of manifesting endless enthusiasm. This does not mean that you can't have a really useless lesson, hungover on a Monday, Tuesday, Wednesday, Thursday or Friday morning, or that it is apocalyptically bad to find yourself just not really in the mood to be brilliant today, sir, but over the space of a full academic

---

7 Actually, leading kids into thinking you are a borderline psychotic can be extremely useful in terms of classroom management. "Don't mess with sir (man). He's a killer."

year, you should be able to be 'on' more times than 'off', and you will generally be able to find some small thing in the lesson, be it a student's response, or some nuance in the subject you are covering, that will lead your students, eventually, towards this strange, almost Pavlovian response or attitude, which is: because you are able to be explicit about how wonderful you think your subject is, they will slowly begin to share your view.

TOP TEACHER TIPS

- Adjectival poverty is a horrendous disease and can have you marked out as thick, so grab hold of that thesaurus. You will need a full and varied vocabulary of compliments and breathless superlatives to apply to your students, their work and to the subject itself. Type 'em up, print 'em out, bung 'em on the wall as an aide-memoire, so you don't get caught describing everything as being, "Amazing." Kids will soon pick up on this and will take the micky, calling you 'Miss/Mr Amazing' in a mimetic and deeply uncomplimentary bout of affected world-weariness the moment your back is turned.

- You are a performer and your biggest enemy is self-consciousness nagging at you, telling you that you are an idiot, and you said this wrong and that wrong, and you have no place whatsoever standing in front of these impressionable young minds, destroying their chances in life. If that particular devil appears on your shoulder, take a second to laugh at yourself, and then cuff him on the nose and get straight back into the zone.

- Develop a way of appearing endlessly enthusiastic. You must have a practised array of facial expressions and gestures that you can inhabit comfortably without feeling too much like an auditionee for *Blue Peter*. These expressions must convey the impression that you think what your student has just said or written is both phenomenal and original. They may well have been the first person in the world to come up with this particular insight and, as such, you should reward them for it with some equivalent of the clenched fist punching the air and tight triumphal lips against your teeth, as you hold their eye contact to tell them, "That is FANtastic." It is useful practising this at home, perhaps even employing a mirror to check you are convincing enough to fool yourself.[8]

---

8 *This is best done after exactly three large glasses of red wine. Forgive yourself if you are less attractive when doing this than you'd ordinarily wish yourself to be.*

SUBJECT KNOWLEDGE

What is your most embarrassing moment? Before this year, my answer would have been, "Being seventeen". A year long state, which would have been bad enough in itself, had it not been further destroyed by spending much of it sat rictus with social clumsiness in sports club discos watching beery Sunday league footballers shout out the chorus of Kool & the Gang's 'Get Down On It' to entirely different words. The definition of awful. This level of embarrassment pales though, when you put it alongside more recent horrors.

Attain a portion of transient micro-celebrity, and your embarrassing moments go distinctly white collar. I was asked at the end of 2007 to write a new year's quiz for *The Times*. It was to feature over three days, to be on the front cover of the *T2 Supplement*, and they'd pay me enough for a good night out and a slap-up feed. The idea was that it was a 'back to school quiz', in which I'd guide *Times* readers back in the direction of their school days, so they could almost smell the changing rooms. I wrote it over the space of two weeks, entirely in the style of Tom Baker's voiceover in Little Britain, and sent it off, much impressed with my own sparkling wit, shiny brilliance and covert ability to take the mick out of my paymasters. I took a day off to shine my halo before it was printed, so at least had a brief remission before it became obvious I'd made the most monumental and awful tosspot of myself. The letters page the next day was devoted in its entirety to readers writing in with joyful and probably correct claims that I was an utter idiot and entirely unsuitable for a cerebral profession like teaching.

In the grammar section, I did a bit about not ending sentences with prepositions, which is a fairly standard piece of English teaching guff. Apparently, 'after' isn't just a preposition. Oh no. It sometimes wears an all too convincing preposition disguise, when it is, in fact, moonlighting as an adverb. *Times* readers rightly exposed me for a fool, a fraud and a sham; and I am now known in certain sections of the country I shall thankfully never visit as the idiot English teacher who doesn't know the difference between an adverb and a preposition.

The lesson is simple. We are few of us geniuses[9] and rare indeed is it to find a teacher to whom the feel of egg upon face is entirely alien. It may be that you are entering the teaching profession because you benefited from a superb quality of education and wish to pass on the benefits you've received. I came into it for an antithetical reason, having spent much of my time at school very bored, learning nuffink. But it doesn't matter how well educated you are; there is a damn good chance you will get things wrong. At the beginning of your career there is a damn good chance you will get quite a lot wrong. Relax. It is fine and vital to get things wrong; that's how we learn. Besides, not only would we not develop by getting it right all the time, but perfection would make us so smug that we wouldn't be able to empathise properly with our kids' battles.

In all schools you will find that the kids call you on spelling mistakes on the board, on grammatical or factual errors. If this happens, do not attempt to defend yourself. 'Fess up, "Yeh, sorry. I'm really stupid today. Well spotted," and get on with it. And don't be cross with the kid who has called you. If you think back to when you were at school, and the teacher made a spelling mistake on the board, you were rightly proud of spotting that they, supposedly the pinnacle and the font of all human knowledge, were sadly human after all.

The issue with subject knowledge as you enter the career is that it actually means something entirely different to what you might think. You may be thinking that it's all about how much you know about the subject you teach, and that you will be fine because you have a degree in it, and besides you read a lot of books, or you can work a spreadsheet, or you know how to make a really quite handsome cabinet. This is only half true. Subject knowledge in schools is actually about how well you know the administrative side of things.

---

9 If I were I'd be bothered to get to grips with whether this is the correct pluralisation, or whether it should be 'genii'.

TOP TEACHER TIPS

It is vital to familiarise yourself with the levelling or grading criteria for your subject as soon as possible. This can be quite tough as the things are written and defined so vaporously that you'd need a degree to understand them.

This, from the QCA's website, is the description of an 'A' grade student in Expressive Arts:

> They experiment and apply skills, processes and techniques of the chosen art forms with a high degree of precision and control to shape and structure ideas. They make perceptive selections, apply them in a refined and innovative way, and use all appropriate compositional elements effectively. They develop innovative and imaginative responses to the art works studied. They review, modify and refine work in an appropriate, perceptive and creative way, clearly defined by the need to realise intentions.

Which may well be completely Greek to you. It is vital however that you focus on having an analytical engagement with these weird and forbidding little pieces of text as early and as seriously as you can. If we analyse the above, my reading of it is that the A grade student will have some kind of thematic idea for their performance/art piece and will go through a range of options for presenting this idea, before deciding upon one in which they are sufficiently skilled technically to put together a competent and impressive, near-adult piece. They have all the basics to pat, and are at a sufficient point with the form that they are able to break rules consciously; and they don't settle on their first attempt – they rework things.

Which is probably of no more use to you than the original. But it illustrates the process you have to go through with the criteria. You must form a rationalised opinion as to what they mean, so that you are able to bash about whether a piece of work is an A or a B grade in a discussion with a colleague.

A newly qualified teacher whose grading can be trusted by senior colleagues saves those senior colleagues a lot of work, and having such engagement and interest in how to grade will show that you have your priorities well worked out, and are potentially an excellent professional. It doesn't matter if you don't get it exactly right in your first year. The grading is very difficult and works on a 'best fit' basis, (if a kid's work has some elements of a C, some of a B, a lot of an A, they are probably an A minus), which has always seemed to me little more than an excuse to give kids grades they don't deserve. (There is a lot of this in the fast moving, target driven world of British education.)

This applies to all levels, be it GCSE, A Level, or the NCAT (National Curriculum Attainment Targets) at Key Stages 1, 2 and 3. You must enter into a dialogue with these and come up with your own understanding. Your understanding can be as simplistic and reductive as the understanding that I have formed myself of the levels. For instance, the NCATs for Writing are as vaporous and exhaustive as they will be in any other area. I have reduced the exhaustive pieces of text to:

Level 1 – Can't do much. More than nothing, but not much more.

Level 2 – Can use full stops and the odd question mark.

Level 3 – Can use commas, not always correctly.

Level 4 – Can use commas correctly, gets apostrophes a bit wrong.

Level 5 – Can use commas and apostrophes correctly.

Level 6 – Has a bash at colons and semicolons.

Level 7 – Uses colons and semicolons plausibly.

Note also, there is an inherent understanding here that a level 6 will be able to do all the things that a level 5 can manage; so our level 6 in writing will use commas and apostrophes correctly, and will be making fledgling attempts at colons and semicolons. If you are struggling over a decision as to whether a student's borderline work should be one grade or another, have a second look at the criteria, then, if you still can't work it, consult a senior colleague.

Of course, subject knowledge is not just how well you have grappled with the administrative side of things and how well you understand the grading criteria. You must also know what you are talking about; and if you don't know, you'd better be prepared to swot up on it.

Much of my life these days is spent like a vulture in the back of other teachers' classes, judging their lessons and, by extension, their validity as human beings. During my years of doing this, I have seen some shockers: the English teacher who could not for the life of him understand that one of the key parts of teaching is introducing students to things they don't already know; the ICT teacher who couldn't use the add function on a spreadsheet; and the music teacher who couldn't play an instrument, and was tone deaf to boot.

Music teacher: But, my voice is my instrument!

Mr Beadle: Perhaps you should consider taking up the recorder.

Kids love it when their teacher is an obvious expert in their subject, and are pretty good at spotting a bluffer. Last year, whilst taking a year 9 lesson, I apologised to the class for my somewhat shaky knowledge, of *Much Ado About Nothing*. "That's OK, sir," said the class in unison. "Our real teacher knows shit about it" – shit here being shorthand for "shit-all" (meaning nothing), as opposed to "the shit" (meaning lots). The fact that their regular teacher was sitting in the class at the time, and was, at that very moment, subject to a particularly intense form of emotional crucifixion – going on to spend the rest of the hour wishing she could be somewhere (anywhere) else, or that she could manifest a sudden ability to melt into the floorboards – meant nothing to the children. They felt they were being short-changed by their teacher's lack of knowledge of what they were meant to be being taught, and care(d) not for their teacher's ego, sanity or career. The lesson here is clear: if you aren't able to keep at least two steps in front of your class, they will suss you out and it will destroy their respect for you. More or less any class you teach, sometimes despite initial appearances to the contrary, will have a deep respect for their education, and if they feel you aren't coming up with the goods, will provide a summary spanking.

TOP TEACHER TIPS

You may be deeply into Barbara Cartland (an image which, if lingered on for more than a millisecond, brings new meaning to the phrase, "Yeeuuwch")[10] but as a newly qualified teacher, you no longer have time to indulge in your penchant for the romantic novel on the train. Use your journey to and from work profitably, so that when you get home you can relax.

Use your first few holidays as a teacher to combine lying flat in a darkened room with occasionally getting up and practising grading work. For secondary teachers this is a good time to grade coursework, so that you become skilled at it early on.

---

10 *Particularly given the fact she has been dead for some years.*

COMMUNICATING KNOWLEDGE EFFECTIVELY AND ENGAGING INTEREST

This is the great mystery. How do you do this? How can you guarantee that your class will be interested in what you have to say?

It's easy to answer. You can't. But you'll find you do better, firstly, by saying far less than you think you should. The most obvious, biggest mistake that any newly qualified teacher will make is going on and on and on until we're all bored and wish we were somewhere else or that we were dead or that it was four o'clock already and that we'd bunked off, or not come back after lunch and why, oh why, won't you just shut up and let me do something?

If you doubt this, try it yourself. Ask someone twenty years older than you, whose musical taste and clothing you detest, to come 'round your house and either read something you're not interested in to you, or to talk about it for a very long time. See how long you can stomach it before you begin to detest the very hem of their trouser. And then spare a thought for the poor school child, who, when they could be running and playing, or grappling with some profound new poetic or scientific thought, are forced to listen to a succession of superannuated old bores wheezing on about sod-all, while they sit, mute, willing the second hand to go faster, please, faster; watching the minutes drown into hours, and feeling their young lives slip gently away into senescence. You didn't like this version of ejacashun being done at you when you were at school, and you wouldn't like it done at you now. Don't do it at them.

Besides, talkaholism is a particularly foolish trick to fall into. The most substantial concern for newly qualified teachers is about behaviour. None of us leave our PGCEs, B'Eds or short, six week courses for Teach First Graduates or Graduate Trainees feeling in any way sufficiently well prepared to deal with the kind of behaviour we read about in scare stories in the right wing press. But there is a general rule of thumb, adherence to which will minimise problematic behaviour in your lessons. That is not to say it won't occur. It will. But, if you spend your lessons talking at kids, you are not only opening the door for poor behaviour, you are inviting it across the threshold and shoving your jugular into its open jaws. Bear in mind this maxim that I have nicked from someone else:

"Talking isn't teaching, and teaching isn't learning."

No matter how charismatic you are, how funny, how incredible to look at, how successful socially, you'll find that you are able to maintain kids' attention for only seven or so minutes if all you do is talk at them. After such point, they will start to get bored, tune out, drop out and sod about. (This will happen double quick if you are writing on a whiteboard at the same time as you are talking, in that, the moment your back is turned, they will begin their own decidedly off-task conversations, bolting upright into pseudo-obedient body language mode the moment you turn around to face them again.)

So, lesson one, if you wish to gain interest is this: *Shut Up!* If you are always at the front of the class, you are there to be shot at, interrupted and talked over. Absent yourself from the front or find another way to introduce the subject than just talking about it. If you wish the kids you teach to be filled with both awe and wonder, you are unlikely to obtain this by reading a manual to them.

Engaging interest at the start of the lesson is vital. In every lesson you will have a few minutes grace before the kids decide they are for it or against it (or you). You must use those few minutes to let it be known that they are in for an interesting and enlivening time. If you lose them early on in a double lesson on a Friday after lunch, it's a long, dark afternoon of the soul wrestling with class control for a truly agonising couple of hours.

TOP TEACHER TIPS

Use PowerPoint slide shows with pictures only to enliven interest and get students thinking symbolically. Carry these around with you on a memory stick, so they can be brought into action in the shake of a lamb's tail. It's a really good idea if you attach your memory stick to your keyring; that way you will be less likely to leave it at home when you really need it, or leave it stuck in the USB thingy in the computer.

HEALTH AND SAFETY

If you are handing out scissors or compasses to children, it is always a good idea to tell them, (the students, not the scissors; that would be stupid), that they, (the scissors, not the students; though it might be accurate), are dangerous implements which can cause serious damage. With the exception of the two nutcases in the class who will take your warning as a cue to test out the theory's practical application, this will have no impact upon their behaviour whatsoever. However, stating this emphatic warning leaves you covered when they start cutting each other's hair, playing that silly chicken game where they use the compasses to stab the desk beneath their splayed fingers or, worse still, attempting an appendectomy on Howard. If you are tempted to use Stanley knives in a lesson, (and there are certain artsy/craftsy subjects in which this temptation might be a curriculum requirement and, therefore, irresistible), then think deeply before you do so. Count them in and out, and make sure your warnings are delivered straight faced and in your sternest of teacher(ly) voices. Stanley knives really are seriously bloody dangerous. You do not want to be responsible for a child being scarred for life by anything other than your fluid use of advanced sarcasm techniques.

Also, if you are zealous enough to consider planning school trips – they are a pain in the arse and take oceans of planning and paperwork for the sole benefit of you spending a day shouting at kids in a completely uncontrolled environment – avoid large stretches of water. Kids often do this drowning thing, about which, no matter how sensitively you frame it, parents are unlikely to be understanding.

On school trips treat your register as your best friend and take it every time you have finished part of the journey, or at any point there is any possibility of a child becoming lost or deliberately running off to a clip joint in Soho. That way when you lose one (or in the case of a poetry trip I once took the whole of year 11 to, ninety kids), you know as soon as possible, and can ring the school to inform them, before you trundle off to the pub and promptly forget what it is you do for a living.

Stanley knives and swimming pools apart, ignore anything else you are told about health and safety. Managers who are liable to use the phrase 'health and safety', a pejorative and superior sneer on their lips, and who do not have even a Northamptonian mum's idea of biting, satirical humour coursing through them as they utter the phrase, are doing so in order to hide the fact that they are, in all other areas, clueless. They are, in fact, on their fourth 'sideways' promotion having shown over the path of many years in the profession that they are not capable of running a bunk-up in a brothel, let alone a special needs section. 'Health and safety' is the preserve of the bore, and will stop you from standing on desks, kids from standing on chairs and the whole class from piling those chairs up in the corner of the room and pretending you are all in a nuclear bunker. Spurn it as you would a rabid dog.

CHAPTER 3
METHODS AND ORGANISATION

In this section we look at the nuts and bolts, the rudiments of how you do the actual teaching bit of the job. This has changed fairly radically over the years and what I think makes a good lesson and what most senior managers or Ofsted inspectors think, may well be very different indeed. Certain governmental pushes, which seem always to be based on research conducted by people who have no idea of what it is practical to achieve in the classroom, are just plain stupid, and you should spit at them.

Several of the guiding principles behind what is now the state approved method of teaching, the 'four-part lesson', are so clearly a complete pile of cobblers that, if you are going to be the kind of teacher a classroom full of children would want you to be, you should ignore them as a matter of policy. However, a big warning: over the past decade, teaching has become a career in which sometimes it seems the only quality that is regarded as being of any worth is conformity. It may be that the school you work in insists on just such a paleness, and that what they want is a series of drab, identikit automatons delivering lessons in exactly the same manner and naming this stultifying blandness 'professionalism'. Do not let this pale version of a teacher be the thing that looks at you in the mirror every morning. There are times to do what you are told, (perhaps). But there are also many more times when you should routinely ignore the instructions of others and find out yourself by experimenting.

Being a great teacher is about finding your own way with things. And you don't discover new worlds by remaining safe, or doing it by some turgid textbook that comes with the promise that, if you follow it, you will be as mediocre as the person who wrote it. Kids do not want or need indentikit teachers. They want, require and deserve you to be brilliant, and you do not get to be brilliant by following the rules.

When interviewed about the nature of his own creativity, the late Paul Arden, one time creative director of Saatchi & Saatchi, not only answered all the questions by drawing pictures but, when asked to comment on the work of another advertising creative, Tony Kaye, said the following:

> Though I'm far from being in agreement with everything Tony does his courage has produced some very fine commercials, but they're not produced in a regular way. You cannot produce great work by normal means, you simply cannot. If you could produce great work within the rules, there would be a hell of a lot more people producing fine work.

I love this quote and think it can be applied very well to an approach that will, if you follow it, make you a very good teacher indeed. As Mr Arden said, "You cannot produce great work by normal means." You must find another way; a way apart from the way that anyone else does it. A way apart from the way that I do it. Your own unique and special way of teaching. And that way must break the rules, because the rules are negotiated in committees of the bloodless and passed through a series of ever finer sieves designed to make them so blandly characterless that any fool can master the process of teaching.

In my view, teaching is a performance art form – one which ranks with and above ballet, theatre and music – and it could and should contain all the others. It is an art form that can synthesise all other art forms. Treat it as something you will attempt to master all the while knowing you will never manage to. Treat it with an investigative sense of pushing the possibilities. Let yourself be excited by pushing the boundaries of the form. Try to be the best teacher you couldn't possibly imagine. The one you wanted at school but never had.

Listen to those more experienced than you, if they are trying to help you, and take account of the guiding words of wise old lags who couldn't be bothered to graduate to senior management. They are often the masters of the trade. But do not do what you are told just because someone in a cheap suit and a position of temporary authority over you wishes to display that authority. Take suggestion only if it makes sense, and provided you see the person making the suggestion knows what they are talking about and is trying to help you.

But do not believe a single government or Ofsted dictate as to what good teaching is. They have restrictive and formulaic views, and they may not ever have been anywhere near as good a teacher as you are going to be.

Over the space of this chapter I'll be going through the things you will be assessed on when you are observed by management. I'll give you chapter and verse about the rationale behind the methodology and whether or not that rationale is truly sound. I'll present a version of the establishment view, and then look at other ways you may want to view this particular aspect of teaching. Some of my own views on this have been described by commentators as being 'maverick', a term I've always felt is used by those whose imagination is sufficient to allow them only to follow. I'm relatively comfortable wearing this suit, as I've never seen any value in convention itself or in being the personification of it. But there will be rationalised opposing views to those I'll present in this chapter. In the interest of balance you should probably seek those views out.

THE FOUR-PART LESSON

Most lesson plan pro formas nowadays come with some tabular version of the 'starter – guided – independent – plenary' format. You are expected to fill in the blanks with the requisite activity. In its favour, the four-part lesson plan ties the teacher to a structure that, theoretically at least, ensures you do not just write, "I am just going to do lots and lots of very, very interesting talking in this lesson. So there."

Broadly, there are two schools in education. The orthodoxy, who take what is called a constructivist approach, and most teachers, who would probably take a constructivist approach if they could, but for whom the amount of prep involved makes it impossible. The constructivist approach has much to recommend it: its proponents argue that kids construct their own meaning through completion of tasks. It doesn't even really matter what the task is. Anything at all related to what they are learning about will lead kids to interesting discoveries they'll make themselves and which are not pushed down their throat by the teacher. And you know what? They're right.

However, one of the constructivist orthodoxies appears to be that any form of teaching that involves the teacher standing at the front of the class and actually teaching anything is somehow a completely immoral display of pure ego. This is facile. There are times – whilst reading a Shakespeare play with a bottom set who can barely read their own name in their first language – that a constructivist approach falls down and you have to do a bit of standing at the front, translating.

The four-part lesson plan seems to seek to enforce the correct balance of teacher and student activity. The starter, the independent bit and the plenary should all be activities the students complete themselves. It's only in the guided bit that you are allowed to give it a bit of rabbit. As such, it obeys the unwritten rule that the students should have three times as much time actually doing stuff in lessons than you spend chatting at them. Consequently, you might reasonably conclude it to be a well-intentioned and important stricture. You might be wrong.

THE FOUR-PART LESSON – A DISSENTING VIEW

The four-part lesson plan has been argued by some teacher activists to be a naked attempt at de-professionalising teaching. Producing formulaic lessons to such a bland and simplistic formula is not in any way complex, and any government seeking to make cost savings on its teachers (and they are) might argue that, since teaching can be reduced to such a simple process, any fool can do it. The doom-mongers point towards the recent advent of cover supervisors, unqualified teachers who are employed predominantly to cover lessons their absent colleagues would usually have taken, as evidence of this.

Whatever the political agenda, and one is always present behind whatever tinkerings the government of the day does to what goes on in schools, there are flaws in the four-part lesson plan that any teacher who wants to be as good as they possibly can will want to acquaint themselves with.

Firstly, acknowledging the points of the activitists, it is too, too, too, too, too, too, too simple. The endlessly nuanced skill of being a good teacher cannot properly be reduced to such a reductive formula, and a properly skilled practitioner would instantaneously reject it as being a dunce's dictat that defies variety. Where an interested teacher might deliberately choose to run a lesson with fourteen parts or might, alternatively, plan a series of lessons over a couple of weeks, in which the kids all continued on with the same activity, lesson after lesson – in order to get a big piece of work done – and would realise that this is a perfectly acceptable way to conduct business, the four-part lesson plan seems to forbid this freedom, giving kids the pale and pointless guarantee that their lessons will all meet a minimum standard; and only that.

As fairly crass proof of how easy it is to structure lessons in far more interesting ways than the four-part lesson, here is a nine-part lesson on bananas, structured with the aid of Howard Gardner's multiple intelligence theory, which you could have done and dusted within two minutes:[11]

1. **Linguistic:** Think of three words to describe a banana.

2. **Mathematical:** I've got three bananas. I eat one. How many bananas have I got left?

3. **Visual:** What's this look like?

4. **Intra-personal:** Think about whether a banana really feels happy within its own skin.

5. **Inter-personal:** Go and find someone and tell him or her whether you think a banana feels happy within its own skin.

6. **Existentialist:** What religion is a banana?

---

[11] *Linguistic*: Yellow, curvy and ripe will do the job. *Mathematical*: The answer is that you have two bananas left. *Visual*: A banana. Well done. You are on fire! *Intra personal*: it is entirely dependent on the individual banana. *Existential*: Buddhist, unless circumcised.

7. **Kinetic:** Feel my banana, children.

8. **Naturalist:** How many fruits can you name?

9. **Musical:** How many songs can you name that mention bananas? (Answers below)[12]

A further issue with the four-part lesson plan is that it ignores the current fashion for every lesson to be a double. If you work in a school where there is a substantial amount of naughtiness, then it is likely, to cut down on the amount of lesson changeovers, that the head or principal will have made each lesson a near two-hour stretch. A four-part lesson is never going to be sufficiently substantial for such an extended period of time. The double lesson will generally be in the region of one hour and forty minutes. If you spend ten minutes on the starter, a further ten waffling on at the front, and ten checking that no one has learnt anything at all at the end of the lesson, it leaves one hour and twenty minutes to work on the chief lesson task. Dem damn kids dem gwan get bare bored[13], to coin a phrase.

THE STARTER

Starter activities take place at the *start* of the lesson: that's why *starter* has the word *start* in it. Are you keeping up at the back?

They should take about ten minutes and came about to cut some of the dead time at the front end of the lesson. Often, teachers will go through a range of administrative

---

12 *Musical*: There's 'The Banana Boat Song', 'Bananas in Pyjamas', 'Yes, We Have No Bananas', 'Yellow Bird (Up High in Banana Tree)', 'the Banana Splits' Song' and, at a push, Donovan's 'Mellow Yellow'. Award yourself half a point for each one, record the number of points you have scored on a piece of paper and then throw that piece of paper in the bin. If you know any more, please do not write to me. I don't care.

13 *Translation*: Those pesky children are going to get very listless indeed.

tasks at the front end of the lesson: collecting homework, taking the register, asking, "Why are you tardy, child?" This has meant, historically, that in many lessons, prior to the advent of the starter, there were whole rafts of time at the beginning in which no one actually learnt anything at all. When you are waiting for your name to be called in order to say, "Yes, miss" or to bring up the hastily cobbled together excuse for a piece of homework you copied from your mate on the bus in the morning, you are not, in any way, cognitively engaged. Unengaged kids quickly go rogue, and this has meant that in a lot of 'pre-the-starter' lessons teacher's first task was ten minutes in, and that task was to regain control of the class who had already begun dismantling the chairs in abject boredom.

TOP TEACHER TIPS

Take your register in the middle of the lesson and set homework at the beginning. Taking the register in the middle cuts the dead time at the front. You don't need to call out the names, Victorian style. Just take a look around and see who's there and who's not. Setting homework at the beginning, just by having it written on the board, means that you don't add it on as an afterthought or, worse still, forget to set it entirely.

A well-prepared starter activity stops this from happening. It should be laid ready for the kids to start it, immediately they enter. And there should be a routine expectation that they will get cracking the moment they sit down. This way you don't have the education of the eager kids, who always arrive on time, being run at the pace of the tardy kids, who don't. The idea is that a well-prepared starter activity engages cognition; students are required to start thinking straightaway. The DCFS list three major intentions of a starter as being engagement, pace and challenge. Engagement is getting the kids involved in the lesson sharpish, pace is about the feel of the lesson being sharpish too and challenge is not giving them what primary schoolteachers describe as 'busy work' i.e. stuff that teaches the students nothing, but keeps them quiet.

THE STARTER – A DISSENTING VIEW

Another view of the starter is that it is by far the worst of all the horrendously crass ideas the drab and facile bureaucrats at the DCSF ever inflicted on us already hideously over-worked teachers. Don't tell me how to teach you flimsy paper gondolas of stale urine! Go back to another nourishing bout of box ticking and be thankful you can still feed your children.

I don't really hold with starters. For me, they are the ultimate, conclusive evidence that the absurdly patronising and utterly ineffective micro-management the government has sought to impose on schoolteachers in the interests of raising our 'professional standards' has gone way out of control. I have written about this in the *Teach-It* newsletter previously, and I think it bears reproducing:

> The initial reaction that teachers had when this idea was first introduced remains true: where's the time to write, design and implement a whole new additional six lessons per day on top of the lessons I am already teaching? The answer is, "There is no additional time you spineless drone," and so my advice would be, don't do 'em. Ignore the four-part lesson plan until such point as you are being observed, and then slap out a perfunctory starter or, better still, do a lesson without a starter that is so good nobody will notice that it doesn't follow the government's strictures. A decent ten-minute start to a lesson can take a decent hour to prepare. And those who are too scared to call it for what it is end up either getting the Scrabble out and letting the children play with squares of ivory for ten minutes, or plunging helplessly in the direction of the word search.
>
> However, you may be working in one of those schools where blind obedience, from both staff and pupils, is perceived to be a sign of quality; and for you, here is a starter activity guaranteed to get senior staff off your back.
>
> Bring in a small ghetto blaster and play them some music: something lyrical; something that excites a response: Tupac, Bob Dylan, MC Paul Barman, Sparks, The Silver Jews; anything which is of interest linguistically, and get your class to transcribe the lyrics. This is not only a really buzzy way to start a lesson, but it gets students quiet, developing their ability to listen pointedly, and allows

them a brief moment bathing in language; which may just be a reasonable definition of the service we are employed to provide for them.

Ask them to read their transcriptions back after the exercise. You will find yourself in an interesting debate about how language creates meaning.

One starter should be enough to see you through a whole teaching career. The same person will rarely observe you more than once. And the whole nonsensical idea will probably have been dropped by the point that the second observation is booked.

I wrote this a few years ago now. The starter activity is yet to be dropped. It will be. Absurd fashions don't last forever. The starter will eventually go the way of the rah-rah skirt, the puffball and twenty-inch flares, and will be thought of as having been every bit as ridiculous.

GUIDED – INDEPENDENT – PLENARY

The guided bit allows you a brief hour to strut and fret in front of the kids and, erm, actually teach them something, which some teachers find useful. Ofsted would argue that such an approach is anti-constructivist and will likely give you a four for (four denoting 'inadequate') in-lesson observations. The independent bit is where you give them a tawdry comprehension worksheet to fill in, and the plenary is where you ask them what they learnt in this lesson and they reply, "Nothing. You never teach us anything. We just spend our days filling in crap comprehension worksheets after you have talked at us for ten minutes. And aren't these double lessons boring, miss?"

This structural stricture exists to ensure that you give the students something to do in the lesson, rather than doing all the work yourself as they sleep. And, aside from the fact that it is brutally simplistic to the point of cretinism there is not too much to argue with about it. As an idea it is sound. Sound but dull.

COMMUNICATING LEARNING OBJECTIVES EARLY

"Why are we doing this, sir?" God, I hate it when kids ask this.

"Because I said so. Now get on with it." On reflection though, it seems a not unreasonable question for the poor, industrially-alienated student to be asking. What is the point of this? What's in it for me? If they are unable to identify what's in it for them, then there is every chance they won't do it. What's in it for you, the teacher, in going to school is obvious: you get paid. Kids don't. They are in a contract with the school that if they turn up, not only will their parents not be taken to court, but also you will teach them useful stuff. Many of these kids want to know at the front of the lesson what it is they are going to learn in that lesson. Some educationalists will tell you that these children are 'big picture' learners. This means that if they aren't shown the direction they are going in and why they are headed there at the beginning of a lesson, then they'll have a breakdown. It would seem churlish then not to tell them, and so at the beginning of each lesson we tell the kids what they are going to learn.

Practically, this involves deciding what you think the kids need to learn in the lesson, which is harder than you might think (and is explained in Chapter 4 on lesson planning), writing them somewhere the kids can see, and then saying them at the kids in a very loud voice.

As with chewing gum, telling kids not to talk over you and getting up at absurd times in the morning, you will get very bored of sharing learning objectives with the class. It all gets a bit groundhog day, as for the twentieth time that week you launch into the same tired, "By the end of this lesson you will be able to dissect a ... oh, who cares, for God's sake?" The way of keeping yourself fresh with this is by having fun with it. One of the errors I see new teachers make with sharing learning objectives is being apologetic about it. As it is the first thing the teacher does actively in the progress of the lesson, the way in which you share them can set the tone. Be apologetic, shy or evidently bored and this will transmit to the students. Throw yourself into the teaching, aware that you are teaching with your whole body, all of your voice and every bit of your passion, and the atmosphere in the room becomes electric, primed for learning. State them EMPHATICALLY, in large capital letters; point significantly in the direction of the words in the objectives that excite you, your whole arm extended;

circle the verbs with a board marker; stop in the middle of a sentence and ask the naughty boy which word you stopped on; do the newsreader trick and choose words to stress at random – anything, anything that transmits to the students that the teacher is not bored by the prospect of this lesson, or by them. Emotion is viral, and an excited teacher makes for an excited class.

Once you have shared the lesson objectives out loud, check that the kids understand what it is you are seeking to teach them. First, you ask Jemima, the clever one at the front. Being clever, she has worked out that all she has to do to keep you happy is read the words on the board back to you, which she will do in an unanimated and listless drawl. Then you go deeper into the class and ask the same question of a middle attaining kid. If they are able to either repeat what Jemima has done or come up with a decent fist of reforming the information after it has been processed in their whirring cogs, then you ask the dribbler at the back. If he can tell you what he is learning today, then everything's alright. If he can't, then no one is the least bit surprised anyway, and you just tell him again. He won't remember, but at least you tried.

RECORDING LEARNING OBJECTIVES

The idea of the starter activity, as we have seen, is that it forces kids into cognitive activity immediately they enter the lesson. The sharing of objectives should, if you are doing things in the way Big Brother requires, then be done once the starter has run its course. Many teachers, however (specifically those who reject the notion of the starter as being an unworkable impertinence), start the lesson with the students copying down the objectives into their books at the lesson's beginning. Now, strictly speaking, this isn't the way to do it. Any damn fule no[14] that copying stuff down from

---

14 *This phrase is the copyright of Ian Whitwham: the impeccable columnist in* **Sec-Ed** *a free-sheet you will find in the staffroom. Seek out this magazine and read him, for he is wise. His column is a lone voice of old school sensibility. He will forgive me for nicking his words, as I wrote the foreword of his book for exactly no money at all.*

the board teaches you precisely nothing, and if you were ever given the opportunity to do a great deal of copying off of the board during your years at school, you will recall what an unmitigated joy it wasn't.

In fact, kids' attitudes to copying off the board are a very good signal as to whether the school you have started work at is a good school or not. If they complain when you ask them to do so, protesting that they don't learn anything from it, then it's a good school. If, on the other hand, they complain when you ask them to do anything more than copying off the board, you have walked into the educational equivalent of Accrington Stanley Reserves. If, furthermore, they get postively angry until you ask them to copy off the board, and the moment you give in to them, start purring things like, "'Ear me now. Dis is da real ting. Dis is da proper teaching innit," then you have made a Faustian contract, signed in blood, to stay at that school and change it.

I once witnessed a conversation between a person who was observing my lesson and a student. Ordinarily, Ofsted inspectors seem to have an almost supernatural ability to zone straight in to the one kid whose books you haven't marked for three months, as you scream internally. "He's never in. And he always takes his book home. Not him! Not him! I spent the whole weekend marking every single other kid's book in the class. Why him, God? Why me?"

On this particular observation the inspector's supernatural abilities to hone in on the dull-witted beserker seem to temporarily desert him, and he sidled up to the most spectacularly brilliant, magnificently articulate and wonderfully loyal student I had ever taught at that time. I had cast Dwayne as Macbeth the year before and he had been magnificent; and he manifested a subtle, yet unmistakably arrogant curl of the lip as the inspector asked him, "What are the learning objectives, young man?"

"They're da ting da teacher put on da board, and he aks us to copy them down, cos he kyan be boddered to do a proper starter activity," replied Dwayne, before casting another infinitely disdainful sneer and going back to sculpting a further piece of his customarily elegant prose.

Dwayne had a point. Many of us still get the kids to copy off the board because our supply of near genius, creative ideas isn't inexhaustible, and producing yet another resource for the lesson – other than the five you've already created to use in the main body of the lesson – is a ridiculous request too far. In practice, though, getting the kids to copy down lesson objectives and key words has many benefits. No, it isn't the optimum way of inducing learning, but what it does for you is provide a routine that kids understand; that all of them, even those with no literacy, can manage. It also has the added benefit of settling the class. It is the fact that it is not a cognitive task that causes many teachers still to use it. Cognitive involves some kids not being able to do it: non-cognitive means you get a calm lesson start. Perhaps you shouldn't. Or maybe you should. It works and it's easy.

SHARING LEARNING OBJECTIVES – A DISSENTING VIEW

I met a very impressive, learned and intelligent woman this year. Prior to sitting with fellow talking heads on a panel in a posh building, we spent a few minutes in as animated a discussion about ICT in schools as was possible given that I had been awake since 1974 and it was now nine o'clock at the very least. During this conversation she revealed an intriguing perspective on what she took to be the biggest nonsense in modern teaching: the sharing of learning objectives. "How do we know what they are going to learn at the beginning of the lesson?" she railed. "It's preposterous." Slowly, I began to see her point. If we take the constructivist viewpoint as a start, and accept that kids create their own meaning and learning if we just give them a series of tasks to do around the subject, then actually defining what they are going to learn in a lesson before it takes place is necessarily going to be inaccurate. We will only ever know what the kids have learnt after the lesson has progressed. Therefore, whilst plenaries still remain a valuable concept – "Just, out of interest, class: what did you learn this lesson?" – telling the kids what they are going to learn is a fatuous piece of egotism on the part of the teacher, and perhaps the statement of learning objectives should always be accompanied by a caveat: "In this lesson I will teach you this, that and the other … but you will learn something else entirely different. And, no, I haven't got a clue what it is going to be."

I heard tell of a teacher who always put the 'hidden third objective' on the board, and pupils were asked to guess what this was at the end of the lesson. This seems a pleasing compromise between doing what you're told and doing what's right. In spelling out two objectives at the front, the teacher ensures he won't be right royally told off by a senior manager with a clipboard, but in having a third objective that the students themselves reveal at the end, he remains alive to the fact that learning is an investigation, and we won't always get the results we expect at the beginning.

There is also the fact that the spelling out of learning objectives is not only drab, dry and utterly formulaic, it tends to destroy the mystery of the process, revealing the teacher's art to be little more than a set of dull steps any donkey could follow. Additionally, Geoff Petty (whose book *Teaching Today – A Critical Guide* is a very useful text) has spoken of the results of a study where, with the use of various control groups, the authors of the study systematically deleted various elements of the lesson for a period of time to see which elements of the lesson were crucial to optimise kids' learning. They found that all that really counts is the process of practice and review. Not sharing lesson objectives at the front end made no difference whatsoever to the kids' learning.

However, it is the current orthodoxy to spell them out, and you don't get the chance to have a fevered discussion with an Ofsted inspector about why you regard the whole notion as being unsound; they just sit at the back and tick a box that says you are either 'rotten', 'average', 'promising' or 'conforming fully'. There is no dialogue to inform their rapidly drawn conclusions. And so, I'd recommend that, for now, you share them with gusto and vim, but experiment while doing so. It is far, far too monotonous, under-evolved and simplistic to be the optimum way of running things. You may find a better way. But not unless you have the guts to try it from different angles.

DO YOU REFER BACK TO THE LEARNING OBJECTIVES IN THE LESSON?

This is something really good teachers do. It's a simple enough trick, but can be unaccountably difficult to remember to do sometimes. If you are interested in being seen as outstanding, though, then you'd do well to put it in your armoury of tricks on the first day and persist with it so that it becomes second nature when you are teaching, observed or not. It is an extremely simple little technique. Halfway through the lesson you go back and ask the class what they are learning today? They will reply, "Nothing. The activities you've set us appear to have no link whatsoever to the objectives." You will cuff precisely three of them about the head, and go back to what you were doing.

Another cunning way of slipping this technique into the lesson is to plan two plenaries: an end of lesson plenary and a mid-lesson one. This is a technique that will have you marked out as a future advanced skills teacher very quickly indeed. A teacher who is in touch with the genius of the form might even plan a mini-plenary every ten minutes, or might experiment with running the whole lesson back to the front, so that you ask them what they are going to learn at the beginning, give them some independent work to do, then teach them something and follow this be telling them what they have learnt. Try it. It'll probably work in a more interesting way than running the four-part lesson in the order you are meant to run it, you'll learn more about what works and the kids will probably have a markedly more interesting time.

KEY WORDS

Allocating a set of key words for each lesson to introduce the kids to seems to have had its lard[15], and I note, with not a little consternation, that many schools don't even have a box for them on the lesson plan pro forma any more. They should.

---

15 *Northern dialect for 'had its day.'*

If we traipse off into a brief philosophical diversion for a minute, I have always felt the process of giving kids key words for each lesson was actually, in condensed form, what we are there for. Equipping working class kids with high order vocabulary is, if you think about it, the most profoundly political part of the job. In introducing kids to higher order language, you are enabling them to convey an increasing complexity of thought, and, besides this, you're also teaching them how to talk in the language of the orthodoxy – those who hold the reins of power. In enabling them to speak this language (whilst letting them know that their own cultural mode of expression is also entirely valid and effective) we give these kids a chance to grapple on even linguistic terms with those who would be their oppressors. In enriching kids' vocabulary we give them a fighting chance, if they wish to take up the reins, of changing the world.

And so, while I am, at the very least, ambivalent about the function and necessity of the learning objective, I tend to regard bringing in five or six new concepts, as embodied by specific pieces of vocabulary that you'll make vivid in some way, as being almost a moral responsibility. I also tend to use them as the key drivers of learning in a lesson.

If you are working on a normal whiteboard then it is useful, at the lesson's start, to have the objectives written out on the main body of the board, but to save a column on the right hand side to record key words. If sharing learning objectives on an IWB (through a PowerPoint you have been up half the night creating), then you just have them on a second page after the one detailing the objectives. Then, probably after having had the kids' record them (which though it is more copying, actually gives them a record in their books of all the new vocabulary you've taught them), you launch into some vivid illumination of the words' definitions.

There are two main ways in which teachers get key words wrong. They either set vocabulary that is far too simple, and that everyone already knows in any case, or they just leave them hanging on the wall without bothering to mention them at all.

With the first of these: remember, kids live up (or down) to the expectations you set for them. If you give them complex vocabulary to illustrate intriguing technical ideas, they will become fluent in both the words and the ideas they represent. This year, for instance, I witnessed a lesson where a newly qualified teacher, a Ms Green, had evidently got this so right: a top set, year nine science class, in discussion, used language I didn't know existed. I sat with a member of the class as he explained to me, at length and in detail, exactly how *positron emission tomography* worked, unaware that I didn't have the merest clue what it was. It's a good teacher indeed who can lead her class to a blithe expectation that such high-order language is merely a matter of course.

If, however, you set them a load of words that illustrate little other than a certain intellectual sluggishness, then you will get a classroom full of intellectual slugs. Key words need to be high order, subject specific, technical vocabulary that they will probably not get from any other lesson (unless we are talking about some of the rhythmic terms that cross over in all the performance related subjects). If you are a science teacher, for instance, you should consider 'diffusion' a decent key word, and 'bucket' a shocker; an English teacher would consider 'homophone' to be of use and 'book' crassly simplistic; maths teachers might find 'numerator' worthy of consideration, but 'protractor' a waste of everyone's time and energy.

The second greatest sin in setting key words is doing it in an entirely tokenistic manner. It doesn't take a long time to think of some double interesting, high order, conceptual stuff related to whatever you are studying, but many teachers do it as a, "Oh bugger I've got to think of something to stick on the board" add-on. They display the words on the board and then … nothing. They don't even go as far as bothering to define them.

Key words are best used immediately after you've shared/shouted the objectives, as the key drivers of the guided bit of the lesson. As they are merely signifiers for a concept, then you'll find that in defining them in interesting ways, you are delving into the good stuff. The key is in what method you use to define them, and this is where your creativity comes in – find your own way. However, just so as to give you an idea of the kind of thing you might want to be looking at, here are a few stock techniques I'll use to define some of the key words that come up with regularity in my subject.

Empathy – I'll sit on a chair next to a young man who's been seated facing the rest of the class, and proceed to give him pretend slaps on the leg. (He has agreed to this before the class, choking back his obvious scepticism in order to show sir his bravery and passion for education.) On every cod slap he lets an agreed mewl of "Ouch", and I improvise a feigned display of sympathy. "Oh. Is Mr Beadle hitting you in class in front of all your mates? That must feel terrible." We'll repeat the exercise with a subtly amended script. "Oh. Is Mr Beadle hitting you in class in front of all your mates? The bastard did that to me too. I hated it, and I hated him for doing it to me. I know exactly how you feel." I'll then ask the difference between the two scenarios.

Juxtaposition – Take one student and get them to stand at the front of the class, and then ask the other students to say what they notice about him. The responses will be pleasingly banal: "He's tall." "He's got his hands in his pocket." "He is black." Then get another student, who is neither tall nor black, and is not prone to putting her hands in her pockets, and ask the students what the differences are between them, or whether indeed they can notice any striking similarities. Suddenly, the answers are more perceptive and analytical: "Well Lou Ann hasn't got her hands in her pockets, which suggests that she is, perhaps, more relaxed than Cedric." "She's staring straight at us, whilst his head is slightly downcast. It's obvious who is the more confident of the two." "Despite the fact that they are different size, gender and ethnicity, they're both students at the same school." Explain that the process of putting two things together for effect is called juxtaposition and that by going through this process of juxtaposition, poets allow us to see things in a new light, just as we saw new detail about Cedric by putting Lou Ann next to him.

Beat – Get the class to hold down a straight four-four beat by clicking their fingers. (They will speed up and you will have to do it about four times before they are able to do it properly.) Then separate the class and get half of them to hold down the beat and the rest to write a sentence defining what they are hearing. Laugh loudly in scorn at their awesomely inaccurate definitions, until such point as a child says the word, 'repetitive'. (Actually, this one serves to illustrate a useful process with key words: rather than telling the kids the definition you set up a situation where they involve themselves in investigatory thought and come up with their own. Once a student has come up with the definition, and has been rightly praised for it, then we record that definition.)

The issue with spraying all these higher order pieces of language at kids is that, if they don't get to use them almost immediately, then they will promptly forget they ever existed. This is where good planning comes in. When you get to the independent part of the lesson – the bit where you actually do things with the new information you have introduced to them – make sure that the activities you plan explicitly require the students to make use of the new language. You might set them a ten-minute essay in which they are required to use all of the terms you have introduced correctly; you might ask them to draw the key words in animal form; or to act out a scenario where the key words are personified and they have a mild disagreement. Whatever works for you and is not a horrifically dry comprehension worksheet. Again here, the setting of the task is where your creativity and wild-eyed interestedness in everything comes in. The more creative you are, the more risks you take with the form, the better time everyone will have. Just be assured, though, that if you haven't given kids the opportunity to use the new information they'll lose it before they've even left the room.

PACE

Pace, unutterably vital in lessons, is a confusing concept. Initially, we tend to think that by making our arms and legs move faster, delivering the whole thing in a mad, teacher-led rush that we're delivering a seriously pacey lesson; and our assessors will be ticking the 'pace' box because of the amount of sheer hard work we've put in during the lesson. In fact, the opposite applies. The more conspicuously you sweat, the less pacey it gets.

By showing everyone how hard you are working – by running everything at a million miles an hour, running around every table, desperately supporting students with task, whether they need you to or not – you actually destroy pace. The key word here is 'purposeful'. Purposeful in no way suggests mad, frenetic or fevered. It is a far calmer, even slightly sedate way of doing things. You can semi-ensure this purposeful nature in lessons by sharing the expected timings for each activity and giving time checks. In setting an activity, you build up with, "OK, and for this activity I am going to allow you exactly ten minutes, no more and no less, you may start ... now." It helps to emphasise the urgency required from your students if you clap your hands at this point. When the activity has run for five minutes you give a time check, "You've now had half the time available for this activity," and it is probably best to give time checks with two minutes and one minute to go as well. The time checks let kids know where they should be on the activity and, generally, at least, they make some kind of contribution to keeping them honest on it.

A pacey lesson is identifiable by its lack of dead time at the front end, its well established routines, the teacher's incisive management of transitions and, particularly, in there being a number of different activities for students to complete. As a rule of thumb, the more activities that you somehow find the time to prepare (or, when pushed, to jot down in a planner) for your class, the pacier the lesson will be. It's a substantial bind preparing a variety of activities for each class and it is perhaps this more than anything else that makes your early years of teaching very difficult indeed. You are continually having to come up with new ideas and worksheets, finding that neither idea nor worksheet actually work, and that it all goes wrong, and they all start shouting at you; never once giving any indication that they care a fig for the fact that you've worked really hard preparing the lesson that didn't work. Remember though, if you have a decently organised file management system on your computer, then the first time you produce a resource may also be the last time you'll have to produce it. You can use it next year, and the year after and all the way through into 2050 when you won't be able to retire.

So, eventually at least, it is well worth the hassle of over-preparing for lessons in your first year. Lots of activities equals engaged kids: in that, if one isn't working, you've always got something else up your sleeve with which to surprise and delight your charges. With a seriously well planned lesson you will witness their innocent little faces light up with gleeful awe and wonder as you pull a fifth, no, even a sixth, succinct and engaging activity out of the bag. The lesson will never go completely flat as, if kids appear to be stone bored by the task, or complete it far quicker than you had planned, you just reach in the direction of your toolkit and pull out another task. What is more, in over-planning you won't find yourself in the ultimate of teacher nightmares: a double lesson on a windy afternoon, treading water in front of a fractious class for whom you do not have enough work prepared, wildly extemporising, flailing, hoping beyond desperation that time will somehow speed up, as you realise that you have a half an hour left – and that all you have left in your armoury is talking to them about something they don't want to know. This situation sucks very badly. You'll find yourself in it a few times. If you had planned a series of activities it wouldn't have happened. You'll learn your lesson. Eventually.

ENGAGING INTEREST: VISUAL AIDS AND DEMONSTRATIONS

I observed a Portuguese maths teacher (a maths teacher who was born in Portugal; not a specialist in an obscure Iberian branch of sums) last year who had cut up a series of shapes on coloured paper – triangle, rhombus, even a trapezium – the whole ball of string and the full nine yards! She kneeled behind her desk so that the kids could see neither her nor the shapes, until such point as she poked the shapes up slowly from whence they were hidden. The kids saw them being slowly revealed and had to shout out what they were from their initial glimpse. Oh, how we all laughed to discover what we had taken to have been obviously a circle – couldn't have been anything else – to be a crafty semicircle in cunning disguise playing tricks on us. How we squealed when we realised that the rectangle was actually an oblong. Hold on ...

This for me is what teaching is all about. Toying with expectations. Maintaining mystery. Guessing and getting it wrong.

THE HARRIS TECHNIQUE

A trick that relates well to that of our Portuguese, maths-teaching friend – and which has always worked well for me both in and out of school – is pretending to be Rolf Harris. When creating one of his master works with either board marker or paint, Rolf, an educational giant if ever there was one, would turn, at carefully pre-prepared points, to his awestruck audience, and with a gleeful, Antipodean twang, mouth the question, "Can you guess what it is yet?" Met with several completely wrong answers, he'd go back to puffing and panting, imitating a poorly played didgeridoo as he etched more lines on canvas. This, 'the Harris Technique,' is best employed at the front of a lesson, just as the kids come in.

Standing at the front of the class with a huge piece of sugar paper in your hands which you are slowly cutting into the shape of a vulture, a kite or an ox-bow lake, stopping after every couple of cuts to ask the kids, "Can you guess what it is yet?" is a very effective way of obtaining a class's immediate attention and interest. If deployed with the right questioning technique it can also get instantaneous access to the best of kids' thinking. To start off teaching a certain section of *Macbeth*, I'll take a huge piece of black-as-pitch sugar paper and begin cutting out the shape of a cauldron, whilst asking, "Can you guess what it is yet?" Of course, in the initial stages of the exercise it doesn't in any way resemble a cauldron; after a few cuts it may look like I'm cutting out a fish. When the kids shout out in expectation of getting the right answer, "It's a fish, sir. A haddock, no less." I'll use their responses as a springboard to a series of comparisons.

"Compare a fish to Macbeth."

"They're both wet sir. He gets bullied by his missus," says one bright spark.

"What about his memory, sir?" asks another.

"What?"

"Well, fish don't have very good memories."

"What? Are you suggesting that they've suffered traumatic childhoods?"

"No, sir," he repositions himself, "Fishes forget things quickly, and so does he. He promised her he'd kill Duncan, but he tries to go back on that promise within hours. He's got a short memory."

"Compare Lady Macbeth to a fish."

"Emotionless," shouts one.

"Scaly," pipes another surreally.

"Bog eyed," says Dwayne Dibbly. It is the first time he has ever made a vocal contribution.

"Can you guess what it is now?"

"It's a severed head."

"Compare Banquo to a severed head."

"It's not the same, sir. He doesn't get his head chopped off, he gets thirty odd gashes," says Rod.

"Yeh, but you could say he has been cut off from life like a head cut from a body," counters Antony agreeably.

"What could a body mean other than a body?" Thirty guttural voices intone en masse: "Huh?"

Sir carries on ...

You can use the Harris Technique with the whiteboard too. It's always good to have stocks of different coloured whiteboard markers in your room: firstly, so you're able to ensure your whiteboard work isn't dull, functional and monochrome, and secondly, so you can use the Harris Technique as you draw an exquisite, multicoloured map of the Urals, or a divine fresco of a Roman orgy. (This, of course, is contingent on you still being allowed a whiteboard in your classroom. Many find they have been utterly marginalised or replaced by the idiotic primacy of the interactive dumb-board. Nice one, central government: thirteen hundred gazillion pounds spent just so every class-room can have a piece of kit that ruins the spontaneity of lessons.)[16]

The guided bit of the lesson should have some form of visual stimulus for the kids; and one of the key things that you will be seeking to achieve with its introduction

---

16 *In your first two weeks at school spend every walk from the school gates to your classroom intoning the phrase, "I will not use a board marker on the dumb-board." If you do commit such a crime, you will feel a seriously bad chump, and will have a permanent reminder of what a chump you are, as it is impossible to get indelible marker pen off the dumb-board. You will have to leave school. In shame.*

should be the inducement of not only awe in your pupils, but wonder too. Principally, your mature understanding that the cliché "a picture is worth a thousand words" is actually true should be your guiding motif here.

All the really, deeply silly Americans who sport hair so starched it looks like Barbie's boyfriend's, and who write books entitled *How to be a Great Public Speaker*, *Win that Crowd* or *How to make PowerPoint Really Funky and not at all Boring (Honest)* share the same principle: if you stick words up on a screen and then read those words to your audience, really slowly, then that audience will rapidly get busy with the yawning. If, however, you stick a picture on the screen and ask the audience to think about it, then you will have them engaged, interested and stimulated.

The primacy of the IWB in classrooms doesn't mean, however, that you should dismiss more analogue ways of bringing images into lessons. Cut up Sunday supplements, stick the pictures on the wall, number them and get the kids to tour the classroom on a treasure hunt in the order they are numbered. Give them special things to look for in each image and ask them to report back. Type up a series of words onto a PowerPoint and stick them up with Blu-tack, rearrange them to illustrate a point. Buy a plant pot, fill it with soil and stick into it rulers with words or pictures on top of them; rearrange these to illustrate a point. If you are a scientist show them the cool things you can do with a Bunsen burner and magnesium. Bring nature into the classroom. What could you do with leaves? Is there a way that you could use the swingers' party game, Twister, to demonstrate what you are teaching (generally, there will be). Could you profitably be using a space hopper at this point, and if not, why not? Is there any way we could cut out life size paper footsteps and illustrate the key learning by having kids place their feet in these in order?

The point is that you should always be seeking to bring props in and forcing the issue, making (occasionally) tenuous links between the objects and the subject. Creativity is all about finding links between things, and you should model this to your pupils. I use Buckaroo to illustrate the use of adjectives, Twister for spelling tests and a series of naked, hermaphrodite Action Men to model sentence construction. These are probably not things that the duller teacher would reach for immediately and, as such, are heading in the right direction. By pushing the limits of what you think should be possible, you will be doing your class a favour. They will come into your lessons with an expectation that they are not going to be bored. And that, dear reader, is half the battle.

TOP TEACHER TIPS

Use the Harris Technique at the front end of lessons to elicit awe, wonder and bad guessing.

Use multicoloured whiteboard techniques.

QUESTIONING AND DISCUSSION TECHNIQUES

What initially appears to be the simplest, and is certainly the most overused, of all teacher techniques is, in actuality, the most technically complex piece of pedagogy that you will ever have to employ. The teacher-led discussion is a series of rock-strewn shallows in which your career can come adrift seriously if you continually fail to get it right. Running one successfully is enormously challenging and very difficult indeed to do well, and, sadly, there is a degree of natural to this technique that, if you haven't got it, can take a long and jagged path of tears to acquire.

Firstly, do not go into a teacher-led discussion blithely, thinking it is easy and that you are going to win as a matter of course. You will have to employ rigour if the win is to be yours. Key here is to apply every letter of the law of Rule 6 – One Person Speaking at a Time, Subsections B – D on pages 21–24 of Chapter 1. Before launching into a teacher-led discussion you must set the expectations for that discussion sternly at the very beginning. Without these expectations being rigid, it'll not run at all smoothly, and you will find that not only does it not go in the direction of kids sharing a genuinely exciting series of ideas they have generated, but that it's complete and utter bloody chaos. So ensure, first of all, that you have insisted on pens down, all students are looking at you and no one at all has a pen in their hand. Pause before you launch into it, and then fire off a question.

Be aware of the fact that certain questions will prompt better answers than others. Open-ended questioning requires kids to indulge in exploratory thought (which is a good thing) and to articulate those thoughts (good too – it develops oracy, which, in turn, will lead to them becoming more literate). Closed questions will generally elicit a monosyllabic, one word grunt (which is less of a good thing).

"How?" therefore, is a good way to start a question; "What?" is not. "Why?" is always a doozie; whereas "Where?" gives little back to teacher. "Does?", "Did?" and "Do?" are all stinkers, as they can be answered with either yes or no.

"Does it do what we expected?"

"Yes."

"Oh ... right ... erm ... Did we like the fact that it did that?"

"Yes."

"Do we expect it to do this again?"

"No."

"Oh, bugger."

It takes a lot of mental dexterity to run a teacher-led discussion well. Start with the knowledge that you've got to ask questions that won't elicit dumb, one word answers that require no thought on the part of the students, then build on this by applying the 'praise and build' technique. The key skill here is to genuinely listen with all your attention focused on the thought the student is exploring and, as they are speaking, pick out the thing that they have said that is worthy of praise – that either shows insight, or is articulately expressed – and dive straight in after they have finished with a pointed piece of descriptive praise: "What I love about what you said there is ..." Then, having given the child-who-has-spoken's ego a well deserved polish, you build on what they have said, using it to prompt another question, "But why is what Mark said, brilliant as it was, only half the answer?"

Sometimes, however, as much as you are actually really interested in the thoughts of all the children, and as focused as you are in finding something to praise in what the child is saying, you lose the plot halfway through the listening process, start thinking about something else entirely and forget where you are. The child may be going into a vastly erudite disquisition on exactly why there are no more fish in the North Sea, but you have, by accident, drifted off onto a sunlounger in Ibiza, being waited upon by a host of lovelies. No matter how genuinely interested you are in your students' thoughts and ideas, it happens. In this situation, you are left with a dilemma. Through your demeanour in previous lessons you've set up an expectation that any contribution a child makes will be greeted with positive affirmation, but you've corpsed and are now left in a situation where all eyes are on you and you can't think of anything at all constructive to say. In this situation the clever/expedient path of action is to just repeat back what you remember of what the child has said back to them, in the tone that suggests that what they've said is a really substantial contribution.

The manner in which you run a teacher-led discussion gives you ample chance to make your students feel good about themselves. It also offers a whole slew of opportunities to upset them deeply, mortally; to damage their nascent self-esteem; to pour ordure on their fledgling attempts to communicate their deepest thoughts. I read somewhere that normal human beings have, on average, about six social interactions during an ordinary working day: teachers, as distinct from normal human beings, have in the region of two thousand. It is due to this that you will come home feeling crucified in your first few weeks of teaching. Human beings, despite being social animals, weren't built to be quite that social! It is the social part of the job that will render you near mute and almost impossible to live with when your lover, partner, friends, spouse or anyone else seeks to communicate with you. You will be all communicated out. Furthermore, if you cogitate briefly on this idea, you'll realise that not only does it give you two thousand possible points per day of changing a child's life for the better, it's also two thousand opportunities to get it totally wrong, screw it all up and do some real damage. So, in a teacher-led discussion beware the following.

DO NOT EVER EVEN THINK OF CORRECTING THE WAY A CHILD SPEAKS

You have to know this deep in the very core of your being. It must be part of your core set of values. The way a child talks is who that child is. It is his cultural heritage. It is the way his family talks. It is what defines him as being who he is. And who he is, is OK by you.

Counter-intuitively, this is especially vital with white kids, specifically those of a working class stripe. They are acutely aware that they are perceived as being somehow 'less than', have probably endured years of well meaning arseholes telling them that how they speak is not correct and are sick of having their culture, their families and their fathers' jobs being denuded of value. If you correct how they speak they will hate you with a concentratedly cold globule of anger burning at a still and focused point behind the middle of their eyes. And they will be right to do so.

BLANKING A KID

This, in the unique anthropology of the school society, is a really naughty sin, and it's something that you'll catch yourself doing inadvertently on occasion. Where you have asked a question that is so scintillatingly exquisite it should be displayed inside a glass case in a museum, the words 'the quintessence of open-endedness' emblazoned beneath it, and this question has made every single child in the class raise their hands and do the 'I am going to wet myself' dance, you have to choose a few kids to speak. You won't be able to choose every child to answer the question; otherwise you'd still all be there on Tuesday. So you go through a process.

Firstly, as a matter of policy, you never choose the ones who are going "Oo oo" and jigging up and down as if they've just soiled themselves, as that's no way whatsoever in which to behave, and shouldn't be rewarded by being given the attention the behaviour seeks. Instead, you zone in on those kids who rarely speak, as giving them an opportunity to do so and being supportive of whatever they say will possibly give them the confidence boost they require in order to contribute more often.

But you must ensure that, unless the pant-wetting dance is being performed, you somehow manage not to ignore any child in the class; through an almost super-human display of flitting eye contact, micro-nods, slightly raised index fingers and the application of the single hand, directed at a forty-five degree angle, palm outward technique, you acknowledge every single owner of each upheld hand. By not acknowledging, you are ignoring the fact that they want to bring some positive contribution to the learning. For some kids, who may be totally turned off by education, attempts at a positive contribution will be very rare indeed. You owe it to them, to yourself and to your colleagues to reward that positive contribution.

Ignore or *blank* such a kid and they'll give up. Once a child has totally given up on education, their chances of going full rogue, nicking cars, collecting Asbos and murdering decent, innocent family men are enormously enhanced.

Another way of doing things that works very well to quell the over-excited class, all of whom are clamouring to be heard, is the 'You – then you – then you' technique. Where the discussion has outlived its usefulness but kids are still indicating that they want to make a contribution, or where you need to regain control of the over-animated class, you go into game show host mode and, in your best Dimbleby-lite, patrician accent, say, "I'll take contributions from Antony, then James, then Samantha," indicating where they are sitting with an index finger pointing down from an arm, upwardly angled to forty-five degrees in their direction. You continue, "And then we really must move on. Everyone else, I'd love to hear your contributions, but I'd like all hands down please." This regains your control of the class, calms the kids down and still keeps the lesson purposeful.

In many ways, running a teacher-led discussion can be likened quite accurately to the job of a game show host. (In some schools your client base and the audience of the *Jeremy Kyle Show* will be markedly similar.) And there is a definite performance element to it. During the running of a teacher-led discussion you have to teach with the whole of your body, and it is here that your gestural skills have to be quite finely honed. You might get away with the performance skills of the ham repertory actor, but it will run far better if your gestures are practised and nuanced, and you understand that to communicate with any sincerity you must continually seek eye contact with the kids you are teaching. Rehearsal at home will make you feel like a complete moron, especially if you get caught doing it by someone, but it will help you inhabit the gestures more comfortably. All other performers rehearse their act. Why should teachers be any different? After many years of being in the classroom, I still get caught by the missus sat in my study chair animatedly rehearsing the particular arm movements I will use if I have to do a speech to posh people, or a lesson to a class who present a specific challenge, as either there are absolutely loads of them, or they are famously naughty. Neither of us is embarrassed by this any more. I don't feel like I've been caught fiddling with my johnson, and she accepts that rehearsal is a key part of the job I do that puts the bacon in our kids' bacon sandwiches.

It is also useful in a teacher-led discussion to resist the temptation to tell kids stuff. You are not a combatant in the ruck. You're officiating it. It is OK to throw in the odd piece of information to move things forward, but in the event of a child asking you a question, it's always best to reply with, "Well, what do *you* think?" – The word education comes from the Greek term for 'drawing out', not for 'pushing in', and Geoff Petty's concept of 'teaching without telling' is a useful maxim to bear in mind whilst running a discussion.

THE CARDINAL RULE OF THE TEACHER-LED DISCUSSION

You must insist that any child who wants to make a contribution to the discussion raises their hand and you shouldn't consider ever taking a point from a child who shouts their ideas without teacher's permission to speak. Should they do so, you may commit the chief sin of running a teacher-led discussion, blanking a child, with impunity.

This insistence makes the whole enterprise feel as if it belongs to some time back in the age of flared trousers, paisley shirts and free love, and you will feel, whatever the age of the kids you teach, that you are patronising them; treating them like babies. There is a solid argument that you are (see Teacher-led Discussions – A Dissenting View, below). However, if you don't insist on this, and try to play it all a bit freer, a bit more 'jazz' so to speak, then things soon run out of control, particularly with the younger class. Turn-taking is a vital skill for human beings to learn. We cannot communicate efficiently or effectively without some understanding of the fact that it is not always our turn to speak. (The bore sitting alone in the boozer nursing a lacerating sadness over his utter isolation did not learn this lesson at all well – and look at him now.) And so, one might argue that it is important that kids have a lesson in this every day.

Stapled to the wall in pretty well every classroom in the country is a routinely ignored, dog-eared piece of laminated, coloured paper displaying the school or classroom rules. Somewhere near the top of this will feature the line, "Only one person speaking at a time." You cannot have discussion where this rule is not enforced without it going in the direction of chaos. Teacher you may be; clever enough to deal with three simultaneous conversational inputs you are not. A key technique, which seems to work quite well in this instance, is using praise at the same time as referring to the notion of respect. If Jemima is in the middle of a sentence, and Maxwell, forgets both his manners and his comic timing, and interjects right in the middle of Jemima's sentence, then we stop the whole thing and calmly point out that what Jemima was in the middle of saying was really apposite and telling, repeat a section of it so that she remembers where she was, and then inform Max he is not giving her the respect that she richly deserves. The mention of the word 'respect' (often pronounced without the 't' in schools) with some kids seems to have a near magic effect. It is the parlance of da yoot on da street, and is a telling – though somewhat sloppily defined: those who most often refer to the concept appear to have the least understanding of what it means – concept in street culture. By informing Max that respec' mus' be given, you are telling him in a manner that lets him know he has broken the rules of engagement in a language he understands. He'll allow it.

The issue with the hands up and only one person talking at a time rules is that they seem to be lessons that, for some kids, are absolutely impossible to comprehend. Consequently, there is a sublime futility to the practice of running a teacher-led discussion. All day, every day, every teacher in every school spends every lesson saying the same thing. "Hands up please. Don't shout out. One person talking at a time." And all day, every day, every class in every school starts shouting out the answers to every single one of the many closed questions they are asked in the lesson. This absurd ballet stuck in a time warp is the current and the historic status quo, and as things stand, by not insisting on hands up on all occasions, because you just can't stand hearing your voice say it one more time, you are not only opening the door for chaos, but you're also undermining your colleagues, who cannot understand for the life of them why, despite their fascistic adherence to this rule, kids in their classes still think it is OK to shout out the answers.

Or you could take the dissenting view on teacher-led discussions ...

TEACHER-LED DISCUSSIONS – A DISSENTING VIEW

No one actually ever learns anything from a teacher-led discussion. You get to prance around at the front of the class, being all-seeing and all-controlling, but no one learns anything. At all. Hands up those of you who can recall a single, particular piece of information you've retained from the, no doubt, thousands of these you participated in during your own schooling. Scans for hands. Finds none. Gives up and goes home.

If you think about it with any degree of analytical prowess, the teacher-led discussion is merely an unthinking default setting; its existence in a lesson could be taken, by those who have no idea how hard a teacher's life is, to prove that the teacher isn't really giving of their best.

And so, a dissenting view would be ... don't do them. They are an utterly inefficient way of running a discussion as, referring back to one of the two cardinal rules of the TLD, only one person is allowed to speak at a time. Whilst in the midst of such a discussion this seems a sane and vital rule. If you step back from it, however, and gain even a smidgeon of perspective, it becomes quite obviously completely insane. Only one person speaking at a time leaves thirty others in a state either of utter passivity or, worse still, totally zoned out. This can't be the way to do things, but in pretty well every lesson ever taught the teacher-led discussion is employed as a vital piece of kit that any teacher would be deemed daft entering the lesson without, and yet it leaves 96.7741935484% of the class doing pretty well nothing.

Often in class you'll only really get behavioural issues when kids are left without anything active to do or when you stand at the front trying to dictate things. The teacher-led discussion combines these two risk factors: leaving a group of inactive kids with a teacher at the front to be shot, or ignored. Consequently, the teacher-led discussion actually causes half of the behavioural issues you are ever going to get in your time as a teacher.

The solution is simple. Don't do them. If you want to run a discussion do it in pairs, threes or groups, so that more people get a turn to say what they think, and you don't have half the room turned off of learning and anticipating roguery.

The strategies you can employ to ensure that all the kids in the room contribute to speaking and listening activities are manifold, and this is an area where a whole lot of really classy work has been done to create learning formats or opportunities that not only really work, but are fun and easy to arrange. It is in the setting of paired or grouped discussion work that you can mark yourself out as the kind of teacher who has thought properly about how learning works, and who is in possession of a special level of super-cool, advanced pedagogical skills.

This book is intended as a guidebook to every aspect of working in the classroom and not a collection of various pedagogical techniques. (If you want to stock up on these buy Paul Ginnis's *The Teacher's Toolkit*.) However, in this particular area, I am of the mind that you really do need to know the full range of ways you can run a discussion, as these form a philosophy of teaching and learning that will enrich your classes. Ensuring you use a great deal of paired and group work is, at the risk of sounding slightly Stalinist, the teaching method employed by the 'ideologically purist' teacher. All group work is underpinned by the notion of giving kids equality of opportunity to contribute; it removes the teacher from being the sole acceptable source of knowledge in the room; and if you plan it well, it gives kids the chance to teach each other, which is actually the most efficient means of ensuring that information is retained.

All human beings possess something that academics helpfully describe as, 'existing schema'. This is the stuff we already know about a subject. In allowing kids to collect those schema in either grouped or paired work, we not only respect their existing knowledge but, in getting them to recall it, we can use it as a bedrock on which to connect the new knowledge they are going to be introduced to or discover.

Aside from this, it is extremely effective in ensuring that you don't have behaviour management problems. Put yourself in their place. You are in a room with all your best mates, sitting around the same table. It's not difficult to work out that, given an option, what you'd want to do is to have a nice little gossip with them. Yet we put kids in this exact situation and then explicitly ban them from doing the thing they most want (indeed are compelled) to do. We actually stop them from communicating with each other. Why? Because the nature of the teacher – student relationship is that you must talk and they must listen. Is it any wonder they kick off? If, on the other hand, you give them permission to do exactly what they want to do – to talk to each other – then you'll find it'll all go swimmingly. They are not being forced to fight against their instinct or desire, and so find the rules of engagement easier to follow.

So hand it over. Let them talk. And instruct them, as you give them a paired or grouped speaking and listening exercise, to make a lot of noise. "I want to hear you speaking … (clap hands) now!" If they don't make a lot of noise they are not learning. So stop them, tell them off for being too quiet and start the activity again.

WAYS OF STRUCTURING PAIRED DISCUSSION (1) – THINK – PAIR – SHARE

This is one of the key ways that learning is structured in pairs and is, I think, used quite often in primary schools, (though I haven't seen it used too often in the secondary school classroom). We start off either by giving a piece of individual work (analysing a text, for instance, highlighting various parts of it) or, better still, we just ask the kids to sit in a space away from their desks and to think about something. (In the fast moving,[17] highly pressurised, Ofsted regulated, target driven world of education, where it seems, at points, that teachers' accountability can be so extreme that we dare not set an activity we cannot rationalise as making an exact, pinpointed contribution to exam results, we fail to give kids the chance to sit still and think often enough. It can be really valuable to sit them away from each other, ask them to close their eyes and just give them a subject to think about for a minute.)

---

17 *This phrase would have been ironic in the seventies. It isn't now.*

You then ask them to get into pairs and compare the results of either their analysis and highlighting, or of the thoughts they were having when sitting individually with their eyes shut. Animated discussion ensues (note) with every member of the class actively involved. No one has been given implicit permission to zone out.

WAYS OF STRUCTURING PAIRED DISCUSSION (2) – PAIRED TASK

A paired activity is simply getting kids to do something in pairs, on which default setting, you would get them to do individually.

You could put a reasonable argument together that there's never much point in setting individual tasks, unless you are assessing (formatively or summatively); in that sitting, either being able or not able to complete the questions etched out on a bland worksheet, is not going to help you retain the information as well as working with your mate would. If he is higher attaining than you, then he'll help explain the things that you can't grasp, probably better than the teacher does, in a language you can understand; and if it's you who's the higher attainer, you'll be caused to clarify your thoughts on the subject by explaining them to your more needy chum. By having to express those thoughts in language rather than just go through the internalised cognitive process that individual work involves, you'll have processed them into a form that you'll find is more readily available come the time you have to recall them.

It's always worth your while challenging the accepted notions. Your bog standard lesson will involve a teacher-led discussion, followed by some work to be completed individually. And, if I might set you a little thinking homework, how would this differ from replacing this with two separate activities to be completed in different pairings? What are the technical difficulties with both former and latter? Which is likely to induce the most learning and be more likely to keep the kids on task? Why? (This question is not rhetorical, by the way.)

WAYS OF STRUCTURING PAIRED DISCUSSION (3) – FACE-OFF

More homework, I'm afraid. "Desks are the enemies of learning. Discuss."

They exist solely so scared teachers have something to hide behind, to separate them, the boss, from *them*, the students – potential anarchists all. If you are secondary trained it will seriously help your development as a teacher if you ask the drama teacher whether you could come to see him or her teach a few times in your first term. In a drama studio you will see teaching without fear. Kids sit on chairs in circles, there's not a desk in sight and the children actually get to use their bodies and to move around in the lessons. Every lesson in every school should have the philosophical freedom of the drama lesson.

A method of getting kids to talk to each other in pairs, which has just such a philosophical freedom to it, is to shift the desks to the side of the class (if you can get used to doing this on a pretty regular basis, you'll be a very good teacher indeed) and just get them to sit, facing each other, knee to knee, with a Rizla's width between those knees. Hand them out a piece of work (Collect ten reasons why Macbeth/Hitler/Tinky Winky was responsible for his own downfall, for example) and just let them get on with it. You'll find that they engage almost instantaneously. What is more, the flexibility that your new classroom organisation has given you allows you to move on to ...

TWOS TO FOURS

Referred to by circle averse Americans as think – pair – square, this is every bit as uncomplicated as it sounds. The pairs join with another pair into a four. At this point you can ask them to compare their ten reasons and consolidate them into the best ten, or you can give them a completely new task. When you run this successfully for the first time as a teacher – and it is very easy indeed – you begin to get the sense of how much can be achieved without the desks clogging up the room. The only technical issue occurs when the number of kids in the class is not divisible by four and you have two kids left out who do not have a four to join. In that case, you just separate that pair and allocate them each to a separate group of five.

FOURS TO EIGHTS

I'm not sure think – pair – square – octagon scans well at all, so we'll leave the Americans to play with whatever amuses them and tell you that this is a step you can take after twos to fours. It creates bigger groups who can all have a lovely chat about something curricular. Maybe even in a circle.

WAYS OF STRUCTURING DISCUSSION IN THREES

In many schools the concept of 'learning threes' is held to be a valuable means of developing staff. You might find that, on your first day in your new job, you are given two names of staff that you are somehow magically able to find the time to spend afternoons in fevered consultation with about the best way to induce 'deep learning'[18] in your charges. It doesn't work, as there is never any time spare to devote to it.

However, this slightly perverse concept of educational troilism is of value for your students. There are several reasons why working together in threes has value. It is particularly useful if you have a high proportion of kids at an early stage of developing English as an Additional Language, in that with individual work there is every possibility, unless you have differentiated properly, that they won't be able to access it at all, and, in pairs, they'll either sit mute letting the other person do the work, or

---

18 'Deep learning' is a concept that appears fashionable at the moment. It is merely a bullshit pairing of two words that some bright spark came up with, thinking it made him or her sound revolutionary or clever. It signifies nothing. Treat anyone who uses this term as if they are riddled with syphilis.

their partner will just do it without attempting to communicate with them. If you put these students in threes with one native English speaker and someone from their home culture who has slightly better developed skills in speaking English, then they get to involve themselves in a way that they wouldn't in pairings or bigger groups (where they can disappear).

WAYS OF STRUCTURING DISCUSSION IN THREES (1) – ALLOCATING ROLES

When in learning threes, it can be a good idea for the teacher to allocate roles to each person in the three: one might be the scribe, one might be the reader and another the leader – any role that your teacher creativity can possibly define. For instance, it can be a useful activity to set up a competitive structure between A and B (an argument perhaps), and to have C referee or judge it. From thence, it is very easy to change the roles around, twice, so that everyone gets to have a go at performing each role.

LARGER GROUPS – OPTIMUM GROUP SIZE AND RELATION TO CLASSROOM ORGANISATION

As we move to groupings larger than threes, which are always, somewhat paradoxically, referred to as being 'small groups', the range of ways of structuring this become dizzying. There is a question, though, as to what is the optimum grouping for the small group discussion? For me, this is heavily influenced by class size and classroom organisation. Generally speaking, if you work in the state sector you will have a class of thirty kids and you will be teaching them in a way too small box that goes by the name of a c-l-a-s-s-r-o-o-m. There's a bewildering array of expectations as to the number of differing methods you will employ to teach the thirty or so children that have been squeezed into this box. You will be expected to use the space to get them to write essays, individually; to sit in pairs and collect their combined thoughts; to try out different roles in threes; and to have big discussions in small groups. Then you will be told they must have the opportunity to role play, to move around in lessons; they must be able to access your display as a learning tool; you must be flexible about the use of desks and be prepared to push them all to the side of the room to create suffi-cient space for them to do fours to eights activities. And this overflow of information, of new techniques that you are never in your life going to be able to master (despite the fact that individually they all appear to be pretty simple), will cause you to bash your head onto your teacher's desk, sobbing.

Relax. There is an optimum way to lay out your classroom to ensure that all these things and more are possible. And that is, have your tables in five groups of six. There are thirty kids in your class: the simplicity of the sum 5 x 6 = 30 solves everything.

In groups of six, all the above groupings are possible without huge rearrangement of tables, or what an old head of department of mine used to describe as faff. Faffing in lessons is not what we want: no one ever learnt anything from an extended faffing session. So, in order to prove we are not at home to either Mr or Mrs Faff, nor indeed any of their charming yet dithery children, we leave the tables so that six kids can sit around them in five different groups. This way, individual work can be done, by just focusing ahead of yourself onto the page teacher has lovingly photocopied from a textbook; paired work can be done by turning to your neighbour; learning threes are half the kids at the table and small group work is done in sixes. Voila!

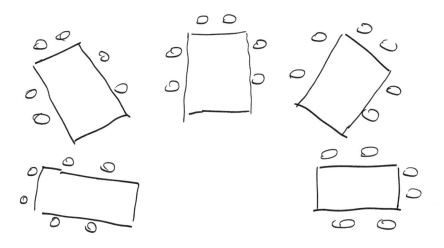

It also makes it relatively easy to have the same seating plan for every lesson. (For more information on these see the sections on differentiation in Chapter 4.)

Once you've got your tables set in five groups of six then, should space allow, it's a good idea to create a mini-performance space in the middle of the class. There's a really hot teacher tip about classroom organisation that takes seconds to do at the beginning of the year, but pays off in terms of making your classroom the optimum learning environment, (which, I'm aware, is the kind of crass phrase you would expect to be coined by some bureaucrat 'stakeholder' working in an office trying to tell teachers how they're all doing it wrong): you push the tables as far as you can to the sides of the room without actually asphyxiating the kids as they try to sit behind them. In doing this you are maximising the space in the class for learning. There's no space wasted behind the kids and their tables; all of it (and in some classrooms the use of the word 'all' here is perhaps a substantial over-estimation) is available for the kids to do a presentation at the front of the class, or for them all to get off their chairs and perform a fantastic role play about algebra.

STRATEGIES FOR SMALL GROUP DISCUSSION (1) – JIGSAW METHOD

You need to know this one. You will (hopefully) have been taught it on whatever course you studied to become a teacher, but it's a method that has to be used in the classroom quite early on, as it takes a substantial amount of preparation and you will need to know intimately that the benefits of employing this method are such that they make the work setting it up well worthwhile.

First, you divide the subject you are teaching into five different areas that your students need to know about, then source some materials either from the internet, a textbook or, more excitingly, through the use of artefacts. (I've taught with this method quite effectively using a series of antique dollies.) You then distribute these items, one per group. (Remember, we are seated in five groups of six.) They then enter a discussion in the initial groups about the source material you have given them, either according to a sheet of questions you have handed out for them to research in the groups, or even a series of roles within the group that you have pre-allocated. Having been given a defined amount of time to complete this initial study, they get busy with the chat.

Whilst the initial chat is going on, teacher either takes a rest, puts her feet up and just observes how well it is all going, or you might want to make that much needed trip to the toilet – they won't notice you've gone. If you are being observed, however, you might want to tour the groups pretending to take note of what they are saying, and randomly ticking a piece of paper to show the observer that you are involved in a continual process of assessment of your students. At this point, if I don't need to go to the toilet, I'll tend to stick sticky labels on the kids' upper arms. Y'know just for the fun of it. Labels that say 'kick me' or, in the case of the child sporting the ripest aroma in the class, 'I need a wash'.

Before you pick up the phone and report me to the GTC police, the labels don't actually say this. They say, 'Expert Group 1', 'Expert Group 2' all the way through to 'Expert Group 6'. (If you are feeling particularly creative you could have the stickers say something related to the topic: 'Positron Emission Tomography Group', 'Radionuclide Group', 'Fluorodeoxyglucose Group', but the educational benefit the kids receive from this is negligible and it looks like you are trying a bit too hard.) You can pick the labels up quite cheaply from WHSmiths, and they are a useful thing for the improvising teacher to have in their desk in any case.

Why the upper arm? Because you can't be arrested for sticking something on a child's upper arm.

Once all the kids have the labels, and have progressed sufficiently with the initial task, call time on it. (With grouped discussions, however, you will often find that where you think the natural break comes is way too soon, and that the kids have way more to say, so take your time here – let it develop.) Having called time on the first activity, you point out that the groups they have been in are their 'home' groups, and that they are now to move to their new 'expert' groups. Point to which tables host expert groups 1 though to 5 and allow a little faffing as they negotiate where they are going next, and do the walking and bumping into each other thing as they get there.

Whilst in the expert groups they take turns in sharing what they learnt in the home groups. When you judge that this activity has come to its logical end (generally when you see that one group has run out of conversational steam – so that no one group is left there, bored, ready to kick off while they wait for the others to finish), you ask everyone to return to their home groups wherein a further grouped discussion takes place about what they picked up in the expert groups.

And that, as they say only rarely in Luxembourg, is that. In completing a jigsaw method for the first time in class you'll come to an understanding as to why it is held by those in the know to be the ultimate of all teaching techniques. Kids learn enormous amounts from this activity: it develops skills of oracy and of turn-taking; they also learn predominantly from each other. You are not involved in any way other than as a facilitator, and, as such, it is a serious, über-constructivist, Ofsted pleaser. I will admit that in the many hundreds of lessons I've sat in the back of I've never once seen it used, which is an indication really of how risk-averse teachers are in this country.

The jigsaw method looks difficult to administer at first, so many teachers don't get so far as to doing their first one. If you are reading this book prior to starting your first job at a school, do yourself a favour. Do it in your first lesson. There will be the odd, slight technical issue, but I guarantee your first lesson as a teacher will have set the agenda for the pupils. It'll either be a great lesson and you will instantaneously be regarded by your class as a teacher who is worthy of respect or, less likely, it'll have some serious teething problems, in which case, it's still all good. You will have learnt pretty well all you need to know about how to run a jigsaw and will have it in your teaching armoury for all time.

STRATEGIES FOR SMALL GROUP DISCUSSION (2) – CAROUSEL

A carousel is phenomenally simple, both conceptually and in terms of its management in class. The issue, again, is that you have to prepare five separate activities, but if these five activities give you an easy, exciting lesson in which the kids learn loads (and they do), then it's well worth the extra prep. Basically, you give separate activities to each group at the beginning, along with an allotted time frame for their completion, say five minutes. At the end of those five minutes you move the activities one group to the left or clockwise, so that all groups immediately have a new activity. Do this five times and you've got a smashing twenty-five minute 'independent' section for your lesson.

You can also carousel the students instead of the activity. The activity stays rooted on the same table and the students move around to work on a new table on each transition. Carouselling the students is riskier in terms of managing the behaviour, as it will often involve kids jostling for position literally and figuratively, and can get ugly. However, in its defence it allows kids to use their legs in the lesson, which stops them from atrophying. It's particularly useful carouselling the students if you are working with car engines or combinations of heavy bricks, as these can be more stubborn when you try to move them from table to table.

COMPLETELY MENTAL STRATEGY FOR SMALL GROUP DISCUSSION – ATTITUDE CARDS

This is really just me being silly, but if your class have worked really hard on some grouped discussion activity and it's all getting a little Friday afternoon and we've been here too long this week, this activity brings a little energy and laughter into the room.

Over the next few pages are a series of cards: photocopy five or so sets of these, cut them up and put them in envelopes. (As a tip, anything that comes in an envelope is likely to elicit an all too brief outburst of temporary excitement from your students.) Hand the envelopes to a responsible member of each group, and ask them to hand out attitude cards, face down. The students read the cards, without telling the other group members what is on them, and in the ensuing discussion they take the role outlined for them on the card.

Say nothing until the very end. If anyone asks you for an opinion, shake your head and refuse to communicate until such point as they have tied it all up. Then add a telling contribution that you have boiled down to two sentences.	You are David Cameron.
Say the unsayable.	You are utterly supportive of the presenter. Whatever misgivings or criticisms of their work that you (or they) may have find the positive and praise it to the skies.
Try to take the lead.	Use this strategy to come up with other, new, fresh ideas.

You are Jesus.	Draw your ideas as they occur. Share them when you've finished drawing them to your satisfaction.
The wild card Join in perfectly normally, but time the session, and two minutes in, stand up and turn your back to everyone else. Stay like this 'till someone addresses you directly.	Try and involve other people. Try and avoid expressing your own opinion, but make sure you get everyone involved.
You are clinically depressed.	This idea completely fires your passion. Get really into it.

How will this impact on future employment?	You are Adolf Hitler.
Take notes and share these at the end of the session.	Assume the body language and attitudes of the naughtiest boy or girl in the school. What does he/she think of it?
Impersonate the teacher you least like at your school: voice, gesture and all. What do they think of it?	Impersonate the teacher you most like at your school: voice, gesture and all. What do they think of it?

Listen for any errors in expression (grammatical, mispronunciation, etc). on the part of the speaker, and point them out. Even if they threaten to hit you.	Pick one person in the group and disagree with everything they say.
Find the positive in everything anyone says.	Say what you really think. Don't censor yourself in any way. Don't spare the feelings of the presenter. For once in your life, tell it like it is.
Over-intellectualise everything.	Take a fundamentalist Christian viewpoint.

What is (perhaps) lost in the learning in this technique (because, in truth, no one learns much from it – I think) is more than made up for by the fact that it is pant-wettingly funny. When you are not being observed give yourself permission to do things just because you think that you and your class will have a good time doing them. They must be related to the learning of course, but don't let the continuous pressure and the talk of standards, standards, standards grind you down. If something promises to be fun, but you are struggling to put what kids learnt from it into a quantifiable box, don't worry too much. The people you are teaching are children and childhood is meant to be a time when you should be allowed to laugh fairly freely. Some kids don't get too many laughs in their home environments. Let them know that, within certain boundaries, they have permission to laugh in your class. And give yourself permission to do so too. The better time you are having the better time they will have.

BRAINSTORMS AND SPIDER DIAGRAMS

We all know what a brainstorm is. You sit in a pair, a trio or a small group, and collect ideas, probably even going so far as to record those ideas on a piece of paper. What you may not know is that the phrase was banned by the Department of Enterprise, Trade and Investment in Northern Ireland as it was deemed as being potentially offensive to people with epilepsy! "The DETI does not use the term brainstorming on its training courses," a spokeswoman said at some point, "on the grounds that it may be deemed pejorative."

It'd make a dog cough up it's dinner with laughter.

They replaced it with the phrase 'thought shower', which, to me is dimly reminiscent of showers of a more golden variety – and is not a picture I want to have in my head when in charge of a classroom full of bright-eyed and impressionable small people. So, we'll stick with brainstorm and the accompanying instruction that if you catch a colleague using the phrase 'thought shower' you have my permission to point at them and guffaw like a drain.

The grouped brainstorm is a pretty dog-eared teaching technique, and kids are generally very well practised at doing them. Often they'll be used at the front end of a scheme of work to collect the kids' schema. The theory being that new knowledge embeds better in your cranium if it is connected to existing knowledge, so teachers the world over who have some idea of what they are doing start off schemes of work by collecting the stuff the kids already know with the aid of a grouped or paired brainstorm and a spider diagram.

For a spider diagram, the bossiest kid in the group grabs the pen and writes the subject, (Shakespeare for instance) in the middle of a landscape piece of white A4. They then draw five or six straight lines coming out of the subject and record their thoughts at the end of these.

The issue with the idea of collecting their schema is that, often, it doesn't exist or isn't worth existing. Get a year 7 class to collect their existing knowledge about Shakespeare and it'll usually look like this:

Which is rubbish.

Where a spider diagram can get interesting is if you put circles on the end of each line rather than just words. You put the words inside the circles, and then (are you keeping up?) 'explode the node'. You take a further two lines off each circle and put circles at the end of these, in which you put a further level of detail from the initial circle. Where a child has written, "Boring" on a spider diagram about Shakespeare, you get them to fill in the two further circles with the reasons they find him boring. You can repeat this process until you have either run out of space on the paper, or your students start threatening suicide; whichever is the expedient option.

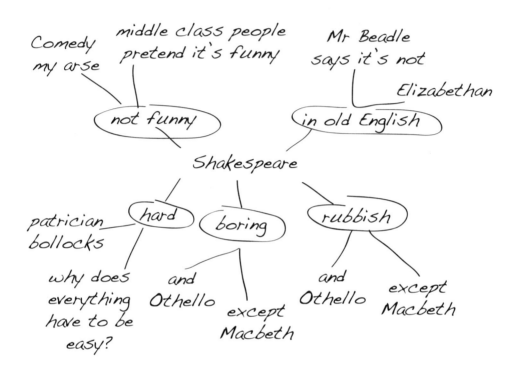

We tend to look at spider diagrams as being a bit babyish in the later years of secondary. As kids have been using them since they were but small, they can get sniffy about being asked to do them when they are fifteen or sixteen. But they are actually very useful as essay planning devices. Using this process of exploding the node[19] and then numbering the ideas in the order that you want to cover them in the essay you

---

19 This was invented by either Oliver Caviglioli or Ian Harris. Not sure which, but as they are mates with each other, I'm sure they can find a way of fighting over who gets the credit in this book that doesn't involve too much blood.

have a really easily constructed essay plan. It is extra good for planning under exam conditions as it can be done so quickly.

As an example, here is a spider diagram turned into an essay, about whether Steve McClaren was a good choice to be manager of the England football team.

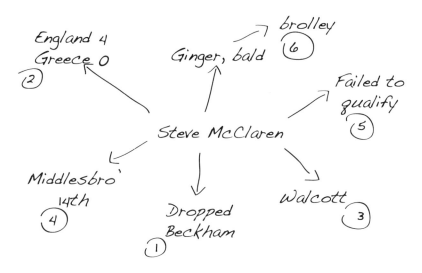

① The alarm bells should have started ringing markedly earlier than they did during Steve McClaren's ill-fated reign as England manager and should have been caused by his infantile decision to drop David Beckham in order to prove he was his own man to the press. In doing so, of course, he succeeded only in proving that he wasn't and was prepared to take populist decisions entirely to please journalists.

② The first game under his leadership was a four-one thrashing of Greece, which leant an illusory impetus to his stewardship ③ and it must be remembered, of course, that he gave Theo Walcott his full debut, (though it is not as if he discovered him, as he had already be in Sven's World Cup squad).

④ However, the idea of picking a boss solely on the basis that he was English (he had managed Middlesboro to 14th in the table the previous season – hardly a phenomenal sucess) soon proved disastrous ⑤. Results went awry, we failed to qualify for Euro 2008 and ⑥ McClaren is now synonymous with being the 'Wally with the brolly' with hair, both ginger and balding, plastered to his anaemic scalp as England bowed out of qualification with barely a whimper.

MIND MAPS

These were invented by a guy called Tony Buzan, who claims them to have almost supernatural powers and, for him, at least, they have — as they've made him richer than Croesus. His invention is brilliantly simple, trademarked and copyrighted. But I doubt he'll read this so here's risking everything ...

1. Grab a load of coloured pencils, or better still felt-tips, and introduce them to a piece of white A4. Make sure you have your paper turned landscape style (because, apparently, we are radiant thinkers and our thoughts need to radiate outwards from a central point), then draw a picture related to the subject you are going to mind map bang in the centre. (In this instance we'll mind map the concept of family and, to help, I have drawn a picture of my own family to help you.)

2. Then using shedloads of colour and being creative with your concept of line, draw five or so curvy, coloured lines coming out from that central point. You might want to put arrows on the end of them.

3. At the end of these lines draw a smashing little picture of five further things that relate to the initial subject. Once you have done this you write a word on (or beside) the curvy line that relates to the picture. (I have drawn crap caricatures of each individual in my family and cleverly written their names on the lines.)

4. Then you take a further three or so lines out from each satellite image and put pictures at the end of these, again writing something related to the pictures on the stubbier lines. You can go as far with this process as you feel necessary, by adding more lines and pictures, even going so far as to Sellotape loads of further pieces of paper so that you have a mammoth mind map that could constitute the display work for the whole wall of a classroom.

The process of creating a mind map is utterly simple; the 'science' behind it equally so. Buzan claims that in combining language (which is processed in the left hemisphere of the brain) and image (which is processed in the right) we are using more of the functionality of the brain than we would with just image or language alone. Consequently, retention and recall of information recorded in the form of a mind map is all the more effective. I've no idea whether this is true, and the claim certainly gives off the fishy waft of abject tosh, but they look pretty on the classroom wall, and kids seem to enjoy doing them. So they're a perfectly decent teaching tool without you necessarily having to believe in any of the CSE level neuroscience.

The uses of the mind map are legion. Firstly, you can use them as a more colourful substitute for the spider diagram when collecting schema at the beginning of a unit of work. If you teach your classes how to do them at an early stage of your relationship, they can be used for manifold functions: to support speaking and listening activities, as a visual script for presentations and, specifically, for revision purposes. Ian Gilbert tells of a story that I've always been tempted to try out, but have never had sufficient energy come May and June. If you teach kids in the room in which they will eventually take their exams and have mind maps on the walls illustrating the key concepts of your subject, they will become so used to these being there they will have an internal visual map of the pictures and come exam time, when you take them down, you can just ask the kids to project their own internal map onto the spaces where the mind maps have been all year, and that way they have access to the information on them whilst in the exam room. It's plausible, captain.

THROWING IN GRENADES – STUFF TO STIMULATE SMALL GROUP DISCUSSION

Buy yourself a copy of *The Little Book of Thunks* by Ian Gilbert. The quality of student chit-chat you'll get out of it is priceless. With Ian's permission I'll quote a couple of his 'thought hand grenades' at you: "Is the gap between the notes music?" and "If I take a photo of a photo of you do I have a photo of you or a photo of a photo of you?" Imagine briefly the quality answers that sparky kids come up with to these questions and buy the book.

There are grenades you can throw in other than thunks though. Odd one out, for instance – see if you can work them out yourself. The idea is that you find a reason that each of the three options could be the odd one out, but in order to justify it you must find something the other two share that the third doesn't. So, what's the odd one out between ...

- A car, a baby and a fridge?

- A cello, a saxophone and a trumpet?

- Albert Einstein, Louis Pasteur and Stephen Hawking?

- Your mum, your dad and your nan?

- Chocolate, crisps and radishes?

- Russia, USA and UK?

- Miss Russia, Miss USA and Ms UK?

- A xylophone, a bag of chips and a surrealist painting?

- Macbeth, Lady Macbeth and Shakespeare?

- An accountant, a bricklayer and an actor?

- A cod, an artichoke and a chicken?

ARGUMENT TUNNEL

Think of this as a classroom version of speed dating. Sure, it comes without the accompanying decimation of faith in humanity and stomach-churning disappointment of speed dating, nor does it do to your self-esteem what 'Bomber' Harris did to Dresden, but it operates on the same principle. With each turn you are introduced to a new person to whom you must speak.

It is pretty adventurous in terms of classroom layout, so, first off, you'll need to push all the desks to the side again. Best, though, that you wait for the kids to arrive otherwise you'll do your back in, or tire yourself out, or give yourself a hernia, or something. Having pushed the desks to the side you line up two lines of chairs along the longest axis of the room, arranged so that those two lines are directly opposite each other.

You give either side a point to argue for or against. The kids sitting in the left hand row might argue that smoking is a good and socially responsible habit, those in the right row argue that it isn't. Any portentous issue for which two arguments might be rationally advanced, no matter how surreal, will do. Asking kids to argue against their beliefs or instincts is a valuable exercise in how to construct a rational line of argument, and also gives insight into how views other than their own may have value or substance. Kids aren't often great at seeing another's right to hold an opposing view – if you doubt this try asking a Christian kid how they know God exists: you'll get the answer, "Because he bloody does, right?" – and experimenting with this vital life skill in the safety of the classroom can only be a good thing.

They are to argue only with the person directly opposite them, and to be reminded that, if they all shout at the top of their voices, not only will they not be able to hear each other, but they will cause the grumpy senior teacher in the next room to come in and shout at sir or miss, and that can only be a bad thing. They must stop arguing the moment they notice you have raised your hand, and then raise theirs too to show that they have seen you.

Once the arguments of the first pairings have borne whatever discursive fruit you think they are going to yield, you raise your hand. They accordingly totally ignore you. Wait it out, they will notice eventually and will raise their hands in a mini-classroom version of a two-dimensional Mexican wave. In most transitionary matters it's better waiting for silence than shouting for it. Shouters have lost control *publicly*. And if you think your colleagues can't hear you, you're wrong.

Having managed the 'everybody shut up' part of the transition you move to the very genius bit of an argument tunnel. Ask the person at the far-left end of each line to stand up and everybody else to move their bums – not the chairs, their bums – one seat to the left. Once they have all moved, you have two people still standing up and two empty seats at the far-right of each line.

Become the mystical weaver of solutions here and put the standing people together with the empty seats so that you have no more of either. As a result of having arranged this movement every child in the room has a new person opposite them. Hurrah! At this point award yourself a free smug expression and instruct them to continue the same argument until such point as it's time to prompt the mini-Mexican wave again and everybody has to find a new partner. Repeat until bored.

Note, you will become bored of this activity before the students do. The right time to stop it is somewhere substantially after your initial reflux of boredom has set in, and before theirs has started.

BRINGING IT ALL TOGETHER – ARGUMENT TENNIS

You can view this in action at http://www.teachers.tv/video/1399. It's a film of this teacher in action at a time before the wrinkles kicked in heavy and deep, and I could still get away with a second-hand suit. There's also a link that says 'How to play argument tennis', written by a person who did not invent it, and who therefore has the rules completely to pot.

Argument tennis is a series of speaking and listening activities (most of which have already been covered in this section) melded together into the ultimate Ofsted pleaser. It is learning as it should be, buckets of fun, buckets of learning, very little work on behalf of the slack teacher. I recommend it. And wish that teaching techniques brought royalties to the originator every time they are used.

This is how you do it:

1.   Choose a contentious issue. Let's take gender as our example.

2. Obtain some research material. When doing the gender thing I will bring parts of Simone de Beauvoir's *The Second Sex* into class. And yes, with year 7s too. You'd be amazed at what kids can understand if you come in thinking they are capable of understanding anything and everything, and that it's your fault if they don't.

3. Run a jigsaw. Start off by getting them to discuss the material in home groups.

4. Stick the labels on their upper arms, then it's into expert groups to share what they learnt from the source material in the home groups.

5. Then back into home groups. What did they learn in the expert groups?

6. Set up an argument tunnel, and have one side of the room argue for males being the superior, one side to argue for females. Repeat till the class are bored (which will be after you are bored).

7. Get them into same gender pairs: face-off style. Hand out a sheet which says something like 'Ten Reasons the Male/Female Gender is Superior'. Ask them to collect those reasons.

8. Pairs to fours. Boil the reasons down to the best ten.

9. Fours to eights. Ditto.

10. Eights to sixteens (yeh, I know, there's only thirty in a class, and three of them never turn up: improvise, bring in two life-sized dolls, or have groups of thirteen, fourteen or fifiteen). At this point you bring in a new technique. You should have two separate circles of children; in the realms of this particular example one group of boys and one of girls. (Though in single sex schools you might want it to be those who'd look good in a dress and those who wouldn't, and in boys' schools … !) The first thing they do – whatever the thing they are discussing is, or the make-up, gender or otherwise – is to appoint one person to be their champion and one as vice-champion. Careful with this last one in the inner cities, as 'Champion of Vice' is actually a highly coveted position in the school and there may well be many killings if you don't phrase it correctly. Give

them exactly one minute to sort this out, otherwise, should you teach girls, the rest of the lesson will be taken up with them dithering manifestly at the door marked decision.

"No. I think you're the best at arguing."

"Oh, no Jemima. You're far more articulate than me."

"No. Psshaw. Preposterous! You're the cleverest. Isn't she girls?"

"Jesus Christ! Will you give it a rest!"

"Sorry sir?"

"Thinking aloud girls. Sorry."

As they are about to enter the gladiatorial environment of argument tennis, they must be properly prepared. Seated in a big circle of fifteen or so chairs with their teams, the champion and vice-champion stay arguing for the side that they have always argued for; everyone else in the group does a reverse tack and begins arguing for the other side. The idea is that this section of the lesson prepares the champion and vice-champion for what they are about to face: argument tennis – the final battle. In coming up against a range of the counter-arguments to their own line under friendly fire, they gain practice in ways they might respond to some of the lines of argument that are going to be directed at them in the more pressurised situation that comes next.

11. While they are doing this, the teacher picks off kids who are not really involved, one or two at a time, and asks them to stand away from their chairs. Teacher then moves their chairs to mark out the tramlines and baselines of a tennis court, and the students sit on them. Once a critical mass is reached, you ask the two champions to sit on chairs situated in places appropriate to an approximation of the positions that tennis combatants might take on the court. Everyone who is left places themselves at either the sides or the base-lines, and if you have any chairs left over without students to sit on them, then they function nicely in the centre as a makeshift, symbolic net.

12. Battle commences. Teacher sits in the position of umpire and selects one champion to serve. They advance an argument that the returner, in turn, attempts to refute. The teacher awards points as per a tennis match (love, fifteen, thirty, forty, deuce, advantage and game). A point is won when one of the players has argued so convincingly that no return is possible or, as is more often the case, when one of the two says something that is so obviously nonsense that it is indefensible. Teacher's decision is final. Where the game is a mismatch and one player is getting slaaartered, then you may decide, in your wisdom, that a substitution is a good idea, and the vice-champion jumps in.

The many benefits of argument tennis

Argument tennis brings together six (count 'em) different speaking and listening techniques in the same lesson, and at no point does the teacher stand at the front telling the kids things. In fact, the teacher does very little work at all during the lesson, aside from managing the transitions and sitting on a table making deliberately eccentric decisions about which argument won or not. It's a completely constructivist activity, enhances students' ability to articulate and, once you've done it a few times, runs like a dream. Try it out early on, so that it sets an expectation from the kids about the kind of learning that goes on in your classroom. Follow the instructions above, and make sure you bring them in when you try it out first. It takes a few goes to get it bang on.

OTHER WAYS OF STRUCTURING TALK (1) – CIRCLE TIME

Sit kids in a circle and something happens. Maybe they too feel the subliminal transcendental hum of the spheres in an amplified form when they are joined together, unified in the harmonious manner of the stones at the 'Henge, or maybe it's just tougher to talk to your mates in a circle when teacher is looking. Either way, they behave better.

If you are attempting to win over a hard class, and it isn't working for you, give them a surprise: bring in a taser! The electric shock those things can give serves to kill the malignant brain cells that cause all the bad behaviour, though can have some effect on their short term memory. Alternatively, if you work in one of those hippy institutions in which tasers are frowned upon, then put the tables to the sides and create the best version of a circle you can, given the constraints your classroom has you under (if room is tight you can do an inner and outer circle). Leave a seat spare for yourself, and then sit down with them and talk about it. Give a whole lesson over to sitting and talking in a circle, and you'll find that, magically, they open up emotionally and you can look for solutions to the behaviour issues as a team. It may be that there is a reason, which is profoundly obvious to everyone apart from you, that they are misbehaving. You will find that, in the golden arc of the circle of emotional one-ness, provided you are prepared to give of yourself, they'll share this reason with you, and you can either do something about it or, at the very least, come in for the next lesson better informed as to who, exactly, these human beings are who you are standing in front of.

Circle time is hugely useful if there is a particular problem with any of the 'isms' or phobias in the class. Thankfully, I have never witnessed a single racist incident in all my time as a teacher, and to be truthful, until they are about eleven kids see no colour. But, then again, I've never worked in Burnley. It exists and you might come across it. Where racism or sexism manifests, get in a circle and talk about it.

What you will definitely come across is rampant, unrestrained and often completely unchallenged homophobia, particularly amongst boys, many of whom are petrified of being gay, and so are inclined to react very fearfully indeed to any suggestion or mention of homosexuality. Kids use the word 'gay' as an indicator of something being a bit crap, which can seem mildly amusing to an immature bastard such as myself, until you put yourself into the place of the gay kid in the class, hearing on a daily basis that the thing he suspects himself to be is shorthand for rubbish. Schools are rabid with homophobia; the vast majority of gay teachers are not out (which is a shameful state of affairs: sophisticated professionals being put in a position where they have to hide who they are), and you may notice that some communities have a bigger problem with it than others. The temptation when you first hear the repulsive 'battyman' first uttered in your class is to go as nuclear as you would should you ever hear a child use the words 'nigger' or 'paki'; and it is a temptation that I've succumbed to on many an occasion. But the better path with any equalities issues is, provided it does not make one particular child squirm in tortuous embarrassment, to sit in a circle and talk about it. Homophobia in schools is at too epidemic a level to ever let it go unchallenged, but you will not change a child's culturally entrenched and conditioned opinions on this by screaming in their face. Educate them by talking with them, in a quiet, calm and measured manner about what their views and behaviour are doing to other humans.

Circle time is perceived to be solely a primary school technique. It's not. If you work in secondary and you don't have it in your toolkit, you are missing out on a vital tool.

(One technical issue with it: if you hand out pieces of paper as source material for discussion in the session, after they have read them, get them to put them on the floor in front of them. Otherwise the rustling of paper in hand will irritate the piss out of you.)

PHILOSOPHY FOR CHILDREN

This could quite reasonably be described as a movement. It started, I believe, in the United States, when a philosophy teacher, bored by the asinine responses of some of his university undergraduates, started teaching philosophy to smaller, school students. Since that time it has grown into a global movement which is well worth investigating. It is of value in any sector.

What we can take from it that can be applied across the curriculum is a process, and that process is stimulus – questions – connections – discussion. Immediately, on laying it out we begin to see that it creates a lesson structure that, if followed, can be applied to any subject, and will inevitably lead on to some mustard speaking and listening opportunities for the class.

Stimulus

In Philosophy for Children this will generally be a child's fable or fairy tale; something containing an apparently simple moral lesson. We read through this as a group. However, 'stimulus' might equally be taken to mean an artefact, an equation or a painting. Whatever suits. The key to running a lesson to this structure is the second section.

Questions

Kids are asked to record any question that occurs to them during the period they are presented with the stimulus. If you are not cast iron strict with this, or do not present the instruction with sufficient teacherly verve, then they will just sit there doing nothing and, as they haven't recorded any questions, the whole of the rest of the lesson will be screwed. Where you are reading, for instance, a fairy story, then it is easy enough to stop at the points at which you, the teacher, feel should have raised a question in the collective minds of your class, and then gently guide them towards the area in which that question might be hiding. It is of use here to stop at regular intervals, reminding the class that they must record any question that occurs to them, otherwise they'll just sit there and passively soak up the lovely story, learning nothing.

How you ensure that questions are recorded when you are presenting stimulus material that is in the form of an artefact or an equation I am not sure. If, for instance, you are talking through a maths equation or process, then it would be wise to stop at every section and check that questions about that process are forming in kids' minds and that these are being recorded. With an artefact, you might want to give the class a guided tour of it, pointing out its key features and reminding the class that, if they have any questions about those features, they should be recording them.

The idea is that at the end of your presentation, story or talk, all kids should have stained the paper with a series of questions that have come to them during the stimulus stage; and it is their questions that form the springboard from which the rest of the lesson takes off. The fact that they have generated what they want to know about the stimulus themselves gives them a sense of ownership of the lesson and, besides this, they are actually getting answers to things they want to know rather than what you *think* they want to know.

Connections

This section is not compulsory, but forms a useful pre-discussion stage that gets kids speaking to each other and categorising pieces of information. Get them into pairs, threes or small groups and ask them to go through the questions they have generated, seeing if they can put them into categories. One of the many things you are seeking to achieve as a teacher is to get kids to form intriguing connections between things; this is the bedrock of high order reasoning, and it's very useful indeed for children to have practice at this through categorisation exercises.

At the end of the connections section you should have several groups, all of whom have a series of questions about the stimulus material and all of whom have these questions categorised into different areas for discussion.

Discussion

Bring the students into the best version of a circle you can manage given the constraints of the classroom in which you are housed (though if it's a sunny day and your classroom is pokey, don't give it a second thought – take them outside and sit in a circle on the grass). If you have been through the connections stage, then teacher can start by asking, "Who has any questions in the area of … ?" If you haven't been through the connections stage, just ask a kid to fire in a question.

And then, having lit the touchpaper, you sit back and, hopefully, watch the discursive fireworks as they ignite. Your role here is as referee, not as provider of information. There will be times when students ask for your opinion on one of the questions that they have generated: try to avoid giving it. Where a question bombs or seems to be suitably resolved with a one word answer, allow it and move on to another question. The idea is that this process produces quality thinking, which feeds into an interested and sometimes impassioned discussion, which will develop kids' oracy and, in turn, feed into their achievement in the area of literacy. It is also an esoteric, non-standard way of looking at teaching anything. The idea of a Philosophy for Children lesson on algebra is appealingly left field, and I'd be really interested to hear from anyone who has tried it.

INSTRUCTIONS AND EXPECTATIONS (TIME, QUANTITY AND QUALITY)

Let's take the instructions first. There is much, I think, to be learnt from the process of checking understanding of lesson objectives (see page 86 of this chapter). Above all, you must put yourself in the role of the dribbler. Will he understand your instructions and what you want him to do next? If you are confident he can, then all's well. But you should be wary of overestimating your own ability to give instructions that have sufficient clarity to be understood. No matter how good you think you are, you will get this wrong, regularly. However, all is not lost when you have failed to explain a complex task very well at all, as there are two fail-safes. Firstly, there is more than one child in the class, and if they don't understand what is required they can ask their mate who does. Secondly, as soon as you've set the task, you immediately go on tour round each student to check that they have started.

The 'post setting the task tour' is a totally top teacher tip. It serves a number of important functions. Firstly, you are able to check that they've understood the task and have either started it or have some intention of doing so. Equally as importantly, you will be able to check that they are laying the work out correctly. Kids' desire to subvert rules on presentation of work is a strange, self-defeating dance; they all know how work should be laid out, but seem to regard a point-blank refusal to follow those rules as a matter of honour. Generally, these rules will be something along the lines of:

1. Draw a ruled line under the last piece of work.

2. On the same page as the last piece of work, where there is space, write the title in the centre, the date on the right and underline them (preferably in pencil, and definitely not in red – that's the teacher's marking colour).

3. Write only in black or blue pen. Drawings in pencil.

4. Don't put stupid bloody circles, crosses or smiley faces over the 'i'.

If you do not check that these rules are being adhered to with an utterly fascistic lack of empathy, then the following will happen.

1. They will leave every other page blank. This is a chronic waste of resources, and makes a book look like the student gives not two figs for their education and that their teacher allows them to labour under the misapprehension that this is acceptable.

2. Titles are underlined with curly, florid and overly romantic red lines.

3. They write in green or, worse still, yellow.

4. Every opportunity to put a circle, cross or smiley face on the 'i' is taken.

If you go on tour straight after giving the instructions for the task they are to undertake, you can nip these crimes in the bud. You have to do it in every lesson, otherwise things soon fall apart, and it is one of the most important things you will do as a teacher. The kids' books are the best record of whether you are a good teacher or not, and if there are whole rafts of pages with either no work on them, or the presentation is slapdash and shoddy, then the kid's book, which is available to your head of department at any time they wish it to be, is grassing you up. Be a Nazi on presentation and many other things fall into place, including, somewhat improbably, behaviour. A teacher who is utterly stern about presentation runs less risk that other rules will be flouted. The fact that you give no quarter whatsoever in the quality of work in their books suggests that you will be equally uncompromising on other matters.

When setting tasks it is important to give the expected time that they will spend on the activity. This is supposed to lend the proceedings a sense of urgency. In theory kids will actually hear the instruction, "You have ten minutes to do this," and will think, "Well that's not long. I'd better get cracking." In reality, however, this often falls on completely deaf ears. Rather than attack the task with the velocity of a greyhound out of the traps, they idle, tarry even. Here again, the going on tour checking they have started is your best friend.

Regarding the timing of tasks, it is often of use to set a series of smaller tasks: two-minute, timed essays, for instance. A series of these keeps kids' focus and urgency, and a lesson with a series of these shorter activities is generally buzzing with purpose and the pleasing scratch of pen onto paper.

Another useful tip for setting written work is to give the kids a word count. There's a number of reasons for this. Firstly, every piece of paid writing work I have ever been commissioned to do has come with a word count, so in giving students a word count to write to you are preparing them for a future in which it might be possible someone will pay them to write something. You are also helping them to discover the skills of self-editing and running a piece through several drafts. Also, the piece of work has a defined end point. Once they have written, for example, exactly fifty words on a subject (neither forty-nine nor fifty-one are in any way acceptable), then they have finished. The task is no longer liable to teacher asking you to, "Go on, tack on another paragraph, y'know, just for me? I didn't get around to setting a proper extension task." On this, the editing works as an extension task in itself, one that is visible to the teacher. While the majority of the kids are still attempting to sculpt their first few sentences, you will be able to see Fast Eddie, pen in hand, totting up the number of words he has written, ready to start the process of editing. The fact that they have to count the words before editing means that setting a word count gives you an easily recognised visual signal of when kids are nearly finished, and this ensures that you don't leave them doing nothing when they have completed the task.

Another top teacher tip when kids who are undertaking written activities have a propensity towards recalcitrance, is to mark a point on the page you want them to get to. This works very well with the lazier student. You will encounter many students for whom the idea of doing any work in lessons is an extremely offensive piece of cheek on the part of the teacher. One of the key techniques a lazy boy will employ here, and I have this on the very good, expert authority of Mr Francis Prince, is simply to stare into space, pretending to be thinking, when in fact their mind is a white canvas in a well lit room. When you call them on this they will say, "Sorry sir, I am thinking of what to write." If you are not sneaky here, pretty early on, allowing this practice will set the tone for your relationship with that student. You will set the work. They will ignore the fact that it is set. The "Sorry sir, I was thinking," lie must be called straightaway. It's best if you employ this technique in the last lesson before break, lunch or home time. You mark with red pen the point on the page that you think it is reasonable for them to have written to, and tell them they will be allowed to go to break, lunch or their evening meal only once they have written to that point. This technique focuses their mind somewhat and is guaranteed to make the most slovenly of students snap to attention and get something useful done at the pace they should have been working at in the first place.

Regarding quality of work, you really shouldn't ever have to say this, but every piece of work that a child produces in your lesson should be their best work. Some kids will attempt to pull the wool over your eyes by turning in something shockingly slapdash and claiming it was your fault for not telling them that it had to be 'best' work. They are chancing it at this point. Let them know that you know they are chancing it and they won't try the same trick again.

Your expectations of your pupils must be as high as they possibly can be at all times. This is key really. There is really no excuse for setting those expectations anywhere other than the highest they can possibly be. Many teachers do not ever get anywhere near understanding the truth of this over the space of a whole career and, as a result, there are generations of people who do not achieve anything like what they are capable of. They go into the same poorly paid work as their fathers, who too were failed by teachers who didn't have a clue what their students were capable of producing with just a little more effort. This is particularly true of some white, working class children. Their techniques at work avoidance are so refined, so sophisticated, that they speak of serious intelligence at work. It is your job to make sure that this intelligence is used in a profitable manner and not frittered away. You do this by pointing at an imaginary line way above your eye-line and saying, "The bar's there."

"But all my other teachers say it's down there," Michael will reply, miming an attempt at pulling the bar downwards.

"I know how clever you are," states the teacher who is deadly serious about getting his or her students to show themselves at their best. "The bar is there."

They will soon get used to your expectations. And live up to them.

PROVIDING USEFUL ACTIVITIES

As we've seen, constructivists argue that any task that requires children to construct knowledge in undertaking that task will do. Geoff Petty, a major evangelist for this kind of approach to learning, is the high priest of task setting, and there is much that can be learnt from his approach. It is well worth doing a Google search for his 'twenty-five ways of teaching without telling', as this contains enough different varieties of task to keep you in them for a whole career. As an introduction to these, however, here are a few of my own derivations on Geoff Petty-style task construction. Where they are not self-explanatory I have explained them. It's worth photocopying the page, getting the scissors out and doing them. You will learn more if you do this and, what's more, you'll still be able to flog your second-hand copy of this book on Amazon after you've finished it. As you are cutting, try thinking how you could use this technique in your subject or, for primary teachers, what curriculum areas immediately come to mind as lending themselves to these kind of tasks.

MATCHING CARDS

Cut 'em up then, place them face down, then pick up two at a time. See if they match. It's like the 'Go Fish' card game you may have played when you were a child, only more boring.

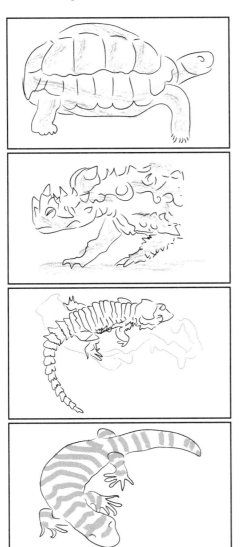

Rolls up into a ball

Colours and bands are a warning to stay away

Stores a quart of water in his bladder

Has a fake second head on her neck

MATCHING QUESTIONS AND ANSWERS

Why do my muscles sometimes burn when I'm exercising?	I don't know, it's really difficult to explain.
Why do I feel sore the day after I exercise?	Because he doesn't let go of the ball until he is on the way down; it looks like he hangs for longer.
What happens to my heart when I exercise?	If you let go of it when you hit the ball you could brain someone.
What is 'VO2 max' and how does it measure cardiovascular fitness?	Build up of lactic acid.
What's the best position for my hands when I swim freestyle?	It reduces the swelling by shrinking the blood vessels.
How high can you jump?	The hitch kick stops the jumper's forward rotation.
Why do long jumpers 'run' several steps in the air after they take off?	It has to pump more blood to bring oxygen to the muscles, so it goes harder, stronger, faster.
How does ice help a sprained ankle or other injury?	They should form an 'S' shaped pattern.
How important is my grip on the bat when I'm striking the ball?	Inflammation/small tears in the muscle fibres.
Why does spinning a ball make it curve?	The number of litres of oxygen a person consumes in a minute.
How does Michael Jordan manage to hang in the air for so long when he goes up for a slam dunk?	Most people can manage in the region of about 20 inches from a standing start.

GROUPING GAME

Cut up each cell in the second table and place each one in the appropriate column in the first table.

Table 1

Nouns	Adjectives	Adverbs

Table 2

Quickly	Bunny	Change
Clever	Arm	Sophisticatedly
Bang	Cherry	Gorgeous
Unpleasant	Never	Only
Custard	Powerfully	Bucket
Child	Cringe-inducing	Dolt
Doltish	Rhyolite	Less
Fewer	Arrogant	Brand-new
Coat	Ear'ole	Olivine

RANKING ON A CONTINUUM

Once you've cut 'em up, put the following (inexhaustive) causes of death in rank order of the number of people they killed in Britain in 2002.

Malaria
Stroke
Suicide
Tuberculosis
Accident
Lung cancer
Malignant cancers
Violence
HIV/AIDS
Cardiovascular disease

The answers for this activity are here[20]

20 1. *Cardiovascular disease* 29.34%, 2. *Malignant cancers* 12.9%, 3. *Stroke* 9.66%, 4. *Accident* 6.23%, 5. *HIV/AIDS* 4.87%, 6. *Tuberculosis* 2.75%, 7. *Malaria* 2.23%, 8. *Lung cancer* 2.18%, 9. *Suicide* 1.53%, 10. *Violence* 0.98%

SEQUENCING ACTIVITY

Same kind of thing, only this time you put the constituent elements of a process in the correct order to make the process work. There may be spurious stages to be rejected.

Locate the phone number of a homosexual Danish man.
Visit the hairdresser and get your roots retouched.
Put on a sou'wester that buttons at the back.
Look in the mirror.
Leave, thanking God you don't have to go through that for another six months.
Be whisked off by a girl and feel vaguely guilty as she massages conditioner into your scalp.
Mouth the words, "Sheesh. What a state!"
Have a pointless conversation about what you want.
Book a cab to take you to Deptford on that day.
Answer a whole range of questions about where you are going on holiday.
Book in for Saturday at 2.00 p.m.

Do keep in mind, however, that having kids sitting down working on either cutting up, filling in, or answering questions on a piece of paper may well be the constructivist way, but it is also known as death by worksheet.

My own view is that there is a definite place for it, but if all you ever do is give kids worksheets – no matter how well done they are and regardless of the fact that you have a full range of worksheet related tasks in your repertoire – then you will only ever be a mediocre teacher. You have to mix it up a bit. Taking kids out for a walk around the school field measuring things is a valuable task, asking them to take notes as you deliver a lecture from the branches of a tree is too. It is of substantial value having a range of worksheet type activities that you can administer, but there is little genius in doing so: try to find your own, more left-field way of doing things and use the worksheet for the drab Tuesday morning or Friday afternoon when you want something that's pretty certain to work well enough without necessarily taxing your intellectual, creative or physical reserves too much.

EXTENDED WRITING

One of the activities no teacher I've ever seen uses enough of is extended writing. Given that kids take exams at the end of their school careers, which decide whether they attend university, and those exams are almost entirely devoted to extended writing exercises, it is astonishing how scantly we prepare them for writing at length. There are a few reasons for this (none of them good). Firstly, it can be difficult to get kids to concentrate for a long enough period to produce a decent and focused piece of written work (which is probably a result of them rarely ever being asked to do so). Secondly, if you set a long piece of writing, you've got to read and mark a long piece of writing, which is clearly infinitely more taxing than just ticking a series of disembodied answers, which are probably not even written in full sentences.

On a more macro-political level it has been the fashion with the National Literacy and Numeracy strategies (cancelled by the time you read this, but all-pervasive for ten years or so) to give children information in bite-sized chunks; to micro-manage their learning so much that the multifariously nuanced and complex skill of writing well has been broken down into teaching kids discrete parts of grammar with little idea of their context. So, rather than writing a series of lovely, imaginative stories and learning through practice and review, kids have had countless decontextualised worksheets about homophones shoved under their noses so the teacher can prove that they are teaching a specific point of word level work. Shocking.

Ofsted refer to 'opportunities for extended writing'. And though the first word in this phrase may initially appear somewhat strange (what kid sees doing a long essay as an opportunity for anything other than a painfully indented index finger and a long slew of boredom), the longer you teach the clearer your understanding will be; if you do not give them the opportunity to improve their written communication you will be selling them very short indeed.

And so, ensure that, in amongst the matching exercises, the grouping, sequencing and ranking games, you make sure that kids either pick up their pens or log on, and are told to write something of a decent length. They may not thank you initially, but if you don't make them do it, there's a damn good chance no one will, and they will leave school without even a half-chance of being anything more than a half-head at a Tesco's checkout.

DO YOU MAKE EFFECTIVE USE OF ICT TO ENHANCE TEACHING AND LEARNING?

My scepticism about the value of some ICT use in schools is a matter of public record. And it has made me public enemy number one with the ICT in Education bloggers (which if you think about it, is a funny thing to want to be).

"What do you want to be when you grow up, son?"

"I'd like to spend half my life recording my thoughts about how excellent ICT is, and how teachers who don't use it very well are demonic."

"Oh. That's nice. What about being a fireman?"

They are a fairly humourless crew, failing to understand that in calling into question the value of much of the ICT in schools, I'm voicing a demand: can we have stuff that works, please?

The IWB has caused a huge issue for newly qualified teachers. Since you have probably not been particularly well trained in its use (though I may be wrong in your case), many/most teachers just use them as a projector. The fact that, generally speaking, the IWB will sit at the central focus point of the classroom means that you will feel an irresistible imperative to turn it on. Few teachers really know how to make those babies sing, and even if they do, the interactive writing function on them is very spidery indeed. And so, what do we do with a piece of kit that many of us can only really use as a projector and that makes demands of us to turn it on? We use it as a projector. The issue here is what to project? And the answer to this question is invariably, "Why a lovely PowerPoint presentation, of course. What else?" And so, the result of replacing normal whiteboards with interactive whiteboards is that where five years ago you could just come into class with a lesson plan (or not), a marker pen and a bucketload of wit and charisma and start improvising, now you have to spend half of your free time devising increasingly complex and ornate PowerPoint presentations. The government might argue that this is progress – going into lessons with a couple of ideas, a dry wipe marker and a bit of improvisatory flair is not their idea of effective planning, and in this they are probably right. But the government does not have to cope with your marking burden, nor do they care to know that it is impossible to plan, teach and mark every lesson perfectly.

So, I give you a revolutionary and, in some circles, extremely seditious idea about ICT in class, particularly in reference to the interactive whiteboard. And that is: only turn it on when you think it will add something of concrete value.

This piece of advice is deemed in some quarters as the epitome of repulsiveness; the witterings of a slack jawed and dribbling Luddite who is resolutely determined not to prepare his students for the twenty-first century. This may well be true, but listening to this one particular witter may well save you your relationship, your sanity and much of your hair. You can teach perfectly well without ever turning the bloody thing on. What do you think teachers did before they were invented? Were all lesson pre the IWB shockingly incompetent? Of course not.

One of the things the IWB's ubiquity and tyranny has done is to promote double boring, front-of-class teaching. If you have ever sat in a business meeting, or a lecture, or, by now, a CPD session, and stewed in an inferno of boredom while someone in a suit read out a set of bullet points on countless slides from a PowerPoint at you very, very slowly, then you'll have some idea as to why you shouldn't ever consider doing this to the children you teach.

How then, given that you should not fall prey to the dictate that you turn on what is, after all, just a piece of kit – the same way as a dry wipe marker or an exercise book are just pieces of kit – every single lesson, should you use it when you do?

I am the first to admit that I am not the world's greatest expert with the IWB. As I resent the fact that my old whiteboard was taken away without any consultation, I tend to cock a sneer at it religiously as I enter the room (much in the same manner the Catholic will bow before the altar on entering the church), but when you do turn it on it is of use to have a few decent reasons to do so: techniques that make it worth its corn. There will be books and software packages that you or the school can purchase if you want to make the most of your IWB. If, however, you just want to get together a few decent tricks that'll get senior management off your back, so you can go back to the grouped speaking and listening work that really does induce the most learning in your charges, then it is worth getting used to the following process.

Getting busy with the Google image search is actually one of the most pleasing ways there is of venturing into the earlier stages of planning a lesson. To model the places this can take you let's take a random subject that this teacher is unlikely to have a great deal of prior knowledge about, or that he's ever taught before: algebra! We go onto the image search, giving ourselves the stricture that we'll only look at the first five pages – otherwise, we will find it is eleven o'clock in the evening, we have done no work at all and we are on page one hundred and twelve of cartoon images of algebraic equations with an observed lesson at nine o'clock the following morning. What do we find? Immediately, on the first page, in amongst the absurdly complicated graphs, crap clip art and covers of forbidding looking textbooks, there are intriguing cartoon images that might lead us somewhere interesting in the lesson.

- A line drawing that looks at the student's fear of algebra, and the overenthusiastic, slightly solipsistic maths teacher's inability to comprehend that fear.

- A cartoon that makes explicit the fact that it is algebraic calculations that calculate how to get exactly the appropriate amount of water to hit the rider on a log flume ride in an amusement park.

- A further cartoon depicting a child at a desk, spewing out a thought bubble, which appears to encapsulate pretty well the thought process required to solve fairly simple equations: "Put the **a**'s together so that 4**a** plus 2**a** is 6**a**. 6**a** equals 12. I need to find out what the variable **a** is."

Each of these could be the springboard or catalyst for a whole lesson. Could that lesson start by examining the students' perception of algebra, sharing their worries and seeking to resolve these? Could it be contextualised by being brought into an environment where it has meaning for the kids, such as calculating how you get the right amount of water on a punter on an amusement park ride? Or could it be used to drill the kids into a formula: a system of processes that they can memorise in order to ensure they have the best chance in an exam?

All these potential solutions to the problem of the algebra lesson are potentially of value, and they would not have occurred without the visual stimulus. I could have sat for an hour wondering how on earth I was going to find a way into algebra other than bringing in a textbook and mouthing the immortal (and should be illegal) words of, "Open your textbooks at page 17. Do exercises one through to fifteen. Oh yeh, and shut up while you're doing it." A quick Google image search gives you an open-ended stimulus that can take you somewhere you would not have otherwise considered and, unlike text, image is not prescriptive. It doesn't tell you what path to follow in the lesson – it just gives your creativity a nudge as to where a previously overgrown path is; one that might be interesting to uncover and follow.

As for bringing these images into the lesson, so that they may do for your students what they have done for you, you simply go to "see full size image," save it in pictures (preferably with a name you'll recall – such images have a habit of being called "154396cviuw4jas," which is utterly useless come the time you want to use them), then import it into PowerPoint, and you have a ready-to-go visual stimulus for the lesson.

Use PowerPoint to show lots of pictures. Loads and loads of them. Get kids to respond to these in oral, visual or written form. Use them as a means of kick-starting a poetic response. Use the pictures to educate without talking over them or defining what they mean. Ask the students to boil their emotional response to an image into one word. Ask them to boil their emotional response to a series of images into a collection of single words. Put these words into columns, then transform the columns into a diagram, a graph, a painting, a ballet. Sort the words into alphabetical order – see what happens. Try starting a lesson, on any subject, with a picture of a bald man or a piece of architecture made out of spent matchsticks. Stick a semicolon in the middle of the bald man's head. Show a series of colours and get kids to relate the subject you are teaching to those colours. Get kids to graffiti (annotate) the pictures with the IWB pen. Enrich their visual lexicon, their experience and their world with pictures. Leave the words for their books.

OTHER ADULTS IN YOUR CLASSROOM

There will be a variety of different people, other than Ofsted inspectors or members of senior management assessing your worthiness, who will sit in your classroom from time to time. The number of these is dependent on the school's profile (i.e. what kind of kids go there) and, in some ways, the efficiency of senior management in securing the funding for these teachers' little helpers. Broadly, they will be there to provide you with support with kids who have specific difficulties accessing education, either because they have English as a second language, special educational needs or they are presenting behavioural issues. The people in your class will either be specialist teachers or teaching assistants, and their roles will break down into the following:

EAL support teacher – to provide specialist support to children at an early stage of learning the English language.

Behaviour support teacher – to provide specialist support to children who exhibit behavioural issues.

Learning support teacher – to help kids who have specific difficulties in learning to access the curriculum.

Learning support/teaching assistant – either attached specifically to a child or to the class in general. There are also higher level teaching assistants, who are like the bosses of the normal teaching assistants (kind of).

All these people are potentially invaluable to you in your first year, and you must make it a matter of policy to make friends with the teaching assistants especially. The first and most obvious reason that you should do this is that, despite their lack of professional status and in spite of the degrading, sweat shop salaries they command, every one of them is more experienced in a classroom than you are. The older teaching assistants, those who have been at the school for years, will have seen it all – from breakfast all the way through to Christmas. They will be able to smell how good/bad/nervous you are, and if you are totally emotionally honest with them, they will help you. But you must treat them with respect, perhaps even, at an early stage of your career, with deference; you are being paid graduate wages to do roughly the same hours they are working for a pittance. Ergo, they are more passionate about the kids' education than you are. Most of them have taken the job because they have had children at the school, they will know most of the kids at the school and, as such, they will have mature, to the point of fruity, opinions as to how to deal with them. Whilst they may indulge in the odd, quiet snicker to themselves whilst you are drowning (though I have always found teaching assistants to be the model of professional discretion), if you do find yourself in this position, then the teaching assistant is your lifebelt. Speak honestly with them about the difficulties you are having, ask politely for help and they will work with you, in the trenches, covering your back as you go over the top. Treat them as if you are in any way better than them (you are not – they have probably seen and dealt with things you couldn't imagine) and your best friend and chief support will down tools, and may even tell all their mates how rubbish you are.

One problem is that you and your teaching assistant never get any time together whatsoever to plan what you are going to do. Theoretically, you are supposed to do this, but there is no time allocated for you to do so. The best you will be able to manage is a quick two minutes in the staffroom before the staff briefing. If you do get such an opportunity, however small it is, take it. Your teaching assistant is the only other professional in the room on a regular basis. They will have the same degree of emotional engagement with your classes as you and if you want to discuss strategies, share how much you adore a pupil or just want to scream at how unjust it all is, your teaching assistant will listen.

There are technical issues with the appropriate deployment of teaching assistants that a decent, mature, adult relationship with them will help. Teaching assistants, though the funding for them and the reason they are actually there may be because of the unique issues a single child with severe difficulties has, are required to be there not just for that child, but for the rest of the class also. It may well be that everyone knows Sandra sits helping out the kid with cerebral palsy, but she also has a responsibility towards everyone else. As a top teacher tip, and this is a doozy, when being observed, order your teaching assistant about a bit. You have to negotiate this with them first, as it may and should be totally against the code of your previous working relationship, but it impresses the observer. They will not know that the whole thing is a ruse that you have cooked up together, and will note approvingly that you have 'deployed' the teaching assistant to do something other than sit having a chat with the child with special needs.

On this, it is OK to ask your teaching assistant to be quiet. Often, as they are probably older than you, and undoubtedly more experienced, you will find that when you are asking the class for quiet and the teaching assistant is in the role of sitting next to the special needs kid, helping them out, your teaching assistant may not think that the request for quiet extends to them. It does. Be respectful as you do so, but you must ask for quiet from everyone in the room. Otherwise, you will find that you are attempting to introduce a class to some grand new idea, with the constant underhum of two people in the room – one adult, one child – ignoring you, and sending out the message to the rest of the class that it is OK to do so.

The same two rules apply with learning support in the guise of someone in your class with qualified teacher status: do a bit of tokenistic ordering about when you are being observed and insist that they button it when you are trying to speak to the class. There are nuances though in the way that you deal with the different types of support teacher.

EAL – These people are experts in something you know nothing about. I have been teaching for a substantial number of years in schools with a plethora of kids for whom English is a second language, but I still know very little about the techniques one should use to help these kids access the curriculum. An EAL support teacher will generally know the lot. Take their advice, and if they offer to create resources for you for Ahmed, Sigrida or Praveen, all three of whom have recently landed in your class with very little English, say yes, and try to disguise the tears of gratitude.

Behaviour – Behaviour support teachers range from committed geniuses with vast vats of inexhaustible patience, reserves of charisma and a deftness of conversational touch that could tame an angry leopard, to the brutally hungover Aussie temp, who is only spending time at school as something to do during the day when there are no women in the pub. Judge this one for yourself. If they are the former, worship them (they enjoy this) and ask them for whatever tips they have. If they are the latter, then they'll generally be a laugh and, more often than not, they'll be well able to stand their round in the boozer. The point is that these guys can vary substantially in quality. If they are a guru, soak up every piece of knowledge you can; if they are a temporary peer, then help each other out; if they are a lazy bastard who used to be a proper teacher but can't be arsed with it all, then remember they've probably got a family reliant on their salary.

Learning support – See behaviour support above. Though there are fewer gurus in this area, a lower number of Australians and more ... well, you get the point. I have worked with one, Sue Latham, who was absolutely great. And some others too.

PLENARIES

These are more important than you might think. As they are part of the four part government stricture, there is a temptation to put it in the same box as the starter activity (i.e. pointless waste of teacher time) and to either leave them out altogether or to lob one out in a perfunctory, cursory and utterly half-hearted manner, simply trawling through the same tired, couldn't-give-a-toss question at the end of every lesson, "What did we learn today kids?" They will make a gainful, though usually bravely and utterly inaccurate, fist of an answer, until such time as Ofsted are in. At which point they will all answer, as one, "Nuffink. You never teach us nuffink. And don't think we haven't noticed that our books have all been properly marked for the first time in the two years we have suffered you as a teacher, just cos speccy is in the back with a clipboard. You are a bastard and a rubbish teacher too."

It's worth putting a bit of thought into plenaries, as they are actually vital for pupils' retention of the new information you have introduced during the lesson. Think of them as the varnish that seals the learning: without it it'll wash away within seconds of them leaving the classroom. In truth, there is a more than good chance that it will wash away anyway, but the plenary at least gives the new learning some faint hope of sticking.

The standard, couldn't-give-a-toss plenary is to ask kids what they have learnt today, hoping grimly that this question will suffice. There are several reasons not to do this. Not the least of which is that it's boring and formulaic, and kids will soon learn to ignore it, as all it does is signal that they will be free from the classroom in a minute or so, and will have switched off by the last consonant in the 'What'. To have the optimum effect you must obey a couple of rules with the plenary:

1. Don't pack up first.

2. Devote a full ten minutes to it.

3. Do more than one.

4. Take an interested and engaged approach to coming up with interesting new ways of performing it.

Not packing up first is pretty obvious. If you insist that everyone puts on their heavy coats, put their rulers into their bags and turn their mobile phones from silent before you launch into the plenary, then you are sending a message that the lesson is over and they are free from you. Trying to regain a class's attention when they are already in an entirely different world, somewhere in the playground, concocting new ear-clunge tortures for Howard, is a battle of the losing variety. You can avoid entering this no-win situation simply by not packing up before the plenary and running it in pretty seamlessly with the last part of the independent section of the lesson.

You'll also find that it is more effective if you don't run it too close to the bell. Kids are generally acutely aware of the time, particularly towards the end of a lesson, and by skirting too close to the lesson's temporal edges with the plenary you'll be inviting a similar effect to that you cause if you pack up first. It'll go awry. Best to discipline yourself to devoting a full eight, nine or even ten minutes to the plenary. This way, not only do kids not see it as a perfunctory waste of time before the lesson's end, but you also ensure that you put a bit of creative thought into it. Devoting a decent fist of time to the plenary gives teacher a problem, however, in that you'll often find that one activity is not enough to fill this time. If we take one of my favourite plenaries, given to me by David Keeling, as an example, you'll see how this can happen.

"Think of a number between one and twenty. Now write a sentence with that exact number of words that sums up what you have learnt in the lesson. Now share this with three other people in the class."[21]

It's a goodie, but it can take between two and five minutes, thereby leaving four minutes at the very end of the lesson in which to string out precisely nothing. Better to have two plenaries planned; that way you never find yourself in the situation where you have a potentially unruly class anticipating release, with nothing whatsoever for them to do. The question is, though, what activities make for a decent, engaging, cognitively challenging plenary?

---

21 *From The Big Book of Independent Thinking (Crown House, 2006).*

Here are a few.

The frozen picture

This is a drama teacher technique, which transfers fantastically well to other subject areas. Basically, a frozen picture, which goes by several other names, takes four people, who freeze in tableau form, thereby capturing a split second of time in physical form. There are two versions of this: the naturalistic and the symbolic, and it is the second that we are interested in for the cross-curricular plenary. Where a naturalistic frozen picture will be a scene in the Queen Vic, caught as if someone has stopped time (Phil with his pint half-cocked and his fat gob open, Dot caught mid moan, Peggy's brow furrowed as she reaches towards the London Pride pump and Nasty Nick Cotton, just about to open his mouth to intone the phrase, "Leave it out, Ma"); the symbolic frozen picture will take a more left-field approach, with students using their bodies in tableau form to express an abstract idea, spatially. Students' imaginations when given this task can be awe inspiring; they will naturally, and without so much as a question, get themselves into shapes that represent a piece of architecture, a specific sentence structure technique, a philosophical premise; even a mathematical or scientific equation.

As a plenary it is an invaluable device. Ask your students to create a frozen picture that sums up what they have learnt during the lesson, and rather than have a group of tired students routinely going through motions they were bored of before they were even born, they'll jump up, snap to it and create a mini-piece of abstract art. Reprocessing the information from the concrete to the abstract is a pretty high order thing for them to be asked to do, in terms of its cognitive demands, and, as such, should help embed the information from the lesson in a lively and exciting manner.

Drawing the learning

A derivation of this, which is of near equal value, but is easier to achieve if you are the sort of teacher who sees physical activity in lessons as being difficult to manage, is to get kids to draw the frozen picture they would have done, if you hadn't been such a scaredy-cat and had let them leave their desks. The singular advantage of this technique is that you get some interesting display work out of it. You can also use a less structured drawing activity, which sometimes has interesting results, and just ask them to draw what they learnt in the lesson or to plot a graph representing the learning. This, in theory, has the same 'concrete to abstract' benefits as the frozen picture, but can confuse pupils, and the work they produce is generally not quite of the same standard as when they are allowed to get physical.

The kinetic

Put simply, the kinetic is a technique whereby you give short pieces of information and they, in fours, devise a series of moves or gestures to accompany that piece of information as they recite it. Let's take a science formula as an example: "Speed equals distance over time." The students might accompany the word 'speed' by whirring their arms round and round very quickly indeed; 'equals' by holding their hands out horizontally in front of them, one twelve inches or so above the other, in the shape of an 'equals' sign; 'distance' by pointing at an imagined point a long way away; 'over' by pointing directly at the ground with their index fingers; and 'time' by pointing at their, now outdated, digital watches. Or, they might do something completely different. The beauty of this, and of all open-ended tasks, is that you are not defining the outcome for them and, consequently, having given your students opportunity to vent their creativity, you get some really exciting, interesting work out of them. I have lost count of the number of different solutions a group of kids will come up with, for instance, when asked to do a hand gesture that imitates the equals sign.

As practice, see what movements or gestures you would come up with for the following formulae: '"Power equals work or force times distance over time" and "Kinetic energy equals half mass times velocity squared." You can use this technique as a plenary, either by defining the learning for them into a few discrete sentences that they can put a kinetic to or, better still, by getting them, in groups, to write three sentences that encapsulate what they have learnt in the lesson and, having done this, design a kinetic to accompany the sentences. They then perform these to the rest of the class.

Key word storytelling activity

If you are introducing new vocabulary in each lesson then for this new vocabulary to enter kids' lexicons, they have to be given the opportunity to use it as soon as is possible. If it hasn't been employed during the lesson, then it's a good idea to design a plenary around them.

Here's a version of this that I designed recently for a group of FE lecturers. They report that the stories they produced with it were rubbish and repetitive, but that it worked well as a plenary in that it got them to focus again on the meanings of the key vocabulary.

Get in groups of four. Number yourselves one through to four. You are going to tell a story in tag form, sentence by sentence. Number one starts, and says a line of a story, which includes the first of the key words in their column below (in this case phallus). Number two follows, using the first word in their column (the adjectival version of phallus) within their sentence. Numbers three and four have their go, then it goes back to number one who delivers a sentence that builds the story and includes the second key word in their column.

Number	Number 1	Number 2	Number 3	Number 4
	Phallus	Phallic	Signifier	Juxtaposed
	Compari-son	Similarity	Difference	Rhetorical
Key Concept	Inverted commas	Title	Irony	Speech marks
	Clarify	Confirm	Discursive	Relevant
	Conjunc-tion	Connective	Flexibility	Mandelson

Young inspectors

Take two students outside the class at the beginning of the lesson and tell them that they are now Ofsted inspectors. They are to tour the class during the lesson, taking notes and inspecting the learning. At the end of the lesson they must present their findings, as to what people learnt in the lesson.

Wandering plenary

Get the kids to walk aimlessly around the room. Every time they bump into a person they tell each other what they learnt.

HOMEWORK

I heard an interview with a famous actor from the East End of London on the radio recently, relating his father's attitude to him coming home with a bagful of homework. "Y'know what son?" he exclaimed, no doubt brushing his slicked quiff back from his forehead as he did so, "If they can't teach you all the stuff you need to know during the day, they can't be very good at their jobs, can they?" (Why-oh-why-oh-why did they not immediately make him Education Secretary?)

You may well have hated homework as a child. I guarantee you, you'll despise it more as a teacher. Our workload is absurd enough without the existence of homework. Homework tips the work required from a teacher somewhere beyond the absurd into the abject, the surreal even. I have never found a method to make the management of homework in any way near manageable. It is impossible and, if you get it right, then you are a better, more organised, more disciplined, more dedicated teacher than I. (Which, in truth, isn't really that difficult.)

There are people who do seem to manage it though, and they have every reason to be proud of finding the will and the time to do so. Let's start looking at how you administer homework with a brief delve into some of the differences between sectors and subjects.

In primary it is unlikely that homework will be such an intolerable burden. My experience of this comes from helping with my own children's homework, which comes in the form of a weekly spelling list to be learnt, the odd science experiment, an occasional leaflet to design and not a single piece of extended writing ever. If you are working in the primary sector, there are substantial issues with workload, but homework is not the biggest of them. A tip here would be that if you want your students to be effective writers, then they have to have as much practice at doing it as possible, and setting stories or the like for homework will really benefit them.

Within the secondary sector there are significant variances between subjects as to the marking and administrative burden that homework presents. A drama teacher for instance might set 'thinking' or 'rehearsal' homework: "By the next lesson I would like you to think about how animals move, or rehearse an animal move in front of a mirror." This suits the drama teacher very nicely indeed. Since there is no outcome to be checked, all the kids can claim they have done it and you don't have to set detentions as no one (surely) would be stupid enough not to go through the easy pretence that they had done their homework.

A maths teacher might set a page of questions from a set textbook: these are generally easily marked, and perhaps it is better for the kids' learning that teacher gets the kids to check each other's answers – for them the issue is keeping a solid record of who has and has not done it, and who is to do detention for being lazy or troubled.

For science teachers the same monitoring systems are used, but their making burden is likely to be a bit heavier in that a good science homework might be to perform a cooking experiment at home and then to write it up. This requires more than giving the kids each others' books and asking them to check the answers. It requires (though rarely gets) diagnostic marking – some evidence that the teacher has read it and has done more than just thoughtlessly put a tick at the end of each paragraph.

Where setting homework gets to be potentially a completely counterproductive exercise is when you are teaching one of the subjects – geography, history or, particularly, English – which rely on a lot of extended writing. In your first year as a humanities teacher you could plausibly have as many as twenty classes of thirty kids each. If you set each class a homework task that requires all the kids to have produced an extended piece of writing, you are taking a revolver and pointing it directly at your own head. No man, woman or dog can manage marking an extra 600 pieces of writing every week without going completely insane. There are solutions to this, which it seems most primary teachers (and all drama teachers) are already hip to: set homework that doesn't involve kids producing vast swathes of writing – storyboard activities, maps, annotations of existing diagrams, 'thinking' work, internet research (though bear in mind if you work in a school in a poor area many of the kids won't have internet access); anything that does not produce the outcome of a piece of written work that has to be marked with a fine toothcomb.

Another issue you will find with homework is that if you let them take their books home that is the last you will ever see of half of them. It can be dispiriting, having set homework, to find that all of them have done it (honest sir), but can't prove it, as they have conveniently left their book at home. The solution here is simple: don't ever let them take their classwork books home. The dedicated professional will implement a system where they all have a homework book, as well as a classwork book. But guess what happens with these? They get lost too. Till such point as you are being observed and then they all magically appear, revealing that the child has done every piece of homework you have ever set to a high standard but, because you have never seen the books, you have not marked them. Really, the best bet if you are to set homework is to get kids to do it on pieces of paper. That way, if they don't bring it in, then you haven't lost a valuable and expensive resource in the form of an exercise book. Additionally, there is no document containing an evidence base of whether you have marked that homework or not. Nothing speaks louder to an observer or parent of your uselessness than an exercise book containing loads of work and no marking. It is genuinely offensive to them, and for good reason. However, having twenty classes worth of homework books marked in peachy keen order is beyond even you. Get the homework in, or not, on paper, and then the document that is proof of your uselessness can easily be made to not exist.

WHAT TO DO IF KIDS FAIL TO DO HOMEWORK?

There are two main schools of thought on this subject. The orthodox view is that homework must be used to extend what children learn in class and, moreover, to involve parents in their child's education. As a parent I see the point in this view and in homework itself, and since the consumer is allegedly always right ...

However, Alfie Kohn, in his book *The Homework Myth: Why Our Children Get Too Much of a Bad Thing,* makes a compelling case that it is all an unbelievably time consuming, futile scam. I tend to lean (at quite a dangerously acute angle) towards Mr Kohn's viewpoint. The benefits of homework are vastly outweighed by the cost of administrating it, particularly in terms of the amount of lesson time that is lost. The creativity involved in the setting of imaginative and useful tasks, combined with the detentions you must set for the vast hordes of kids who are either too disorganised to do it, too overworked, or who have responsibilities at home, and the vast swathes of time you have to spend marking it, do not equate to benefits that will accrue for your students. Most teachers reach in the direction of the photocopied and badly thought out worksheet, rather than expending extra creative effort designing a fulfilling, beneficial homework experience, differentiated for SEN, EAL and G&T students (now often called gifted and able – and therefore substantially less satisfying in initial form).

I tried an experiment in school this year (one which I don't recommend you try in your NQT year). I set the kids homework, letting them know that it was entirely at their discretion if they did it. If they did it I would mark it with a degree of passion and interest but, if they didn't, I wouldn't chase them up for it. This spared up acres of time, relieved a substantial plop of entirely unnecessary stress and affected the kids' attainment how much? Not a jot.

You will be told off right royally by a functionary if you try this out yourself, so don't. But it suggests an approach to homework that will be of value to you in your first year, which is, *do not be its slave*. The workload in your first year would have been ridiculous enough if some bright spark had not dreamed up the idea of setting extra tasks that are of little educational value. So recognise that they are generally an exercise in ticking a box, and get that box ticked by taking a lesson from our drama teacher friend a couple of pages back. Set homework tasks that have minimal outcome in terms of the marking burden and if kids don't do them, then forget the detentions. It is plausible that this course of action will have someone breathing down your neck at some point. (Plausible, but unlikely.) School systems tend to check only on whether you have set homework, not whether it was of any value, and not if you set the appropriate time wasting detentions when kids didn't feel that they could be bothered to spend their time at home with their families sweating on what a homophone was. By ensuring that kids have homework of some sort recorded in their homework planners every week you will likely escape the beady eyes of Big Brother who, in any case, has no mature understanding whatsoever of the cost-benefit analysis you have been though to come to this decision, and, as such, it is worth getting one over on in any case.

So if setting homework is merely about keeping out of trouble with the internal pseudo-standards police, how do we ensure that we are on the money in doing so, and that we don't forget to set it? Two ways: one of which is pretty standard, but makes sense. If you don't want to have homework as a mere afterthought, hastily scribbled into planners at the lesson's end, then you set it at the beginning of the lesson. Having homework on the board to be recorded, perhaps alongside the lesson objectives, adds the routine element that keeps kids feeling comfortable as they develop an expectation that it will be there ready to be taken down every lesson. It also ensures that you expend a little creative energy on task setting. Since you are including the setting of homework with your forward planning, then there will be thought attached to it, rather than, as is often the case in lessons, just snatching the first idea that comes into your head at the end of the lesson.

If you want to plan further forward though and dispense with the whole rigmarole for a whole term or half term, then a brilliant idea is to use at least half of your first lesson with any class scribbling down the homeworks for the whole term in their planners. This has a number of advantages: firstly, once you have done this, you are safe from the pseudo-standards police for a long time. Should they call for kids' planners, so as to undertake a spot check of which teachers are setting homework regularly and which teachers should be subject to a jolly good telling-off, then having set all the homeworks in advance and seen them recorded in class, you are not only in the clear, but liable to be mentioned in dispatches as having been a good boy or girl. This technique also saves a lot of teacher time, in that you will not even have to think about setting homework for another three months. Furthermore, there is a decent argument that you could use homework as its own, independent scheme of work, with which kids might be able to investigate a complementary subject to the one that you are studying in class, which will inform and enrich their experience of lessons.

CLASSROOM DISPLAY

The phrase 'learning environment' is worryingly redolent of dungaree clad thesps who don't work on a stage, no, they are gainfully (un)employed in a 'theatre space'. If it's a classroom, call it a classroom. Give it a rest with the talk of 'learning environments'. This is an entirely reasonable reaction to what appears initially to be a piece of politically correct, linguistic weaselry; until, of course, you give a second thought to the ideological shift that calling it a 'learning environment' represents. Classroom is a nineteenth century word. It brings to mind a grey and Dickensian vision of the lofty pedagogue sporting a handlebar moustache intoning a series of facts at rows of scared children who are fed solely on gruel. The only part of this picture that is still present in the twenty-first century is the diet of the pupils (though, there are times when I long to share a staffroom, just once again, with a colleague who has a handlebar 'tache). The bit that most certainly shouldn't appear any more is the adjective 'grey'. There are vast swathes that one could write about display, and there is a book in it should someone wish to write it, but it is important that your classroom is not a monochrome environment that sends kids to sleep the moment they enter.

The head teacher who is responsible for many of the views I have directly imported from her and pretended were my own, Linda Powell, said something to me once that chimed loud and true: if you respect the school environment, you respect the child. And the obverse applies too. Give a child a shoddy environment in which to learn and it is likely that they will behave shoddily. Why else are many of the schools that feature the worst behaviour problems coincidentally those where ceiling tiles hang down and in which bare walls feature peeling paint? There is a solid argument, therefore, that if you lavish attention on the learning environment and show that the place in which the kids learn is important and cared for, they will feel important and cared for too.

Your job here is to make your classroom what Linda describes as, "An Aladdin's cave of learning," and which I have updated as a "Mini-academic Euro Disney." You do this by always having a tiny percentage of your brain on the lookout for things you can stick on the walls to animate them; and by taking something of a magpie approach to your home life. See a pillow? Teaching *Othello*? Take one in and staple it to the wall. Your partner may nag you about it, but teaching is a job that requires great sacrifice on the part of the spouse. They'll have to get used to sleeping without a pillow. It's not as if you can. You've got to be up in the morning. It will also be a huge help to you if you are able to put your hand in your pocket to the tune of about twenty quid or so, and buy your own mini-laminator from WHSmith. That way, when you are reading the Sunday supplements and come across an image or piece of journalism that immediately fires the thought that it will illuminate the curriculum for your charges, you can get busy with the tearing and the scissors, briefly heat up the laminator and have a piece of display work ready made for stapling to the wall come Monday morning.

The chief thing that you should be using your display for is showing off the work of the class to the class themselves. There have been studies making correlations between students' self-esteem to their having a piece of work displayed on the walls.

If you think back to when you were a kid, then you may remember your parents going to parents' evening without you. When they returned, you were as disinterested in what the teachers had to say about you during parents' evening as you generally were during lessons. Had you a piece of artwork or an essay on the wall, however, and your parents had failed to notice it, you may well have been inconsolable. So ensure that you display students' work – with their name emblazoned on it in large point size – to show that you value it and, by extension, them. Importantly too, don't just put up the best work in the class, as this will generally always be done by the same three or four candidates, and their work's absence from the wall will give the lower attaining kids yet another undeserved lesson that they are not important. They get enough of those. Show a range of work. Everybody's in the class. Even Melvin's picture of a spider, with the word "Spydr" underneath it.

The issue you will have on entering the first term is that, if you have are lucky and have a fairly sizeable classroom, there will be acres of space to get covered with multicoloured visual noise, and that classroom may recently have been departed by another teacher who has a different specialism to you, who is still in the school and was very handy with a wall stapler. There is no way to be subtle about this. They will just have to watch on and sob silently as you rip down the display that they have lovingly cultured and curated over so many long years. One of the key things about display that tells a story is its age. Inspectors will notice all too quickly if the walls are covered with work, on which there is a date telling the tale that it has been on the walls since 1985, and most of the kids who did it are now senior figures in the civil service. And they will judge you on it. Adversely.

The size of the job of decorating the classroom can be off-putting, but you'll do best by having an initial splurge in the first few weeks, then adding to it on an 'as and when' basis. The first few weeks of a school year, particularly with the younger children – reception, year 3 and year 7 – can be a honeymoon period in which your classes will give you liberties you will not get from them at any other point. Use these liberties to have display lessons, in which there is no defined learning outcome, other than getting the walls covered in nice looking stuff. Raid the display cupboard, divide the class into various groups and set them distinct display tasks. One group might be writing up their autobiographies in neat, another will be doing bubble writing of key terms on coloured paper; others creating storyboards, or adjective displays animated in the style of the adjective. The two naughty boys will be employed helping you to staple oceans of coloured sugar paper to the walls, and the whole room will be a feverish hive of industry. Display lessons can be extremely stressful indeed for the teacher, as you have to keep interrupting what you are doing to find new jobs for idle hands that have finished the job you gave them at the beginning of the lesson. They leave a substantial mess too, which can make you immediately unpopular with the cleaners. But they are worth the effort and the stress. Once you have braved five or six of these you have a classroom that has been decorated, and what is more it has been decorated by the kids themselves. The theory here is that it will give the students a real sense of ownership of the classroom in which they are taught, and this being so, they will be more likely to respect not just the school fabric, but also the learning that takes place in the room they have ownership over. Just don't let them date their work. That way you can leave it up for a few years without anyone noticing.

Display can be used in a really show-offy way in lessons. If you have a decent amount of notice of the observation – and you are a real teaching spod, desperate for your brilliance to be noticed – then orientating a lesson so that it references a recent piece of display, or even allows students to travel the room on a learning related treasure hunt, in which they have to notice things about images you have stapled to the walls for this purpose, it is likely that you will be adjudged something other than 'inadequate'. Above all, remember that there are few things in teaching likely to instantaneously win you a decent reputation with your colleagues, or with management, than a committed and imaginative approach to animating your classroom. If you wish to delve into the murky world of impression management, and you will find this is sadly unavoidable in the profession, then display, as it is visible, is the quickest, most certain way of creating that favourable impression.

"Have you seen the new girl's display? She's as serious as cancer.

And about as easy as a nuclear war!"

CHAPTER 4
LESSON PLANNING

Increasingly, there is a formal and written expectation that newly qualified teachers will have a completed lesson plan for every lesson they teach. I am not sure what to think of this. When I first started teaching, this expectation was outlined to you on the first day of term, but no one checked up on it. Consequently, you'd get away either with a few ideas sketched out in a planner or, in moments of supreme lassitude, the four-step lesson plan (made up in the four steps you take towards the classroom door). Allowing the teacher to decide how detailed they wish their planning to be strikes me as a fairly civilised way of doing business. Since you, the teacher, are responsible for the amount, or lack, of planning you put into lessons, you, the teacher, will be on the receiving end of the consequences if you attempt to wing it. If you don't have sufficient reserves of energy or charisma, and you enter a difficult class with a totally unplanned lesson, you are likely to be eaten alive.

And so, if only for this, I would advise that you make a decent fist of planning something for your classes for every lesson. The well planned lesson is key to keeping your students in decent order. Even if it goes pear-shaped you still have a script that you can cling onto grimly as you wade through the treacle of time towards the end of the lesson. But by 'decent fist' I don't mean that you should spend your whole life lesson planning. You'll soon come to the understanding that planning a really excellent 'bells and whistles' lesson that completely engages, as well as ticking all the banal boxes you are required to acknowledge exist by an education system that has no idea of what it is humanly possible to do in an allotted period of time, takes the best part of half a day. You do not have that amount of time to plan a single lesson. It may be that you have six lessons a day – to plan bells and whistle lessons for that day would take three days itself. Erm … this equation is entirely insoluble unless you learn a few advanced skiving/workload management techniques.

You cannot plan every lesson to be as good as you can possible make it. Neither will you be able to fill in every single one of the silly little boxes asking you whether you have cross-checked your art lesson for links with numeracy, or what ICT skills the kids will be learning in your PE lesson. So don't try. If you do, you will give yourself a nervous breakdown.

Remember that it is only a job after all, and have three different versions of lesson planning readily available, knowing when it is appropriate to bring them into operation:

1. The 'it'll do'.

2. The 'I did my best'.

3. The 'full Ofsted'.

The first of these is the only time you really bother with the notion of the four-part lesson, only you don't bother with the starter, so it is, in effect, a three-part lesson plan. You teach them something new, give them independent work to investigate this new concept, and then check whether they learned anything at the end. You will find that most of your lessons will follow something related to this pattern.

The second is when you really want to give a class a decent learning experience, because they are either really nice or really horrid. You sit with a piece of paper for five minutes (you will be surprised how rarely you will get to do this), come up with three or four ideas as to activities you can use to teach the kids the subject, and then hastily scribe these onto a lesson plan, checking whether you have some differentiation for the SEN kids and an extra task for the higher attaining.

The third version you do 'as and when' someone else is in your classroom, and it is worth going to town on it. As I said in the display section in Chapter 3, if you want to be *seen* to be a really good teacher then you must focus on the parts of your teaching that are visible. You therefore pay a great deal of attention to getting your learning environment sorted, and come to a pretty quick and certain realisation that you must take observed lessons deadly seriously. You will be able to get away with a couple of dodgy observations at best nowadays, before you are identified as being, 'in need of support'. You don't want this. 'In need of support' is shorthand for, 'Senior Management are not sure you are up to the job'. You will be allocated a more experienced member of staff to sit in on more lesson observations, then sit with you in hushed and darkened rooms delving into your 'development needs' (the things they think you are rubbish at). Should you have two or so shoddy lesson observations, then this procedural will be instituted, and there is no guarantee whatsoever that the more experienced member of staff appointed to help (for which read – monitor) knows what they are doing, nor any guarantee that they aren't a pocket fascist, who, for some deeply sad reason, are envious of your relative youth, and who will drink enjoyment from your tears as they drum you out of a profession you have dreamt of since childhood. You can avoid all this unpleasantness by ensuring that when someone is going to sit in the back of your lesson with a clipboard, you spend half of Sunday ensuring that your lesson is supremely well planned, that every box is ticked and, specifically, that you take an entirely constructivist approach (i.e. you don't perform – observers don't like this).

The full Ofsted is not to be brought out every day, however. You will not be able to do this, as it is entirely impossible. There will be managers who pay lip service to the idea that you are expected to prepare every lesson down to the last degree. Check their timetable in the staffroom. They may very well be able to do this (but probably don't), as they don't actually teach very often. Your job is to give of your best and much of this is realising, in your early years, that teaching is, to regurgitate a cliché, a marathon not a sprint. You can't give of your absolute best to every class, every lesson. If you attempt to do this you will find that you have exhausted your physical and emotional reserves within the first two or three weeks of term, and will have a long distance to drag your still breathing corpse to the holidays. As a rule of thumb, it's probably a good policy to give each of your classes a version of your best at least once a week. If that runs over into twice a week then all to the good, but don't expect to be able to turn in the full Ofsted every lesson.

As regards the four-step lesson plan, the completely unprepared improvisatory session, it is possible to do this. However, what tends to happen with the entirely extemporised lesson is that, as your adrenalin is raised by the high risk nature of the strategy, you teach entirely from the front. You can get away with it. But in getting away with it you will find that you have destroyed yourself. It is a reasonable experiment to try a whole day teaching unplanned lessons from the front of the class just to see what happens. You may well find that you've taught some quite interesting lessons. It is possible, if you have the ability to think quickly, to invent interesting activities without prior thought or planning, and have the confidence to follow your nose down interesting directions. It is also possible that the kids didn't get really bored by your blatant display of an ego, which strictly they would really rather prefer you took outside and shot it like the sick doggy it is. However, the cracked and broken shell that will stare back at you as you glance at the mirror at the end of the day will tell you that, perhaps tomorrow, you should come into the lessons with at least an 'it'll do' version of a lesson plan.

SETTING LESSON OBJECTIVES

This is way more difficult than you would think. It appears (and should be) an extremely easy concept to grasp. The objectives are what you are going to teach the class or, in modern day speak, what the class is going to learn (since teaching itself is now regarded as somehow an outmoded notion). You may hear someone tell you that you should be a 'facilitator of learning', you may even hear the stock codswallop claiming that you should be, 'The guide at the side, not the sage on the stage'. Anyone who even thinks of uttering this phrase without contemplating their immediate suicide should be summarily sectioned, and if you hear it, it is in your contract that you are fully entitled to mutter the word "twat" under your breath without any possibility of anyone calling you on it.

The issue is that deciding what it is that the class is going to 'learn' is way harder than it seems and, oddly and annoyingly, there are various schools of thought on what constitutes a decent learning objective. One which appears regularly in school lesson pro formas nowadays is the *know – understand – be able to* format. This format requires you to set an objective for something you want kids to *know*, something you want them to *understand* and something for them to *be able to* do. This format seems to have been instituted as a reaction against the predominant form used in the past decade which was to have objectives only of the *be able to* variety. The precedence of *be able to* was, I believe, to ensure that teachers focus on inculcating skills in their students; in that you can *know* something simply by the teacher telling you it, you can *understand* things this way too, but to *be able to* do something you have to be active, doing something – and that activity is likely to require some technical skill, be it writing, drawing, talking, acting out, designing or calculating. Having *be able to* as the sole format with which we recorded objectives also served to relegate knowledge of a set body of facts to the past. The British education system is in constant internal dialogue as to what it thinks of 'facts': there are classicists, the like of Chris Woodhead, who believe, not unreasonably, that it is an entirely appropriate objective for an education system to equip students with a body of knowledge, details and dates that they should know in order to properly understand the world in which they live and will one day work. Others see filling kids with facts about things as an outmoded, even Dickensian, idea. They point out that delivery of facts can reduce students to being seen as passive, empty vessels to be filled with a set of dead knowledge, which has been filtered through the countless biases of governments, exam boards, writers of textbooks and, finally, their teachers.

In the 1990s and early 2000s the latter view prevailed – and it was considered somehow politically incorrect to incorporate teaching children things you think they needed to know, without this being couched in language that suggested they would also be taught some skill of analysis, with which they could process or re-use this information. Consequently, you could not write, "By the end of this lesson you will *know* how the caste system works" on your lesson plan. This would be regarded as being evidence of unacceptable didacticism; of a teacher who has not caught onto or understood the brave new world of ensuring that children are equipped predominantly with skills over knowledge. You would have to write instead, "By the end of this lesson you will *be able to* recount the inequities in the caste system." This way, the bunging in of the, arguably tokenistic, 'recount' ensures that the students must reprocess the information. They cannot just sit listening while you waffle on about what you believe is wrong with the caste system, they must talk about it themselves locating their own views on it. All this seems entirely reasonable until you ask yourself the question, "Well, just what is so wrong with kids being in possession of discrete pieces of knowledge or information?"

It is in answer to this question, I believe, that the *know – understand – be able to* format was introduced, to validate teachers introducing their students to new knowledge. Which, again, seems reasonable, until such point as you give it a second's thought, and realise that knowing something is entirely implicit in understanding it, and as such the objective *know* is entirely superfluous. This idiocy is further compounded by the presence of the *be able to* objective. Equally, as you must know something in order to understand it, you must be able to demonstrate understanding in order to reprocess it. As an example, here is a set of objectives in the *know – understand – be able to* format:

By the end of this lesson you will:

- Know that a bear shits in the wood.

- Understand why they don't use toilet paper.

- Draw and annotate a picture detailing the reasons a bear doesn't use toilet paper.

Bear

unsuspecting
rabbit being
used as
toilet paper

If we take this admittedly over-serious example, we can see that the first two objectives are contained within the third. In order to draw all the reasons bears don't use bog roll, you must first of all, as a fundamental to the task, know that they shit in the woods. Further to this, you must understand all the reasons that they are unable to use Andrex. And so, we see that the *know – understand – be able to* format is somewhat pointless, in that *know* and *understand* were always implicit in *be able to*.

Given this analysis, how do we go about setting lesson objectives for our students that are appropriate and of use? What is the process? There are two ways of doing it. The orthodox is just to refer to the scheme of work, which has been completed, of course, either by yourself or a head of department, and has been mapped to the national curriculum, so juicy and useful objectives are ready to hand. If, by some astounding miracle, you find this document doesn't actually exist, then there is a second approach that I have always found helpful. You find out the stuff that they don't know, and teach them it!

In order to find out what they don't know you have to mark their books. Whilst marking you keep a blank piece of paper at your side and, as you are reading through their work, you'll notice things that no one seems to be able to do. You might notice that no one can use the possessive apostrophe, that their understanding of the build up to the First World War is missing a few details, or that their ability to create a functional frozen picture is not sufficiently nuanced spatially. Whatever it is you have found they can't do, you make that one of the objectives for the next lesson. After you have taught the lesson you mark their books again, and check whether they learned what you taught them. If they have, look for something else they can't do or, as is often the case, you'll realise that the fact that you have taught them something does not mean they have learnt it, and you must go back to the drawing board, finding a new way of teaching them the thing they are struggling with.

The key to objective setting is the verb that you choose to start the objective with. This must be active. And so, we spurn *know* and *understand*, look askance in the direction of *realising*. We head, instead, towards verbs that suggest that students will have to employ a skill, and we not only teach them the knowledge they are missing, but the skill with which to investigate that knowledge. Consequently, we are able to distinguish between a useful objective, "By the end of this lesson you will be able to draw the reasons a bear doesn't use bog roll," from a shoddy one, "You will understand why a bear doesn't use bog roll." And this affects the lesson we teach them, as not only are they to soak up the knowledge and understanding implicit in the objective, but we must also teach them the skill (in this example drawing and annotation) that will help them to achieve the task.

Here is a table with a set of useful verbs that you might want to use to set objectives:

Evaluation – appraise, argue, assess, compare, conclude, contrast, criticise, describe, discriminate, explain, interpret, judge, relate, summarise, validate
Synthesis – categorise, combine, compile, compose, create, design, devise, explain, generate, modify, organise, plan, rearrange, reconstruct, relate, reorganise, revise, rewrite, summarise
Analysis – analyse, break down, deduce, detect, differentiate, discriminate, distinguish, identify, illustrate, infer, outline, point out, relate, select, separate, subdivide
Application – apply, change, choose, classify, compute, demonstrate, develop, discover, employ, manipulate, modify, operate, organise, predict, prepare, produce, relate, restructure, show, solve, transfer, use
Comprehension – convert, defend, distinguish, estimate, explain, extend, generalise, give examples, give in own words, illustrate, infer, interpret, paraphrase, predict, read, rearrange, reorder, represent, restate, rewrite, summarise, transform, translate
Knowledge – acquire, define, describe, identify, label, list match, name, outline, recall, reproduce, select, state[22]

22 Available from –
http://www.tlc.murdoch.edu.au/gradatt/verbs.html

A further important piece of information regarding lesson objectives is not to do twenty of them. You'd do better to focus on teaching the class two or three things well, than a thousand things poorly. You will destroy the clarity of the lesson if you attempt to teach too many things. Also, it is entirely reasonable to teach a lesson that only has one lesson objective. Don't let anyone ever tell you otherwise.

CROSS-CURRICULAR OBJECTIVES

Here's a thing. The CBI, the employers' organisation who are indirectly responsible for much of government education policy, do not think that school leavers get to them with a sufficient grasp of the basics of literacy and numeracy. What they base this on, other than finding the impulse to tutt like an embittered old lady on a bus muttering something about the kids of today irresistible, I don't know; but as a response to the CBI's dissatisfaction with the educational state of school leavers, functional skills are coming to get ya! For a substantial time there have been boxes on lesson plans asking you to define objectives (as appropriate) for literacy, numeracy and for ICT, the idea being that all lessons should have at least some cross-curricular application, and should contribute towards kids' acquisition of functional skills in these areas. The fact that an English teacher teaching quadratic equations as part of a scheme of work on Anne Frank is as absurd as a maths teacher asking kids to improve their use of connectives whilst doing those very equations seems to have passed policy makers by. And so, these pretty but pointless little boxes have remained on lesson plan pro formas, wasting space and teachers' limited thinking time for any number of years.

The reason behind the ICT box is slightly more understandable but, as always, there is a political agenda behind it, which reduces quite neatly to the fact that we are a nation of xenophobes, quite petrified of both the Chinese and Indian tiger economies. Britain's manufacturing base is spent and government wishes to turn us into a 'knowledge economy'. With the most lucrative economic knowledge being that which comes in the form of interfacing human beings with computer screens, our rulers wish us, as a society, to be the most ICT literate in the world. Fair enough. Though there are further agendas behind it, particularly in its interface with the personalisation agenda. The strategic objectives of Becta, the government's lead agency for ICT in education, include: "To save the education system £100 million over three years" and to "double the number of teachers using technology to support personalisation". These two objectives are linked – given that software salesmen do not flog their wares for nothing, the way in which Becta will save the government such a substantial sum of money is by using computers to replace one-to-one support for kids with special needs. Rather than have someone sit with them and explain how the phonetic code works, for instance, they will be stuck in front of a generic computer game; it will shut them up, stop them complaining and teach them nothing.

The CBI's agenda has resulted in a recent change to government policy: in order to qualify in one of the new vocational 16 – 19 diplomas, students must also pass exams in functional skills in ICT, English and maths. There was also talk of making passing these functional skills qualifications a prerequisite to passing GCSE English and maths, until such point as they realised that you cannot have one qualification dependent on passing another (and entirely unrelated to the fact that it'd result in half of the students who currently get C grades failing), and so a swift U-turn was performed. It is intended, however, that this will be the case at some point in the future and, as a result, the boxes on the lesson plan asking you to cross reference your lesson to literacy, numeracy and ICT objectives will not only remain, but will be an increasing focus over the next few years.

You will be increasingly required to make spurious correlations between things that have little inherent connection. "In this lesson on Joseph Conrad we will waste half our time plotting a timeline of his life, when we should have been reading the bloody book." Or "In this lesson in which we were meant to be doing impressionist painting with paint, we will improve on the working methodology of the greatest artists of all time by using clip art." What one could say in defence of this practice, which I have perhaps over-satirised, is that there is certainly a substantial issue in this country with students' literacy and with our expectations of what can be achieved in this realm. How the cross-curricular, functional skills boxes on the lesson plan attempt to mediate this is to ensure that there is a literacy related outcome in every lesson. And with the exception of maths, which really is a standalone (in that numeracy is literacy in an entirely different language), it is not unreasonable to attempt to drive up standards this way. If, therefore, you are teaching a subject area that uses the English language you can quite reasonably be expected to have objectives related to improving kids oracy, their reading, or their writing. This seeks to circumvent one of the biggest causes of literacy difficulties in British education: the PE, history or geography teacher allowing spelling mistakes and grammatical errors in written work, as they leave it to the English teacher, who is fighting a losing battle, as all her colleagues give the children implicit permission to make such errors, since they don't correct them.

In terms of practical advice, though, there is a decent rule with functional skills objectives: include them only if you can think of decent ones that will not interrupt the flow of the subject specific stuff you are teaching. Don't force these spurious connections, so that you force kids to do something with ICT when it would have been more efficient to make do without it. Similarly, don't waste time on measuring stuff just so you can add a numeracy objective, when, in fact, doing so will completely ruin the lesson. Have the bravery to leave these boxes blank if you cannot find anything obvious to go in them. Don't bother to go through the pointless process of filling in a box with something useless just so that it looks like you have thought about it. "Not applicable to this lesson" shows you have thought about it properly.

IDENTIFYING RESOURCE REQUIREMENTS

This is simple as a science technician: you write down all the things you are going to need in the lesson in order to teach it and you check that list before you enter the classroom to ensure you haven't forgotten anything. You do this because there are few things in life more irritating than spending ages designing a spangly worksheet, and then forgetting to bring it into class. Logistically it is useful to take this box seriously and, during the lesson planning process, the very moment the need for a resource — be it the empty shell of a tortoise, a vacuum-cleaner or a worksheet on prepositions — becomes evident you write it down in the resources box straightaway. Don't write them down at the end. You will forget stuff.

PLANNING FOR THE NEEDS OF DIFFERENT ABILITY LEVELS

Differentiation, extension or, perhaps nowadays, personalised learning, are perceived to be a very important part of your professionalism. You must differentiate your lessons four ways: there will be the stuff you teach the mainstream kids, harder or 'extension' work for able and talented, easier stuff for the kids with special needs and then stuff specific to children at early stages of learning English. And you must do this for every lesson that you teach. Nothing easier.

Let's be honest here, dear reader: ain't gonna happen, is it? My mate, the teacher and author, Francis Gilbert, is very good on this subject. "The whole thing is a duplicitous gimmick," he says. "In reality, schools just do not have the resources, time or space in the curriculum to implement it." You cannot properly differentiate every lesson four ways. You will go dribbly within your first day of doing it. In order to survive with differentiation without ever feeling you are giving any particular cohort of kids a raw deal you have to be judicious about how, where and when you differentiate. Before I share with you the ways of keeping this task manageable, it is worth going through chapter and verse on the subject to save you from delving into one of the many completely unreadable books that exist on this subject. I've read them so you don't have to.

When I'm presenting on this subject to teachers, I'll ask them to put up their hands if they feel guilty about differentiation. They all do. Then I'll ask them to keep their hands up if they feel guilty enough!

The point here is that the impossibility of differentiating properly for every lesson, for every class, is only matched by its importance. By not differentiating we feel we are letting down the most vulnerable (in the case of SEN pupils) or, paradoxically, the most needy (in the case of able and talented) of our pupils. This is compounded by the fact that the mere presence of special needs staff in a lesson that you haven't properly differentiated lays a covert guilt trip on the poor mainstream teacher, as well as the fact that your training in how to deal with kids with low level literacy will probably have amounted to chucking a Cloze procedure at them and telling them to get on with it. Differentiation may actually make you angry at yourself, as it constantly puts you into a situation where you feel that you are bad at something, and this is prone to making people spiky.

However, I think it's worth looking at the emotional effects of poor differentiation on the students you teach. If you give SEN kids what primary teachers describe as 'busy work' — stuff to keep them from asking for your attention, but teaches them nothing — hoping it'll make the problem go away, it won't work. Because that problem is a child and that child will be back next lesson with the same needs, but with a half a per cent more added emotional damage.

There are two key concepts when we are talking about the emotional affects of poor differentiation: 'susceptibility' and 'anticipatory anxiety'. Imagine please, you are asked to stand, on your own, in front of all of the other staff members at your school. You have your back turned towards them, and they have all been given an instruction on a piece of paper. That instruction relates to you, but you don't know what it is. What you would feel here is called 'susceptibility'.

Now you are in a group sitting down, and the person standing at the front, with her back towards you, is your head teacher. You must write down three paragraphs in which you are completely honest. They can't see you. You are to write the story of the most unprofessional thing you have ever done as a teacher.

How do you feel here? How does the head teacher feel?

How do you feel when the head teacher turns 'round and asks to see what you have written?

All these feelings are, to varying degrees, examples of 'susceptibility'. Learning challenges how we see ourselves. The very process is, by definition, threatening to our self-esteem, as to learn is to admit that you have deficiencies, gaps or imperfections. Given this piece of information, you can see how you must be very careful indeed with the emotional landscapes of your students in terms of how your task setting can impact upon their sense of themselves.

For a further look at the emotional aspects of learning, give a bit of thought to these two fairly easy calculus questions:

1. True or false? The two functions f and g defined by the following equation are equal.

   $f(x) = 3x + 3$ for x real and $g(t) = 3t + 3$ for t real and positive

2. If functions f and g have domains Df and Dg respectively, then the domain of f/g is given by?

   (A) The union of Df and Dg.

   (B) The intersection of Df and Dg.

   (C) The intersection of Df and Dg without the zeros of function g.

   (D) None of the above.[23]

Troubling isn't it? You can't get near locating any meaning in it, let alone get any purchase on solving it. And you've just looked at it briefly or, more likely, skipped down to this bit. Imagine if you were shut in a room with a whole series of these exercises, for a full double lesson. How would you feel? What would be the emotional impact of being made to feel like this all day every day for eleven years? As an example of the potentially destructive impact of school on a young person's self-esteem, have a guess as to the age of the girl who made the following statements?

23 Available at – http://www.analyzemath.com/calculus_questions/ functions.html. The answers, like you are remotely interested, are 1. False. Two functions are equal if their rules are equal and their domains are the same. 2. (C). Division by zero is not allowed in mathematics, you silly.

- I am everything bad that you can say to me.

- I hate myself and what I do.

- It is difficult for me, but nobody realises.

- The horibblest person is better than me.

- I cannot do anything.

- I am a piece of crap.

She is in year 8. You shouldn't give this child a piece of work that she can't do, as it is going to reinforce this view of herself that someone else has given her.

FORMS OF DIFFERENTIATION

Let's start with what you already know. It is generally held that there are three main forms of differentiation: outcome, support and task. You should know this. However, there is also the argument that you can differentiate by assessment, and since assessment of pupil need should be the starting point of any differentiation you will do we'll start with that one.

DIFFERENTIATION BY ASSESSMENT

You can't properly differentiate on the basis of assumptions. You cannot match work to need if you do not know what that need is ... and so all differentiation must begin with assessment of what your pupils require. There is also an entirely sound idea that the best and most effective form of differentiation is decent marking. If you think about it, marking, when done properly, is differentiated to the point of being the epitome of personalised learning. Children are given feedback, praise and targets that will generally be entirely individual to their needs.

Differentiation by outcome

There is, I think, a solid argument that differentiation by 'outcome' is no differentiation at all. If I'm observing and I see the naked and rapidly sketched single word 'outcome' in the differentiation box of the lesson plan, I think to myself, "You're not taking this seriously – either you are already a member of senior management, or you don't care much about the grade you are going to get."

If you think about it, differentiation by outcome is actually a definition of low expectations. They'll all do the same piece of work, and some will do it well, some will do it moderately well and some will do it badly, and that's fine.

So I would advise that it is only really acceptable to put the word 'outcome' in the differentiation box if you are completing a formally, summatively assessed task.

Differentiation by support

The second and, for you, the most useful form of differentiation is differentiation by support. This comes in three fascinating varieties: teacher, support teacher/assistant and peer. The first of these, like differentiation by outcome, is akin to writing on the lesson plan that you couldn't really be arsed to differentiate and that you were just going to let the kid with cerebral palsy sort himself out really. (And can't he wheel himself out of the lesson? It's really beginning to hurt your back).

Differentiation by teacher support can start with the best of intentions and, initially in your career, it will appear to be a completely reasonable thing for a teacher to expect of herself. What are you going to do with the child who is struggling with reading? You are going to give him extra special, one-to-one support during the lesson, of course. What better?

It takes only a few runs at this to realise that, though well intentioned, it is as useful as a strategy as a one-legged man in a bum kicking contest. You will have in the region of thirty children in your class, all of whom see your attention as the Holy Grail. Despite the fact that they are generally enormously open-hearted and generous in spirit, and want the best for their struggling colleague, they will not be able to discipline themselves to be sufficiently quiet, passive or engaged to give you more than about thirty seconds with the struggling kid, before it all kicks off and you have to go and deal with something else.

Where a child has a statement of special educational needs, there is a chance that they will have in-class, one-to-one support, either from a support teacher or a teaching assistant. The temptation here is to just leave them to get on with it. So you teach one lesson to the rest of the class, while the support teacher and the special needs kid enter their own special, ostracised bubble, where, detached from the experiences of their peers, they can get on with creating a relationship of utter dependency on the part of the kid. A warning here: although support teachers are fantastic people, and do their jobs with great dedication, you will be doing the child a disservice if you let them become too dependent on one person. The support teacher will not be there when the child grows to adulthood and has to look after himself. As the support teacher will happily tell you, such kids can develop a learned helplessness if someone else is always there to do their work with them, and so it really is better to not write "support by support teacher" on the lesson plan. Aside from this, if you are in an observed lesson and you write this any observer worth their corn will mark you down as someone who is not thinking too deeply about things.

Differentiation by peer support

This is where the good stuff is – differentiation that actually works and costs you little in the way of hair tearing effort. A teacher who differentiates by peer support and can provide evidence, backed up by data, that she has chosen according to a rationalised methodology – who sits with who, and for what reason – is a teacher who recognises the learning needs of her class, and is doing something about giving them the best experience possible (without giving herself such a headache with workload as to lead to insanity). In this, it has a sublime advantage over differentiation by task, in that it does not involve creating various differentiated worksheets, which can take hours, destroy your health and reduce you to being a permanently embittered member of drudge squad.

Differentiation by support – paired work

There's a nice phrase: what a child can do in a pair today, they can do on their own tomorrow. Differentiation by paired task is the surest, easiest way for teachers to differentiate without actually having to do a great deal of extra preparatory work. It gives one-to-one support – which is what most parents want for their kids. If kids work in pairs they are less likely to rubbish the task, because they are not only rubbishing themselves but their partners also. To set this up properly and effectively they must be producing a joint product or must be given only one worksheet – and the teacher has to be explicit about them taking turns.

There is a pleasing element of safety to it. If we think back to the notion of susceptibility, learning requires a degree of emotional risk taking and this is the environment in which kids are most likely to take risks. A pair provides safety: there's no public ridicule in a pair. There is an argument that if you use paired work in every lesson, you can use your support staff as an additional teacher and not just have them sitting with the one child who becomes increasingly dependent on them.

Paired work can also be set up as peer tutoring: where you use the kids to teach each other. You can reduce this to a model of binary options:

- Most able tutoring the least able.

- Least able tutoring the most able.

- Least able tutoring each other.

- Most able tutoring each other.

Both gain out of this equation. The tutor has to clarify their thoughts and under-standing through expressing them with language. Teaching puts kids in their zone of proximal development, and it is actually the tutor who gains most from this arrange-ment, as it develops their powers of expressing thought rationally and convincingly with language. In order that this is shared around then the groupings must be fluid.

An added benefit is that peer tutors may find ways of explaining things that are bet-ter than the teachers'. If you are going to do this, it is useful to have a circle time session first in which you discuss how to give feedback – you can start by asking how do you feel if someone tells you your work is rubbish, even if you know it is. Training kids to give each other positive feedback will improve the whole class's self-esteem.

Differentiation by support – groupings

It is, I believe, perfectly decent practice to point out (in a class without entirely non-literate pupils, for whom you really should be providing work differentiated by task) that you have a seating plan that has been worked out so that the groupings are sympathetic to kids getting decent peer support. You've already read the key facets of this on pages 7 to 9 of Chapter 1 (Rule 2 – Sort your seating). If you can't remember it, go back and read it again.

Differentiation by task

There are occasions though when you really won't be able to sell it to yourself that sitting Johnny (who can't read) next to Jimmy (who can read very well) is actually benefiting either of them at all, and you will have to reach in the direction of dif-ferentiating by task. Differentiation by task could quite easily be satirised by some unkind cynic as being 'easy work for thick kids'. And despite the deep unpleasantness of this epithet, sadly there is some truth in it. Many of the tasks we throw at kids with special educational needs treat the issue as just that, "Here's your idiot sheet. Get on with it, and I don't want to hear a peep out of you all lesson."

On this subject, an illustration into the awful truth of a phrase which I think, admittedly somewhat controversially, should be tattooed on the inner wrist of every newly qualified teacher. You pick up your QTS certificate, and go directly to the tattooist, who prints a phrase on your inner wrist – and that phrase is ...

NO ONE EVER LEARNT ANYTHING FROM A BLOODY WORD SEARCH!

When filming the Channel 4 series *Can't Read Can't Write* in which I taught a series of spectacularly crude phonics lessons to a group of adults with literacy difficulties, I worked with a young man called James. James started the course completely illiterate. He is a lovely guy, a real grafter, looks after his mum, loyal to his family, gets up at half-five every morning, works for buttons. He told me the story of his school career, and I think it serves to illustrate why you should never, ever use a word search in lessons. I asked him what his lessons were like? He replied that all he ever got was a word search at the beginning of the lesson.

Now you can see the teacher wondering aloud, "What am I going to do with James? I know, I'll give him a word search. That should keep him busy all lesson." Now the thing is James has done so many word searches in his school career that he's gotten really – and I mean really, especially, brilliantly, spectacularly and stupendously – good at them. He can't read, but that does not mean he doesn't want to do well. It isn't his fault that he can't read. He's tried, and he will give his best to every word search they throw at him – he can do the most complex word search you could ever imagine in five minutes flat.

This creates a distressing picture. The teacher has given James work to keep him quiet, but James wants to be an achiever, and he's sweat blood to get the thing done as quickly as he can, and he's up not long after the lesson has started saying, "Look, I did this really good. I am clever. No one can do these as quick as me." He's expecting praise, because he deserves it. But does he get that praise?

No, he doesn't. He's ruined the teacher's lesson. The word search was meant to keep James busy for nearly an hour. So the teacher – maybe imperceptibly, but probably not, because it's a stressful job being a teacher, particularly when you've got a bouncy pre-literate kid who's got no work to do – is angry with James, as he has become a problem for the teacher. What message has this given this young man? He's done his best. He's got the worksheet done, and the teacher is cross with him.

I found this story heartbreaking because I know this child as the man he's become, and I respect him, and I understand why the teacher did it. But it's a disaster all round. It's caused by teachers treating differentiation as busy work. Don't do it.

THE CLOZE PROCEDURE

This seems to be the standard default setting of the shoddy differentiator. You take a piece of text, type it up, then take a few words out, replacing them with gaps and put the now decontextualised words at the bottom of the page. SEN kids then use whatever reading ability they have to see which of the words should go in which of the gaps. The idea, I think, is that it develops reading comprehension, and once they have done it, they also get to do some nice copying in their books. My thought about cloze procedures has not changed since the first time I encountered them, and that thought is: Christ, can't we do any better than this? Surely the finest minds in world education can come up with something that helps kids with low-level literacy more effectively than getting them to fill in the gaps. There's a solid argument, I think, that the cloze procedure is little more than a word search on steroids and should be treated with the same degree of contempt. Don't just give the kids in the class with the most need a default setting. They are worth more.

There are further problems with the Cloze procedure. Giving Cloze procedures is asking kids to work in their area of failure, which is writing. Also, because the language they use is so simple, they give a simplified version of the curriculum. Not being able to read well doesn't make you stupid. Ask Einstein. The Cloze procedure presents the curriculum in a linguistic form which is way lower than the level of intellectual engagement a child may have with the subject when they don't have to read and write and, consequently, it can turn kids off subjects they actually like.

If you are going to use one then there is an argument for you to do it in a slightly different way. Get the kids to make them for each other. Here you would use one of the pairings suggested on page 196 of this chapter, and the higher attaining of the pair would produce the cloze for the lower attaining: the higher attaining student would then mark the lower attainer's attempt at it.

Eventually, if they do this as a paired task, you will be able to ask the lower attaining students to produce their own Cloze procedures – which is an infinitely more cognitive task then just filling one in.

This technique can be made to work with all forms of differentiation by task. Take the lazy teacher's way and get the higher attaining students to do your work for you. Get the kids to differentiate for each other.

SPELLING STRATEGIES

These were taught to me by Cynthia Klein, the flame haired high priestess of spelling. It is a simple enough process to arrange, and gives kids with low level literacy a task they enjoy and that may actually run the risk of teaching them something useful. You simply go onto PowerPoint and print off ten or so words related to the curriculum area you are teaching, in as large a font size as possible. You then give the ten pieces of paper, along with a pair of scissors, to the child who is struggling. From thence they must do three things with each word.

1. Spot words within the word. If we take the somewhat surreal example of 'Walthamstow', then we can see that it contains: Walt, ha, ham, am, stow, to and tow.

2. Cut the word up into sections. Key here is that they must cut it up the way "they like it". They may like Wal-tham-stow, they might prefer Walt-hams-tow; crazies might even go for W-alt-h-amstow. The way they like it is the right way.

3. Deliberately mispronounce the word the way they have cut it up three times. Our crazy friend would be sitting in a classroom saying Wuh-alt-huh-amstow, Wuh-alt-huh-amstow, Wuh-alt-huh-amstow to himself over and over again as the rest of the class look on, eyebrows raised. It helps if, as they go through

the pissmronunciations, they pick up the cut up pieces of paper with the sound they are pronouncing.

This technique will not last an SEN child a complete lesson, but you can use it as an introduction to some written or speaking and listening activity that features the words. It's also of use to mainstream kids who struggle a little with spelling as it does genuinely improve their spelling.

THE WORKSHEET DIFFERENTIATED FOR THE WHOLE CLASS

At the beginning of my teaching career I would seat kids in groups according to their attainment, and give each group a different worksheet: cloze procedures for those scratching away at the earliest levels of literacy; Q&As for the middle attaining; and extended writing for those of higher attainment. It didn't work. Not only was it near impossible to administer, but the middle attaining kids always seemed to get a raw deal from this kind of thing.

You can actually produce a single worksheet that is properly differentiated for the whole class by just putting the easiest questions on the worksheet first, and increasing the degree of difficulty as you go on. This is called a tiered assignment. Alternatively, you can use the same worksheet, but differentiate the point at which they start — Kylie and Jade I'd like you to start from question one, Peyvand from question four and Gulay could you just concentrate on question twenty, it's very difficult indeed.

DIFFERENTIATING BY LEARNING STYLE

In the process of writing in this book, there was a crushing inevitability that, at some point, I would have to brush briefly against learning styles. You will have been initiated into these by someone at some point, no doubt. You may not yet recognise it for the utter crock of methane it is.

My understanding of it, and I could be wrong, is that the idea that each of us has a preferred learning style originated from the Californian proto (pseudo) science called neurolinguistic programming, NLP for short. NLP has always seemed to me to be a set of party tricks, and one of these party tricks is talk of 'modalities'. The NLPers correctly identify that we take in information through our five senses. They then go on to spout the scientifically unproven hogwash that each of us has some form of hardwired preference for taking in new information through either hearing (auditory), touching (kinaesthetic) or seeing (visual) – and therefore have preferred learning styles. The fact that there is not a single ounce of scientific proof for this preposterous theory did not stop the Department of Education from recommending that schools took it seriously. The result being poor, innocent children being forced to wear a silly badge, saying, "Hi. I'm Mike. I'm a kinaesthetic learner," causing him, no doubt, to refuse to take part in lessons where the teaching did not appeal to his preferred learning style. "I can't do this, miss. I'm a kinaesthetic learner and we don't do reading."[24]

So, why is the assassination of the idea of preferred learning styles in the section on differentiation? Because despite the fact that humans don't have hardwired preferred learning styles, it is a useful concept in terms of defining modes or lines of input. If we use the idea of having a lesson with 30% auditory work (talking and the like), 30% visual (looking at or drawing pictures), 30% kinaesthetic – and the left over 10% for sodding about and deliberately wasting time – then you have the basis of a lesson that has a variety of different styles of input, and therefore doesn't completely disenfranchise any child who, for instance, really hates listening because he is deaf. Furthermore, the fact that learning styles are intellectual smeg, doesn't alter the fact that we do not let kids use their bodies enough in lessons, and so whilst the notion of the kinaesthetic learner is to be treated with a snigger behind the hand, the idea of kinaesthetic learning is not to be dismissed so easily. The very fact that it has a label that we can attach to allowing kids to move around in lessons, to involve more dance and more drama in our teaching and to employ muscle memory as a way of

---

24 If you are genuinely interested in why the notion of learning styles is cack, then check out the work of Professor Frank Coffield. He's proved it.

encoding information means that learning styles have made some contribution to our understanding of how a lesson should be run.

EXTENSION WORK

There is differentiating downwards for kids with difficulties and issues, and then there's differentiating upwards for those who are classed as being particularly able or as having some absurdly magnificent talent. First, a word about these children and the process whereby they find themselves being on the list of specially clever or talented students. Excellence in Cities (a programme designed to improve inner city education provision) makes the following definitions:

'Gifted' learners (are) those who have abilities in one or more subjects in the statutory school curriculum other than art and design, music and PE;

'Talented' learners (are) those who have abilities in art and design, music, PE, or performing arts such as dance and drama.

Gifted and talented are therefore pretty well entirely separate definitions: 'gifted' signifies some form of academic or intellectual excellence, 'talented' a particular aptitude in either sport or the arts. You can be 'talented' and be a complete dunce, 'gifted' and a complete and utter physical klutz. There will be some form of downloadable data sheet that will provide you with the information as to which of your class fit either (or both) of these definitions. With regard to how this data informs what you do in terms of differentiation, there are but a few things to consider. Firstly, do not think make the mistake of thinking that you have to differentiate upwards in academic subjects for students who are registered as being talented: if you are teaching history, for instance, then it is of no relevance whatsoever to you that one child in your class once had a gymnastics lesson in which they were marginally OK. You only have to produce a lesson that acknowledges that certain children are registered as talented if they are accorded this epithet in the subject you are actually teaching them. If you are teaching drama and two members of the class are mini-McKellens then you must somehow acknowledge this in your lesson plan by making specific provision for them, preferably by task or by support.

Where children are registered as gifted it means that they are recorded as being particularly bright and, again, you must make specific provision for their recognised intellectual brilliance. The issue here can be that, since a certain percentage of the school population has to be recorded as being 'gifted' regardless of whether there is actually anyone in the school that can spell their own name, then you will occasionally come across children who have been labelled as gifted who stretch this definition to laughable lengths. "You must be joking. If this child is gifted, I'm the bastard offspring of Mother Teresa and a preternaturally myopic chimp!" Once you have given your laughter full throat at such a definition, then you must put your giggles away and imagine it had some substance, differentiating accordingly.

The style of differentiation you map to each 'gifted' child in your class is up to your professional judgement (and this is probably the one time you will get away with just putting the word 'outcome' next to their initials in the differentiation box). Broadly, though, the acceptable forms boil down into:

1. Support by pairing – Sitting the gifted child next to the low attaining child, and getting the gifted child to explain things, may seem to you that you are just fobbing off the bright child, but it is regarded as an entirely acceptable form of differentiation. In theory, the most effective way of learning something is by actually teaching it to someone else and, therefore, sitting the highest attaining next to the lowest is differentiation by support for both of them.

2. Task – If differentiating by task in a downwards direction is unconscionably satirised as easy work for thick kids, then extension work can be equally as easily summed up as tougher work for clever kids. Giving a 'gifted' child an entirely different, much more challenging task makes them feel special, and if you have thought this task out properly, will give them the level of challenge that their superior intellects will thrive on.

3. Differentiation by extension task – This is a subsection of differentiation by outcome, in that the gifted child will perform the same task as the rest of the class but, as they are so clever, they will finish it quicker, and you will have

prepared for this by cleverly providing them with a whole new task just at the point they have put their pen down, having finished the first one. In truth, it is a good idea to have an extension activity in your back pocket for every lesson you teach. All this takes is a (very) brief bit of thought that will reward you sevenfold. If, before every lesson, you grab a pen and write the answer to the question, "What will I get the kids to do who finish the activity before the lesson is over?" you will save yourself from having the aforementioned kids sitting with nothing to do, and a full half hour left in which to do that nothing. You will realise pretty early on that "the devil makes work for idle hands" is not, as you may have previously thought, some crypto-religious fishwives' cliché, but is the most profound truth imaginable. If you do not want Gaz, who has been wrongly identified as 'gifted', using his front door key to undo all the screws in your desk because he has nothing to do, have some extension work planned.

RECORDING DIFFERENTIATION

Schools nowadays are awash with data. Data tells management which of the kids in year 11 are likely to get the grades that will obtain management a promotion, and so we treat data with reverence, as it is likely to be the difference between a Lada and a convertible Audi with 'go faster' stripes for the deputy head. Your differentiation must be referenced to this data. It's simple really, you look at the data sheet for your class and discern which of them are:

1.   On the SEN register, and for what.

2.   Are at Stage 1 or 2 of acquiring English as an Additional Language.

3.   Registered as being 'gifted', or in the case of PE or arts' subjects, 'talented'.

Having done this you transfer the data onto the lesson plan differentiation box by putting the initials of the child next to the special need:

SEN:

CP: Action, learning

PB: Action Plus, reading

CM: Statement, EBD (Emotional & Behavioural Difficulties)[25]

EAL:

MS, GM, SS: EAL 1

G & T:

RM, DR, PP: Gifted

PT: G & T (basketball)

CC: Talented (art)

Having shown that you have a full grasp of the special needs in your class, you map what you are going to do, specific to each child, in that lesson to give them access to that lesson.

This is how not to do it:

SEN:

CP: Action, learning – outcome

---

25 You'll see from this example there are three stages/levels of special needs: Action means that someone has noticed something's wrong and has registered it; Action Plus means that it is being taking seriously and they are somewhere along a process of getting the kid a statement of special educational need; Statement means that they are pucker special needs and are entitled to some in-class support.

PB: Action Plus, reading – outcome

CM: Statement, EBD – outcome

EAL:

MS, GM, SS: EAL 1 – outcome

G & T:

RM, DR, PP: Gifted – outcome

PT: G & T (basketball) – outcome

CC: Talented (art) – outcome

This is more like it:

SEN:

CP: Action, learning – peer support, paired with PT

PB: Action Plus, reading – task, creation of cloze procedure with RM

CM: Statement, EBD – support, LST will sit in group

EAL:

MS, GM, SS: EAL 1 – task, will do exercise in home language, individually, then will translate as a trio

G & T:

RM: Gifted – task, creation of cloze procedure with PB

DR, PP: Gifted – outcome

PT: G & T (basketball) – peer support, paired with CP

CC: ~~Talented (art) – Who gives a monkey's? This is an English lesson~~

HOW TO KEEP DIFFERENTIATION MANAGEABLE

The easiest answer to this is: only do it when you are being observed. It works for the vast majority of teachers in the country.

If you want to make a decent fist of grappling with it though you must find some ways of cheating. Differentiation appears complicated, but is merely a series of very simple concepts and procedures. Where you will struggle, however, is not in failing to understand its myriad complexities, but in keeping on top of it. Differentiating properly (particularly by task) is very time consuming indeed, and you already have enough to do.

The way of making this manageable is by correctly identifying that peer support and paired task is the easiest way of ensuring that you are making at least some provision for the SEN kids: if you sit them next to a clever kid, who is also empathetic and kind, then they will receive some support from their partner. Think carefully about these parings or groupings, match the right kid with the right helper and you will find that lessons go pretty swimmingly. Remember also, that reading and writing tasks actually create special needs. Try and teach a week of lessons where there is to be no reading or writing; but, instead, plenty of drama, speaking and listening and recording in different forms: graphs, pictures, presentations. See what happens when the kids with literacy difficulties are not disabled. Do they fly? Then remember that if you don't grapple with their special need or attempt to do something about it, you will be contributing to their continuation, and mix it up so that their lessons feature bits in which they can contribute equally, and bits where they have to focus on improving their attainment in the thing they struggle with.

STRATEGIES FOR KIDS WITH ENGLISH AS AN ADDITIONAL LANGUAGE

This is the realm of the expert. I am not one. My knowledge of specific strategies that you might use to aid those kids who can't speak English yet is shockingly rubbish, especially so for someone who has spent their career in schools with a high proportion of refugee kids.

As an illustration of what not to do, however, imagine a scenario where you are on holiday in an Arabic country, one in which you haven't even the foggiest chance of understanding a single word that is said, and a local approaches you and asks you a question in Arabic.

Do you understand the question? No. You haven't a clue what matey is saying to you. In fact he is asking if you speak Arabic. You say, "I'm sorry I don't understand Arabic," but he ignores you, continuing to talk at you, but much slower, and this time with bigger gaps between the words. You still don't understand so he starts annunciating the consonant sounds in his language more clearly. This makes no difference to you. He's speaking Arabic, and you don't speak Arabic. "I'm sorry," you say again, "but I don't speak your language." This makes no difference to him. He changes the order of some of the words. "Arabic. Speak. Do you?" then tries again missing some out, "Arabic? Do?" You look confused and perhaps a little scared as he says this again, more loudly with seemingly entirely random hand gestures.[26] You nod wildly, even though you are completely and utterly petrified, as his gestures become wilder still and he starts shouting at you.

"SPEAK IT? DO? ARABIC YOU?"

"SPEAK IT? DO? ARABIC YOU?"

"SPEAK IT? DO? ARABIC YOU?"

---

26 Did you know that the funny hand gesture (looking like a lower case 'b' or 'd') Americans use to signal that things are "A-OK buddy" means "You are a bumhole" in the Middle East. Careful with gestures, now.

How would this feel if you were in a foreign country and you didn't have a clue what was going on? Very scary indeed I would imagine. This is exactly what we do when we try to speak to refugee kids in English. It is called 'revving up' – putting more energy into the interaction – and it doesn't work. It isn't helping the kid, and the teacher is passing some of the pressure they are feeling from being useless onto the kid, in all probability scaring him (no matter how fiercely etched teacher's smiley and understanding face is).

Two cautionary tales here. When but a youth I joined the Penge and Anerley chapter of the Young Socialists. It was like the Hell's Angels in that there was a lot of poorly achieved facial hair, but unlike the Hell's Angels in that none of us rode motorbikes. We were a preposterously badly dressed group of people, clad in parkas and scuffed shoes, who, every Tuesday, would go 'round people's houses to call each other 'comrade'. The woman invested with the job of the looking after these young socialists' development was called Helen. Helen was often referred to by the elders as being a bit 'Mili'. I had no idea what this meant. Military? Millionaire? Millipede? Were there a hundred legs hiding under her voluminous kaftan? I was only seventeen. I didn't know much about anything at all. It turns out it was short for militant. The Militant Tendency was a faction in the Labour Party who tended towards militancy, and were the object of newspapers' weak satire as being the loony left. They were 'Trotskyite', apparently. I haven't a clue what a Trotskyite is, though I am told I have met a few.

Helen was not best pleased at me referring to my girlfriend as being a 'bird'. No. She was not in the least pleased. In a quiet pub on a Sunday evening, full of teachers wishing they didn't have to go to school the next day, in front of my comrades in the struggle, she launched into a venomous attack about my sexism. "What's wrong with being sexy?" was what I wish I'd said. But I didn't. I just sat in a green parka, lower lip quivering, as someone much older than me tore several strips. "Your statement hates wimmin," she ranted, "And so do you." (This was news to me). "Bird is not appropriate language. Can your girlfriend fly? Does she eat seeds? She is not your bird. It's an appalling diminution. She is strong. She's invincible. She is woman!"

My next encounter with the word 'inappropriate' was at a north London council that I will not name, in Haringey. I had lucked into a completely shit job servicing the needs of social workers, many of whom were completely mental. "Can you sort these papers into alphabetical order Phil?" "I should think so, social worker. Nothing to it, really." One of my colleagues, a nice Indian lady called G, questioned the veracity of something I'd said. A working class Londoner's dialect response to someone questioning the truth of what you've said is to hold your hands out, palm upwards, and utter the phrase, "Honest Injun." This did not go down too well with G or the rest of my colleagues, and I was shipped onto a disciplinary as fast as my little legs could carry me.

Again, I felt terrible. I hadn't meant to suggest that G or any Indian people were dishonest. There would be no reason for me to impute this, since I don't believe it. (Besides, north London social workers are too thick to realise the derivation of the phrase is actually from the kind of Indians you see John Wayne slaughtering in cowboy movies). I was just speaking my language.

But my language had got me into trouble. I suppose I could have rationalised it out and realised that it wasn't my fault. But I didn't. I just felt guilty and hurt and abused and really, really very angry. As angry as anyone would feel if someone had punished them for speaking the language of their family, their heritage and their culture.

Bear in mind this anecdote. A kid's language is very, very important to them indeed – be it some regional dialect form of English, or be it an entirely different language to English. It is the language their father speaks. It is what they are. You must respect it, explicitly. Put it on the wall of the classroom. Allow kids who have little English to write their assignments in their home language. It is still writing. It is unlikely that you will be able to read Lithuanian sufficiently well to understand what they have written, but you can still mark their work by commenting on presentation, their performance in class and how hard you know things are for them. Furthermore, there are translation devices on the web (Babelfish) that will allow you to make comments on their work in their home language "Jūs turite padaryti ir apie tai" in Lithuanian means "You have done well on this." "Keep it up" is Lithuanian for "Keep it up." Asking kids to write in their home language shows that you respect them, marking in that language shows them you care. You think they are special enough to have gone to a bit of extra trouble for, and that is a very good thing indeed for a teacher to do.

CHAPTER 5
ASSESSMENT

There are two kinds of assessment: formative and summative. Summative is the kind that you will remember from school tests: you sit in a drafty room answering a series of multi-guess questions, and are eventually allocated a mark that ruins your future. The teacher collects these marks on a spreadsheet and your progress, or lack of it, is put on your school report. Accordingly, you receive an extra sickly kiss from mummy or a cuff 'round the ear from dad, depending on how you've done. We are not much interested in summative assessment in this book. It happens. You have to do it. Ain't no mystery. Formative assessment, however, is a multifaceted and sophisticated beast, and is worth taking very seriously indeed if you are at all interested in seeing your students achieve.

MARKING

Make no mistake: this is the most important thing you do as a teacher. All the other stuff is of no use whatsoever if you don't mark your books properly. You can be endlessly enthusiastic, have great subject knowledge, be fully cognisant of every rule and regulation, manage behaviour wonderfully, teach fascinating lessons at a cracking pace, which feature bucketloads of flannel-free praise, and it will be all to nought if you don't mark their books. They won't progress. Antithetically, you can turn up hungover every morning, wearing the same creased pair of Farahs as last week, with hair that looks like a bird has slept in it, then spend most of the lesson talking at kids about how wonderful you are; but mark their books with dedication and rigour and your class will fly.

There is a substantial difference in the marking burdens of different subjects. Broadly, and obviously, the more writing you have to do in the subject, the more difficult it is to keep up with the marking. Drama and PE have it easy; music, art and D&T

likewise; maths teachers enjoy the blanket ticking session whereas scientists have to be slightly more focused. Where it gets more vital and difficult is when you move from geography (hard, but you can always get them doing maps) through history (harder, but you can always get them doing historical maps) into English (nigh on impossible). However, no matter what subject you are teaching you have a responsibility, and it's a biggie, to your students, your colleagues and to society as a whole, to make sure that you focus really heavily on ensuring that there is a point to the work you are setting your classes.

As an example, I'd like to share with you the story of a young lady I have been teaching this year. Her name isn't Cerise, but we'll call her that to stop me being sued. She is a very bright girl and, as I write this, a few weeks before results day, is expected to get a good grade in English. I have only been teaching her in year 11, but have read every word she has written over those eight months, commenting lovingly on it. By chance I came upon her book from year 10, and was interested to see how she had done that year. Let me take you on a journey through Cerise's year 10 book.

The first thing we notice is that it is covered in graffiti: pictures of love hearts, stars, scrawled nascent attempts at a signature. Then we open the front cover and delve inside: the first page is well presented, but unmarked. The second page has been left blank. Third page: well presented, unmarked. Page four: blank. Five: less well presented, unmarked. Page six: blank. Page seven: token effort from student, unmarked. Page eight: blank. A whole (admittedly pitiful) term's work with no evidence that any teacher has even considered opening the book to read what Cerise has written.

We return from the Christmas holidays and Cerise appears to have a new attitude. Her first page after the holiday, page nine, is covered with work – autobiography. We read it. Cerise writes, "I live with my brother and my dad. My mum died and it's kind of hard at the moment, but as people have said to me, look into the future, not the past, so therefore that's what I must do."

What would a teacher worth their money notice about this? Decent complex sentences, correctly applied commas and ambitious use of a high order, conjunctive adverb, perhaps? Maybe they would notice that, in the line, "It's kind of hard *at the moment*" that Cerise's mum died relatively recently, and that, in writing this, she is telling the teacher that something cataclysmic has happened in her life, and she is struggling. What did the teacher notice? Nothing. She didn't read it.

Page ten: blank. Page eleven: almost blank. Page twelve: blank. Page thirteen: more autobiography. We read. "I live with my brother and my dad. It's good living with them but unfortunately it would be better if my mum was still here. This thought actually touches deep inside, but she died at Christmas, and is therefore no longer living with us. I always thought I was going step-by-step up in life, but this devastating cause, caused me to go two steps back, so eventually I gave up." We look at the date, 12th January. We relate that to Christmas. We realise that Cerise's mum died three weeks ago. We start to hate the teacher who has left this piece of work unmarked.

Page fifteen: unmarked. Page sixteen: blank. Page seventeen: unmarked. Page eighteen: blank. Page nineteen: unmarked. Page twenty: blank. Page twenty-one: organised writing, and finally we note there is a teacher's comment at the bottom of the page. Cerise has written, under the heading 'Bad Day', "One day I woke up for Christmas, and I got a phone call from the Doctor's. My dad's face dropped. I asked him what's wrong. His face changed colour. I tried to ask him what was going on, and he told me that it was something serious, but I was just to hurry up and get ready. We left the house, and I found out that my mum was just about to die. I couldn't believe it. My life had ended. I felt dead. I felt to cry. I was just speechless."

What do we see at the bottom of this devastating cri du coeur? A sympathetic word, a gentle touch of encouragement, the marking equivalent of an arm round the shoulder, an empathetic tear and the warm adult assurance that it will get better, one day it will, I promise you? No. We get none of this. Cerise got none of this. What did she get, as an exchange for opening her heart and revealing the state of utter torment she was in? A single tick in red pen, accompanied by the line, "You need to use capital letters properly."

There is probably a reasonable explanation behind this crime perpetrated upon a vulnerable young lady. There always is. But whatever the reason, it isn't anywhere near good enough.

You will occasionally hear teachers talk of the somewhat vapourous concept of professional integrity. By this most teachers mean that, generally at least, they would regard sharing a needle with a student as being something that they'd move towards being disinclined to do. For me, professional integrity, notwithstanding the fact that taking class A's in the staff toilets is probably more than a few steps beyond the pale, boils down to one key rule: a teacher who places marking their books properly at the heart of their practice is a teacher who possesses professional integrity. Maintaining this integrity costs though. My own life now is a dizzy whirl of teaching, speaking engagements and writing. The selfish swine in me would prioritise the speaking engagements over the fact that I have a pile of books to mark, in that if you go in underprepared to speak in front of two hundred highly intelligent, graduate professionals, who are all secretly hoping that you'll be shit, then you are asking for it, really. However, I find that given the choice between writing another gag that doesn't work for a big speech, and marking Cerise's book, there's only one winner.

The reasons you should prioritise marking above every other facet of the role are manifold, but simple enough. Firstly, what is the point of kids doing the work if no one reads it? None. Like the tree in the forest that falls when no one hears it[27], when a kid writes a piece of work *for you to read*, and you do not read it, it is, to them, like they haven't written it at all. Not reading it sends all manner of negative messages to the child: effort is pointless, their work is of no value to you and they could have got away with not bothering. This is how kids are made to feel in crap teachers' classes. Don't make them feel that way in your class.

Where work is not properly marked or, worse still, is not marked at all, a pernicious negative message gets through to those kids whose work has been ignored in double quick time: they stop trying, stop caring and stop working. Pages get left blank, presentation goes awry, discipline disappears. An unmarked book rapidly becomes shocking, and tells any observer everything about you they will ever need to know. A key observer's trick, with which you can tell whether the teacher is good, bad or indifferent in seconds, is to look at the first page of an exercise book, then the last page. If there is evidence of progress in the standard of the work, then the teacher is a good teacher: if the work has gone downhill, they are not. Simple.

---

27 *Incidentally – if a man speaks in a forest and no woman hears him, is he still wrong?*

Decent marking is *the* key to pupil progress. If you do it regularly and with a degree of professional fascination, proof marking every word and setting gradational targets, you will, whatever else your faults and flaws, be a very good teacher indeed. Your pupils will make exponential gains, the results that they attain will outstrip anyone's expectations and your career will fly.

However, it is a technical exercise, and being such, requires a bit of technique. The next few pages are designed to equip you with all the technical nous you will need to be a great marker of work, and therefore a great teacher.

RED PENS AND THE TEMPTATION TO TICK

Hopefully, your school will allow you to correct kids' work in red pen. It is the classic way. (Some schools, in an outbreak of insanity, insist that teachers mark in green. There is no logic behind this insistence; they are just trying to be clever and, in attempting to do so, succeed in proving they are far from it). The single issue you may have with the red pen is that it can get lost easily. You will need to be ready to get down to a nourishing five minute bout of marking at any point during the school day: it is of no use to you if four of these five minutes are spent searching for your red pen, failing, then rushing to the stationery cupboard, which has just run out of them. It is well worth investing in a box of them out of your own money, and keeping them at home. A box will last well past your first year, and will ensure that you never go to work without a red pen or two in your top pocket.

How you employ that red pen is crucial. There are teachers who think that all that marking requires is to tick every paragraph in sequence, then to write "Very good" at the bottom of the piece of work. Don't do this; even if it means working half of Sunday to catch up with marking your books properly. Random ticking is, in many ways, worse than not marking at all. At least in an unmarked book the child may hold out the forlorn hope that you may one day get your act together and read all the stuff that they have written for the sole purpose of you reading and commenting on it. With a book that has been randomly ticked a child's hope that someone cares about their work moves from the forlorn to the vain. Random ticking is insulting to the intelligence of the children you teach and will be quickly picked up by your boss as a completely unacceptable thing for a graduate professional to be doing.

FOCUSING ON PRESENTATION

Of course we are interested in what the student writes, but before we even get to it there's the whole other issue of presentation – which is actually worth spending a little more rigour and effort on than you would think. Actually, your stance on the presentation of work is pretty definitive: if you are lax with it, the students will take this as an incitement that they can take the mick in all other areas, and so, counter-intuitively, how you challenge the many wheezes they will employ in order to break the rules on presentation actually has a substantial impact on behaviour.

The mortal sins of presentation

1.   Graffiti – The first of the major sins is the book cover of which every inch features the name of a boy band, the child's initials, love hearts or gang names. You go directly to eleven on this. The first kid that puts graffiti on their exercise book, chuck that book straight in the bin. No messing. Stuff protocol. Chuck it in the bin and chuck it in with panache. Let the rest of the class know that the same thing will happen to their book the moment that they too think it is OK to scribble on school resources when they should be working. This may sound a little harsh, but if you don't do it, then everyone will think it is OK to cover their books in scrawl. Think about the image that creates to the parents, to your Head and to any observer. If I am assessing a teacher and all the books are covered in spider poop, then this teacher has not given kids the right message about respect for themselves, their attainment and school resources.

2.   The blank page every second page – I have no idea why almost every child I have ever taught thinks that this looks good, as it doesn't. It looks lazy. It may be that every child in the country thinks that they are somehow putting one over on the teacher by insisting that, if you don't mind, they'd prefer not to

write on pages 2, 4, 6, 8 etc; that by writing on only every second page, they are somehow working harder, as they get through the book twice as quickly. Whatever the absurd mindset here, it is vital that you are both vigilant and diligent in fighting the war against this crime. You will be fighting it for the rest of your career, or until such time that they finally get rid of books (next week, then). You will not win it, in that if you relax for a moment, every child in the class will attempt to surreptitiously miss out whole pages at that very instant. You will not conclusively win the war, but be assured it is a holy one and you must satisfy yourself with being the victor in every small battle.

How you win the battle (and you will probably have to fight this on a daily basis with every second child you teach), is by setting up the expectation that after every piece of work, no matter where that piece of work has finished on the page (within reason), they will draw a single, ruled line (preferably in pencil) and start the next piece of work directly under that line, scribing title and date, then getting on with things. You will have to restate this a few times, but in reality they all know it is an expectation they should be following. The key here, though, is in making the classroom tour immediately after you have given them the title and date to copy down. You look at where every child is starting their work for the day, and, if it is not as instructed, you calmly and purpose-fully inform them where you want the work to be started. If you do not do this, half of them will miss out whole pages and a whole forest's worth of trees will have been cut down for no reason at all. Sadly, you must do this every lesson. The learning on this one, "I must not attempt to take the piss out of miss by deliberately missing out pages from my exercise book," never seems to stick.

3. The ridiculously big margin – Exercise books generally have margins already ruled on the left hand side of the page. Consequently, it takes a deeply commit-ted waster to take liberties on the left hand side. Such a species of waster does exist, but they are rare indeed, given the fact that there are three other margins on the page with which liberties can be taken more easily. These are, in reverse order of popularity:

    a. The bottom of the page – It seems pretty obvious where the page ends to you or I. There is a last line. This fact does not register with some students, who are of the belief that the last line of the page is half way down it.

b.   The right hand margin – Again, obvious to us, madness to them. You will run across one class member every year who is thoroughly committed to not writing to the end of the line. "But that's how I write," they will protest. "No. it isn't," you reply. "Write to the end of the bloody line."

c.   The top of the page – They think we are idiots. We set them a page of work and think, not unreasonably we believe, that the page starts at the top. Not in the surreal landscape of the serial lazy sod. For him, it starts four lines down. That way he'll have to do less writing. He thinks you are stupid. He thinks you won't notice. You do notice. Call him on it. Write, "Do you think I am a complete idiot? Rhetorical!" in the lines he has missed out.

4.   Writing in red, green or purple – Every school insists that its students write in only blue or black ink. Why this is, I am not sure. Perhaps it is perceived that it creates a pleasing uniformity, more likely it is a reflection of the world outside – you write a letter to your bank manager in pink gel pen, and you are unlikely to get that loan – and there is also the fact that if they write in red, then you won't be able to tell the marking from the work. Whatever the reason is, it is a rule and, as such, it will cause kids to attempt to subvert it. You stop this with the 'copying the title down tour'. Any child reaching for the multicoloured gel pen is to be swiftly disabused of their rule breaking intent. This is easy enough in classwork, but can be difficult to enforce with homework. The correct response to homework scribed in purple is to refuse to mark it. Just write something at the bottom saying, "I have not read this piece of work, as it is not in the correct colour. If you want me to read it, you must use black or blue."

5.   Circles or kisses over the 'i' – You may not find that this sends you mental, in which case, allow it. It does send me mental. I don't allow it. This means that I spend an undue part of my rapidly diminishing years left on this beautiful and blessed planet crossing out such kisses and circles when I could be smelling lilac scented blossom. You may find this to be a waste of time. I do too. But it doesn't mean I am able to stop myself.

6.   Errant underlining – Rules is rules. I insist that there is a single, pencil drawn ruled lined under the title. What you get if you don't insist on this is lines in

red, squiggly lines parenthesised with asterisks, titles that are not underlined, or even, heaven forfend, double underlining.

7. Ampersands – This is an ampersand: &. It is wrong.

8. Numbers recorded in numeric form – How are they ever going to learn how to spell eighteen if they always write 18? Make it a policy in any extended written work that does not involve calculations, as applying this policy in maths and science does not work very well.

You may find all these rules, "A bit much, really," and I agree there is a slightly jarring conflict between being libertarian on outlook, wanting to nurture kids' genius and creativity and in being such a complete totalitarian in terms of piffling little rules regarding presentation. This totalitarian viewpoint has been developed over many years of witnessing what happens to kids' books if you don't take just such an approach: they end up a complete dog's dinner, and make you, the teacher, look like a poor professional. As with much of the stuff with behaviour you must know in your soul that your fascism in certain areas is merely there to save a whole lot of bother and bloodshed in others. Once they learn that sir or miss is a complete fascist regarding the little things, then it is less likely that the bigger crimes, such as just sitting there and doing no work whatsoever, will occur. Being a Nazi regarding presentation pays off eventually. What happens is that the kids become proud of their books, as they look orderly and organised. This impacts on the standard of the work they do in them. A decent looking book will invariably have a decent enough standard of work in it. Similarly, open a shocking looking book and, well, you are not going to be too surprised.

MARKING FOR CONTENT

Get this. Kids love having their books marked. They adore it. In the class of a teacher who is punctilious and takes marking seriously, the first thing that they will do when they enter the class is greedily devour the comments that teacher has spent substantial effort and time scribing. It almost makes all the effort worth it. Whatever feeble protestations many of them will make, the vast majority of schoolchildren really want to achieve well at school; they want to learn. And, from my experience, they are pretty hip to the fact that decent marking, in which achievable next targets are set, daily, will give them the equipment they need to improve.

As marking is the key to student improvement it must be something that you take very seriously indeed. And if you are teaching one of the subjects with a particularly heavy burden, I am afraid there is little substitute for time with your books. I wish I could make it easier for you, but this is an area in which the hours you put in will, eventually, pay off big-time for your students. Of course, you may be dead by then, but hey! Everything ends. Being seen in the staffroom every day, feverishly marking, also lets your new colleagues know that you are serious. "Have you seen the new girl? She's always marking!" will be uttered in tones that are slightly scared, not so much for your physical and mental well-being, but for the fact that you are showing everybody else up, and they are slightly envious.

As it is such an invidious task, being permanently under the marking cosh for ten months a year, every year until you die, exactly fifteen and a half seconds after the retirement bash at which people reveal that they never really liked you, you must find a way of enjoying it. This is a question of mind over matter. There is nothing much enjoyable about being always behind on a very important task, and is one of the reasons that the profession you have entered, far from being the cruisey doss you might have imagined, is perhaps the most stressful way there is of making a pretty paltry living, but you must approach it, on a daily basis, as something you enjoy doing.

There is a process for marking, which works well whatever time you are doing it – in that it feeds into your lesson planning, and, as such, is pretty well a decent definition of 'assessment for learning' that overrides the bucketload of impenetrable gruel you may be given explaining what the government thinks it means. First, you ensure you have a pad or a piece of paper next to you as you are doing the marking, and then the process goes like this:

1. You proof mark every word they write. If the title is misspelt, correct it. If their name is misspelt, correct it. If it moves, correct it, if it doesn't, do the same. There are idiots who argue that you shouldn't proof mark, as the swathes of red ink on his work puts poor Johnny off and makes him feel like a failure. You have to ride this instinct out. The thing that has caused little Johnny to be so

shocking at literacy is other teachers allowing him to make mistakes without correcting them. Yes, it is emotionally difficult for him, but not half as emotionally difficult as finding that he is an adult and cannot feed his family because a load of pansy liberal teachers who were worried about upsetting him left him illiterate, as they would not mark his work properly.

2.   As you are reading the work you will notice things about it: some good, some that need improving. It is more than likely that you will chance upon more glaring technical errors than you will things that you feel are worth praising – there is a clever cheat here. If you notice, in the first line, some glaring grammatical, factual or technical 'learning need' way before the prose has even begun to assume anything resembling coherence, then you leave three lines for the positive comment, in which you are going to say what you liked about the work (but haven't found yet), and write the word, 'Targets'. Then number the first of these 1 and, referring to the particular development need you have noted in the first line, turn this into a target that you want him to hit in the next piece of work. These targets must be technical, and, unless they are a generic literacy target, subject specific. As an example, in my subject, English, the targets I most wish I had a stamp for are, "Always put a comma before 'but'," "Make sure you don't start successive sentences with the same word" and "Try not to use the same word twice in a sentence." In maths an appropriate target might be, "Ensure you twiddle with the integers twice before you numerate," and in science, "You need to stop pretending that you know what positon emission tomography means just to impress the inspector."

3.   You should easily be able to muster three or four targets during your proof marking of the work, and by the end of your reading you will have a good idea about what you liked about the work. Record what you liked about the work in the two or thee line space you have left for just such a purpose above the targets. The rationale behind this is that the positive comment, in which you remark in detail about the aspects of their progress you are pleased with and, specifically, make reference to the work that shows you have read it in detail, opens the student up emotionally to the target. In praising first of all, you have avoided putting them on the defensive immediately, and so, shields down, they are more able to take on board the friendly advice on how to improve.

4. When you next mark the student's book, the first thing you do is check what targets you set them last time and mark the next piece against these. If they have hit the targets you set after the last piece of work, then you praise them for doing so. If not, refer the student back to the last set of targets. It's pretty easy to conceive of how this process makes progress almost inevitable. Educational improvement is a gradational process won in small, bite sized chunks; and in setting small targets which we check progress against on a near daily basis, we seize these small improvements for our students. Over the space of a year, such small improvements can mount up into a whole hill of startling progress.

GRADING

You will notice when you are being observed that, at some point during the lesson, the inspector will have a few quiet words with a couple of kids. What they will generally be asking them are the following three questions:

1. What are you learning this lesson?

2. What level/grade are you at in this subject?

3. What do you need to do to get to the next grade/level in this subject?

Ensuring kids give the correct answer to the first of these questions is done by sharing your lesson objectives emphatically and then checking understanding. The third is ensured by regular target setting when marking books. The second you get from regular grading. Many schools have two concurrent systems of grading: effort grades and national curriculum grades. Effort grades came about because Trevor, who has special educational needs, always gets a 1c in the national curriculum gradings as he can't read properly. It doesn't matter how hard poor old Trev works on something, he always gets the same grade: and so, effort grades acknowledge the superhuman efforts that he puts into some lessons. By giving him an 'A' for effort we give Trev a sense of achievement. In reality, however, effort grades are a complete waste of time. Trevor knows very well his position in the scheme of things. He is well aware that he is at the bottom and, in giving him a tokenistic 'A' for effort, you are patronising him. He's not thick. He just can't read very well. Besides, every single student knows whether they worked hard or not on a piece of work. Effort grades are only telling them things they already know.

What is important is that the kids in your class know what level they are working at, and what they need to do to get to the next level. There is a political agenda behind this, of course. The government's reputation in terms of its educational policy pretty well boils the kids down to statistics. The more of these statistical objects (children) that are numbered at the higher level, the better the government comes across, and the more likely it is that certain MPs in marginal seats will keep their jobs. The not unreasonable idea is that, in order to progress to your ultimate aim, you've got to know where you are and what steps you must take to reduce the distance between your current position and the goal. Consequently, inspectors are very hot indeed on kids knowing what level they are working at, and you must grade work regularly, sharing these grades with the kids themselves. Inspectors take a very dim view of kids not knowing where they are in a subject.

ASSESSMENT FOR LEARNING

This is the current vogue. It'll last a few years before the DfE has another wheeze with which to marginally alter the state approved method of teaching. The premise behind 'assessment for learning' is sound, however, and relates quite well to the stuff above about having a piece of paper next to you when you are marking their work, to note what they need to know next. It is about having assessment as an embedded part of the process of learning, not as an add-on at the end.

There are three subsections of assessment for learning: teacher assessment (which has already been modelled above), self-assessment and peer assessment. Let's look at the last two:

Self-assessment

There is a line that if a kid was able to properly self-assess, then they wouldn't have handed in the steaming crock of nonsense that you have just received. If they could self-assess, then their work would be perfect anyway and they would have no need of teachers. It's an easy line to take, but it does no one any real good. Developing students' ability to assess strengths and weaknesses in their own work is actually pretty key to them becoming adept at acquiring the skills they'll need to continue through life's journey successfully improving their abilities. How we do this in lessons is to give them the criteria against which they are assessed, and getting them to mark their own work against it. "If you were an examiner and you had been given this piece of work to mark, what grade would you give it and why? What would you suggest to the student that they do to improve their work?"

The issue with this is that, as we noted in the Chapter 1, the assessment criteria can be vapourous. It is useful, before any exercise in self-assessment, to ask the kids to translate the assessment criteria into a simplified form, in their own language, so that they are better able to map their work to the criteria. The benefits of this are substantial: firstly, they develop the skills of spotting what it is they need to improve upon to get to the next grade; secondly, assimilating the information about how you are going to be assessed in any exam is always going to be of benefit.

Peer assessment

Peer assessment is essentially the same job, but rather than mark your own work, you mark your mate's. The disadvantages are that in marking your mate's work you are not necessarily directly improving your own. The advantage, though, which some-what overrules the disadvantage, is that you have to feedback to your mate your assessment of their work, and this opens up a valuable developmental dialogue. Also, it is far easier to be objective when analysing someone else's work than it is your own and, as such, you may be more inclined to tell the truth to your mate than you are to yourself. Acknowledging this, it is decent practice to run a self-assessment activity first, then immediately follow this with a peer assessment of the same piece of work.

AND FINALLY...

Teaching is a lifetime vocation. It is also just a job. It is entirely possible to hold these two apparently conflicting views at the same time, and for them to not rub up against each other too uncomfortably. You have probably entered the profession because you are following a passion: a passion for the life chances of children; a passion for your subject; or even a a passion for having an interesting job. There are times, however, when you will need more than highfaluting ideals to get you through the day. You must also be able to be realistic – realistic about what it is possible to achieve and what it is right to expect of yourself.

With all the will in the world there will be some kids, or maybe even whole classes who, not only do you struggle to get through to, but may also struggle to like. It comes as a shock this first realisation that there is a child whose educational chances you are responsible for that you find it difficult to like. Forgive yourself for being human, and remember that if you were stuck in a room with thirty adults there would be some you didn't warm to.

There will also be some kids you can't reach. I still have this. However many absurd plaudits I've had thrown at me, on the day I am writing this, after returning home from school, I am struggling, I feel vainly, with the fact that there are three children in a class I am teaching and I have no idea, after many years of experience, what on earth I am going to do to get them to buy into my lessons. I forgive myself.

Be aware that teaching is maybe the hardest job that it is possible to do. Yes, we get long holidays, but the workload in our profession is impossible to deal with. You cannot do the job properly. And you will kill yourself if you try. If you are in a situation where the demands on you are so intense that you feel yourself losing who you are, stop. Go to the cinema, the pub, visit friends, do something that makes you forget about the job. As teaching is a vocation, there are people who think having a vocation should preclude you from having a life. These people are idiots and zealots. Ignore them. A decent teacher has experiences outside of the classroom and these experiences inform the sort of person they are in it.

You will be told, often, by more experienced members of staff that your NQT year is the hardest year of your career, and that it will get better. They are not saying this for the good of their health. It is said to help you. There is a light at the end of the tunnel. It is called your second year of teaching. It is markedly easier. But you have to get there. Make a promise to yourself and keep it. However low you get in your first year as a teacher, you will see it our for a whole two years. You won't pack it in when the going gets tough. And I promise you, if you apply many of the lessons in this book, by the end of the second year you will be walking the corridors of the school and notice the many smiling faces that light up when they see you; the many enlivened voices calling your name and appreciating the fact that it is, as rumoured, the best job in the world.

ABOUT THE AUTHOR

Phil Beadle is an English teacher, a former United Kingdom Secondary Teacher of the Year in the National Teaching Awards, and a double Royal Television Society Award winning broadcaster for Channel 4's 'The Unteachables' and 'Can't Read Can't Write'. He writes a column called 'On Teaching' for *Education Guardian*. This is his third book. His first was serialised in *The Telegraph*, his second has been used by Liverpool and Manchester United football clubs.

www.philbeadle.com

twitter.com/PhilBeadle

YouTube link http://bit.ly/philbeadle

RECOMMENDED READING

Ainley, Patrick and Allen, Martin – *Lost Generation?: New Strategies for Youth and Education* (Continuum 2010).

Beadle, Phil – *Could do Better: Help your Child Shine at School* (Corgi 2008).

Black, Paul – *Assessment for Learning: Putting it into Practice* (Open University Press 2003).

Bukowski, Charles – *The Bukowski Sampler* (Quixote 1969). P. 57.

Collins, Michael – *The Likes of Us: A Biography of the White Working Class* (Granta 2005).

Davies, Nick – *The School Report: Why Britain's Schools are Failing* (Vintage 2000).

Evans, Gillian – *Educational Failure and Working Class White Children in Britain* (Palgrave MacMillan 2007).

Gilbert, Ian – *Essential Motivation in the Classroom* (Routledge 2002).

Gilbert, Ian – *The Little Book of Thunks* (Crown House 2007).

Hodgson, David – *The Little Book of Inspirational Teaching Activities* (Crown House 2009).

Kohn, Alfie – *The Homework Myth: Why Our Children Get Too Much of a Bad Thing* (Da Capo Lifelong 2007).

Petty, Geoff – *Teaching Today: A Practical Guide, 3rd edition* (Nelson Thornes 2004).

Rogers, Bill – *Cracking the Hard Class: Strategies for Managing the Harder than Average Class* (Paul Chapman Publishing 2000).

Willis, Paul – *Learning to Labour: Why Working Class Kids get Working Class Jobs* (Gower 1988).

INDEX

A

ability levels 8, 190–3
    cloze procedure 199–200
    self-assessment 226
    worksheets 201
activities, halting 20–1
argument tennis 136–9
argument tunnel 134–6
assaults 43–4
assertive discipline 26
    detention 37–41
    either/or rule 29–30
    moving from table 31–2
    moving seat 30–1
    standing outside classroom 32–6
    telling-off, in classroom 26–8
    telling-off, outside classroom 28–9
assessment 213
    content 221–4
    differentiation by 193–4
    grades 224–5
    for learning 225–6
    marking 213–18
    peer assessment 226
    random ticking 217–18
    red pen 217–18
    self-assessment 226
attendance
    students 88
    teacher 4–7
attitude cards 121–6

B

bags 9
beat 96
behaviour management 4, 24–5, 47–50, 74–5, 160–1, 163, 218, 221
    attendance 4–6
    chewing gum 10–13
    corridors 43, 44–5
    crisps 13–14
    detention 37–41
    discipline 26–36
    fights 44–6
    group discussion 103–5, 110–12, 114–16, 121, 140
    halt activities 20–1
    health and safety 76
    knives 46, 76
    lies 15–17, 147
    looking at teacher 23–4
    pausing 24, 29
    pens down 21–3
    phoning parents 42
    praise 55–60, 67
    professional distance 60–1
    restraining 43–4, 45–6
    rules 9
    seating plan 7–9, 116–18, 197
    serious situations 43–4, 45–6
    talking in class 17–20
    violence 43–4, 45–6
    work avoidance 50–5, 147–8
behaviour support teacher 161, 163
blanking 106–8
blocking door 35–6
body language 23, 26–8, 30–1, 67, 107–8
brainstorms 126–9

233

V

W

Y